Dan Diaper and Cols

CSCW in Practice:
an Introduction and
Case Studies

Springer-Verlag
London Berlin Heidelberg New York
Paris Tokyo Hong Kong
Barcelona Budapest

Book and Series Editors

Dan Diaper, PhD
Department of Computer Science
University of Liverpool
PO Box 147
Liverpool L69 3BX, UK

Colston Sanger
GID Ltd
69 King's Road
Haslemere
Surrey GU27 2QG, UK

ISBN 3–540–19784–2 Springer-Verlag Berlin Heidelberg New York
ISBN 0–387–19784–2 Springer-Verlag New York Berlin Heidelberg

British Library Cataloguing in Publication Data
CSCW in Practice: Introduction and Case Studies . – (Computer Supported
Cooperative Work Series)
    I. Diaper, Dan II. Sanger, Colston III. Series
    004.01
    ISBN 3-540-19784-2

Library of Congress Cataloging-in-Publication Data
    CSCW in Practice : an introduction and case studies / Dan Diaper and
    Colston Sanger (eds.)
        p. cm. – (Computer supported cooperative work)
    Includes bibliographical references and index.
    ISBN 30540-19784-2 (alk. paper) : $42.00 (U.S. est.). – ISBN 0-387-19784-2
    (U.S. : alk. paper) : $42.00 (est.).
    1. Authorship–Collaboration–Data processing. 2. Work groups–Data
    processing. 3. Information technology. I. Diaper, D. (Dan) II. Sanger, C
    (Colston), 1950– . III. Series.
    PN171.D37C73   1993
    004.6–dc20   92-39255

Typeset from authors' disks by Fox Design, Bramley, Guildford, Surrey
34/3830–543210 Printed on acid-free paper

Preface

Dan, is this book going to provide a substantial, coherent and timely contribution to CSCW or is it just going to be a ragbag of papers from several meetings stuck together?

The latter, of course, Colston. However, ...

... and the "However" was rather long and technical, but not substantially different in overall content from that of this preface. Most of the papers contained in this book were initially presented at meetings organized by the UK's Computer Supported Cooperative Work (CSCW) Special Interest Group in 1991, but the book is not a proceedings, whatever the above quotation suggests. Readers will immediately notice that, unlike typical proceedings, all the references are placed together at the end of the book and that there is a substantial index: the hallmark of all proper, technical books of quality. If you choose to delve further than this preface, you will find that each chapter is cross-referenced, thus you also gain a coherent structure across chapters – an advantage traditionally associated with high quality single-author books. Furthermore, turning apparent disadvantage to advantage, while single-author books must inevitably present the idiosyncratic perspective of their author, in this book, and appropriately for a young area such as CSCW, you will be presented with the views of a dozen CSCW experts who all have considerable, hard-won experience, gained over many years. Indeed, the main title of the book emphasizes that this book is primarily about real CSCW, not arcane academic theories of CSCW. Nor, in general, does it present a merely technocentric rehearsal of CSCW systems that have been developed or claimed to have been developed. Moreover, the book's sub-title allows us to provide an introduction both to the technical and human aspects of CSCW, but still emphasizes that most of the chapters contain reports, admittedly in greater or lesser detail, of the various authors' CSCW experiences.

While we suggest that CSCW is a "young" field, it has been around for a decade or so as something recognizably different from its progenitor fields of research. The authors have at least been CSCW's childminders, if not its midwife. We believe that this book will be of value to those who are relatively new to the field, both students and the more qualified, and to the old salts, because it collects and reports practical experience, something at present in short supply in an accessible form.

We had planned to eschew the conservative strategy of prefaces: that of providing a synopsis of each chapter (presumably so that editors can prove to potential readers that they have looked at their book's content). However, some account of the rationale for the structure of the book (i.e. the chapter order) seemed appropriate, and in preparing this we found it natural to provide such synopses. Also appropriate is a brief description, somewhere, of how the book was produced, since it is itself an example of CSCW.

Ordering the chapters took several meetings between us, since we assumed that a random chapter ordering was not desirable. We had two constraints to balance: first, the material we had or were promised; and secondly, who else did we know who could readily supply us with additional material that would be of sufficient quality? That the chapter authors are all UK-based will be a disappointment, our publisher assures us, to an international technical market. Nevertheless, our final structure is as follows:

1. An introduction to CSCW is provided in three chapters which cover, in turn, three perspectives:

1 Rodden: A technocentric report of CSCW in general, its base technologies and its applications.

2 Brooke: A user-driven view of CSCW requirements, which proposes the style of technology we need for CSCW.

3 Hewitt and Gilbert: An interactional perspective derived from consideration of the user interface to CSCW systems.

2. Next, the most researched and used area of CSCW – collaborative authoring – is described in three chapters that all

contain case studies. Its choice to follow the introduction is obvious: not only is there just more material, but nearly everyone in industry and academia has some experience of writing in collaboration with others. Thus the application area is familiar to all and the problems with using electronic mail (email) to support such writing will be readily comprehensible, although some of the proposed "solutions" to the reader new to CSCW will, we hope, be both novel and informative.

4 Gilbert: Case studies from the early days of CSCW where the people got on and did it (collaborative authoring).

5 Sharples: An introduction to collaborative authoring to allow readers to comprehend the theoretical problems following an understanding of the problems with crude CSCW technology described in the previous chapter. Another case study illustrates some of the issues.

6 Diaper: A practical look at the problems of collaborative authoring using just email and a detailed case study of writing a short journal paper collaboratively.

3. The range of CSCW applications now broadens and the remaining five chapters form a second part to the book and repeat the first six chapters' general structure:

7 Newman: Back to a technological perspective and a description of the CSCW facilities provided in the UK by one freely accessible system.

8 Wastell and White: A theoretical introduction from one perspective to the issues of cooperative working and several case studies for illustration.

9 Benest and Dukić: A particular CSCW system is described. On the one hand (see the next chapter) this system is modest; on the other, it is implemented and usable on widely available, modest microcomputers and is valuable as a description of what is available now.

10 Seward et al.: While narrowing the application to the multi-media support for face-to-face meetings, the high-tech Pod is a system that can be hired, although not cheaply, today.

11 Kirkwood et al.: Finally, one of those rare papers which we need more of (see Hewett 1991 for an argument why), a description of a CSCW system that was trialled and that failed in a real, commercial application. While many of the problems will appear obvious and trivial in retrospect, we

hope those in industry will nod in agreement to an accurate portrayal of the real world and the academics will appropriately shudder and be more practical in their proposals to their industrial collaborators.

Finally, this book is itself a case study in collaborative authoring. Certainly the collaboration is at and above the level of the chapter, but its production has made extensive use of computers. We should remember that CSCW does not automatically imply that computers need to be networked. Posting a floppy disc is an equally valid means of computer data transfer and it has its own advantages and disadvantages. Much of the communication between editors and authors has been by email. The editors collaborated in making extensive comments on all the chapters: firstly we acted as referees, advising how each chapter could be improved; secondly, we produced the high level cross-referencing between chapters. The book may be a multi-author one, but it is possible to treat it as a "proper" book that can be read from beginning to end, being led by the structure described above. Each chapter has the additional advantage that it can be read alone (after all, who has time to read a whole technical book these days?).

For the cross-referencing, we went through all the chapters again and identified all the bits we thought might potentially be cross-referenced. These were at quite a high level, with the exception of references to particular application software ("technology systems"), since the purpose of the exercise was to get chapter authors to make our suggested cross-references explicit in their chapters. We listed the cross-references as mnemonics with a chapter and location ID. We added to the list as we went through each chapter and then finally structured the list into a version similar to the "Hypertext Semantic Net" given at the end of this preface. We present it to provide an alternative access structure to the index prepared by the publisher. While in tabular, rather than graphic form, this is a hypertext net in that it identifies nodes ("Node types") and the links between nodes ("Chapter node referents"). It is semantic, in the jargon of hypertext, in that the nodes are labelled as meaningful entries (e.g. "X.400", "COSMOS", etc.).

Most of the cross-references were suggested to the chapter authors, although not all are actually used in the book. We have therefore presented to readers our original proposals for cross-references, since these are more extensive, rather than the final set, which should be extractable from the index (i.e. where an index item has more than one chapter referent). Our classification still provides a general overview of the book as it can be thought of as having had a voting procedure applied to it (i.e. it lists those issues that are of sufficient significance that they are mentioned in more than one chapter), although such an operational definition of "significance" must, of course, be treated with caution.

The other reason for presenting the hypertext semantic net is that it allows us to comment on the computer tool we really needed for this part of the editors' task. Had we had all the chapters on-line, and a simple hypertext shell such as GUIDE then we could have been even more thorough and complete in our cross-referencing. Furthermore, what we needed most was a string searching capability, since though we had marked page numbers as well as chapters on our original list of possible cross-references, we spent many hours searching for the "right" cross reference.

Finally, on behalf of the editors, we would like to thank the authors for their time and effort, and Linda Schofield of Springer-Verlag, who has helped considerably, both with this book and with establishing the CSCW book series.

Hypertext Semantic Net

Technology Systems

Node types	Chapter node referents										
	1.	2.	3.	4.	5.	6.	7.	8.	9.	10.	11.
X.400	X			X	X						
COSMOS	X				X						X
Information Lens	X	X									
Hypertext	X					X		X			
Post-it notes	X					X					
Quilt	X			X							
meeting room	X								X		
Coordinator		X		X				X			
Microsoft Mail			X	X							
fax				X		X					X
BLEND & electronic journals					X		X				
LaTeX					X	X					
JANET						X	X				

Group Issues

Node types	Chapter node referents										
	1.	2.	3.	4.	5.	6.	7.	8.	9.	10.	11.
chair type role	X		X	X	X	X	X		X		
floor control	X		X								
conflict resolution	X				X				X		
voting	X					X			X		
improve cooperation	X	X									
organizational change		X			X						
increased complexity from single user		X	X								X
tacit, evolved procedures				X		X			X		
face-to-face meetings				X	X	X				X	
other (non-chair) roles				X	X			X			X
group size				X	X	X					
private v. group goals				X	X	X					
social aspects		X	X		X			X			X

Technology Issues

Node types	Chapter node referents										
	1.	2.	3.	4.	5.	6.	7.	8.	9.	10.	11.
speech acts	X							X			
non-action types	X			X							
synchrony/asynchrony	X		X	X	X			X			
pruning	X						X				
private/public views	X								X		
window layout	X		X								
WYSIWIS	X		X								
feedback			X		X						X
shared workspace			X	X					X		
technical standpoint	X		X		X				X		
coordination of work on same parts				X	X	X					
difference single & groupwork		X		X							
locating comments				X		X					
versions				X	X	X					
more email fields				X		X	X				
distributed system environment	X						X				
topic reply structure	X	X		X							
technology push		X		X		X			X		
scheduling	X						X				

User Issues

Node types	Chapter node referents										
	1.	2.	3.	4.	5.	6.	7.	8.	9.	10.	11.
user change		X			X						
different user needs		X						X			
user role change during task		X		X		X					
user responsibility to themselves		X							X		
motivation				X		X					X
affect				X		X					

Application Domain Issues											
Node types	Chapter node referents										
	1.	2.	3.	4.	5.	6.	7.	8.	9.	10.	11.
office procedures	X	X						X	X		
planning v. editing stages				X		X					
geographical disparity					X	X			X		
line management model										X	X

CSCW Applications											
Node types	Chapter node referents										
	1.	2.	3.	4.	5.	6.	7.	8.	9.	10.	11.
conferencing	X				X		X				
decision conferences	X			X			X		X		
collaborative writing				X	X	X		X			X

June 1992   Dan Diaper
                                                                Colston Sanger

Contents

Contents

3 Groupware Interfaces

4 CSCW For Real: Reflections on Experience

5 Adding a Little Structure to Collaborative Writing

9 Computer Supported Teamwork

10 The Pod: A Purpose-built Environment to Support Group Working

11 Usability Trialling for CSCW Technology: Lessons from a Structured Messaging Task

A. Kirkwood, S. Furner, W. Ablard, B. Clark, K. Dickerson,
A. Mercer, S. O'Donnell, Y. Siu and O. Williams 163

Contributors

Wilfred Ablard
British Telecom Laboratories, Martlesham Heath, Ipswich IP5 7RE, UK

Ian D. Benest
Department of Computer Science, University of York, York YO1 5DD, UK

John Brooke
User Information Architecture A/D Group, Digital Equipment Co. Ltd, PO Box 121, Reading RG2 0TU, UK

Bruce Clark
British Telecom Laboratories, Martlesham Heath, Ipswich IP5 7RE, UK

Dan Diaper
Department of Computer Science, University of Liverpool, PO Box 147, Liverpool L69 3BX, UK

Keith Dickerson
British Telecom Laboratories, Martlesham Heath, Ipswich IP5 7RE, UK

Davor Dukić
Department of Computer Science, University of York, York YO1 5DD, UK

Stephen Furner
British Telecom Laboratories, Martlesham Heath, Ipswich IP5 7RE, UK

G. Nigel Gilbert
Social and Computer Sciences Research Group, Department of Sociology, University of Surrey, Guildford, Surrey GU2 5XH, UK

Betty Hewitt
Department of Sociology, University of Surrey, Guildford, Surrey
GU2 5XH, UK

Andrew Kirkwood
British Telecom Laboratories, Martlesham Heath, Ipswich IP5 7RE, UK

Andrew Mercer
British Telecom Laboratories, Martlesham Heath, Ipswich IP5 7RE, UK

Julian Newman
Glasgow Polytechnic, Cowcaddens Road, Glasgow G4 0BA, UK

Sharon O'Donnell
British Telecom Laboratories, Martlesham Heath, Ipswich IP5 7RE, UK

Tom Rodden
CSCW Research Centre, Department of Computing, Lancaster
University, Lancaster LA1 4YR, UK

Colston Sanger
GID Ltd, 69 King's Road, Haslemere, Surrey GU27 2QG, UK

Robin R. Seward
ICL, Beaumont, Burfield Road, Old Windsor, Berkshire SL4 2JP, UK

Mike Sharples
Collaborative Writing Research Group, School of Cognitive and
Computing Sciences, University of Sussex, Falmer, Brighton BN1 9QH,
UK

Yuk Tai Siu
British Telecom Laboratories, Martlesham Heath, Ipswich IP5 7RE, UK

David G. Wastell
Department of Computer Science, University of Manchester, Oxford
Road, Manchester M13 9PL, UK

Phil White
Department of Computer Science, University of Manchester, Oxford
Road, Manchester M13 9PL, UK

Owen Williams
British Telecom Laboratories, Martlesham Heath, Ipswich IP5 7RE, UK

Chapter 1

Technological Support for Cooperation

T. Rodden

The ubiquitous nature of personal computers has ensured that computer systems and tools have penetrated large segments of "traditional" work practice and personal access to computer systems is no longer unusual. However, most of these systems have been considered in isolation, both from other tools and from other people, or groups, using similar tools. The availability of modern networking technology and the reliance of most projects on the cooperative activities of people has led to the emergence of systems that aim to support groups.

Computer Supported Cooperative Work (CSCW) has emerged as an identifiable research area which focuses on the role of the computer in group work and involves researchers across a range of disciplines. Bannon and Schmidt (1991) highlight the roles and issues addressed by each of the disciplines involved in CSCW and emphasize the multidisciplinary approach required in investigating group work. Within this multidisciplinary context, this chapter examines the computer technology involved in CSCW, highlighting the different forms of system that have emerged to support group work.

Two general approaches exist in the development of CSCW systems. The first and most prominent approach has been to develop systems that support the exchange of information between users. A second technique is the development of systems that exploit the sharing of information to allow cooperation. Often these techniques are combined to allow more comprehensive cooperative systems to be developed. Within this chapter we shall consider each of these approaches in turn and highlight the technologies exploited by each approach. Finally, the recent emergence of electronic meeting systems, which combine the sharing of information with informal group communication, is briefly examined.

1.1 Information Exchange

Systems supporting information exchange are arguably the most wide-spread class of cooperative system developed to date. The assumption underlying these systems is that members of a group cooperate primarily by exchanging messages. The assumed model of interaction within these systems lends itself to supporting asynchronous and remote cooperation. Systems based on information exchange have evolved from electronic mail (email) programs, which allowed a user on a central machine to send textual messages to other users on the same machine.

As wide area networks designed to support computer communication became more widespread, electronic message systems increased in complexity and functionality. This development resulted in the formation of a number of standards which provide the basis for most modern message systems. Perhaps the most comprehensive message standard to date is the X.400 (CCITT 1987) standard, which encompasses many of the principles underlying message systems.

The X.400 Message Handling System (MHS) recommendations define a generic architecture for message transfer. This architecture is representative of the techniques used in message systems and is illustrative of the principles employed in message-based systems. Electronic message systems typically consist of two separate components: the user interface which deals with mail preparation and reading, and the message transfer system which directs the mail to the correct recipient (Fig. 1.1). This structure is reflected in the X.400 MHS model, which contains two basic components, user agents (UA) and message transfer agents (MTA).

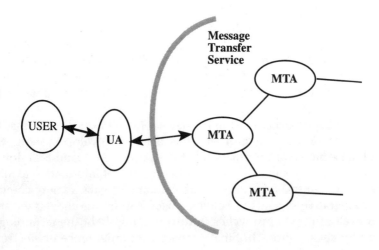

Fig. 1.1 A simple architecture for a message system.

```
% mail
Mail version 5.2 6/21/85.  Type ? for help.
"/usr/spool/mail/tam": 458 messages 55 new 458 unread
 U401 mbt@uk.ac.lancs.comp Thu Jul 18 17:34  28/1214 "blurb"
 U402 S.A.Scrivener@uk.ac.lut Thu Jul 18 22:31  48/2086 "Meeting FEES"
 U403 colston@uk.co.gid Thu Jul 18 22:31  40/1429 "CSCW Book series"
>N404 compsecs@uk.ac.lancs.comp Fri Jul 19 10:53  21/429 "Brussels"
 N405 Simon.Kaplan@fr.inria.sophia Fri Jul 19 13:27  28/1141 "Re: position pape"
 N406 Dianne.Murray@uk.ac.surr.soc Fri Jul 19 14:33  34/1562 "Re: Developers wo"
 N407 jam@uk.ac.lancs.comp Fri Jul 19 15:39  8/211  "pub : Lord Ashton 9:00 pm "
 N408 Dianne.Murray@uk.ac.surr.soc Fri Jul 19 16:33  17/795 "IWC interest in CS"
 N409 Dianne.Murray@uk.ac.surr.soc Fri Jul 19 16:34  48/1402 "Your original IWC"
 N410 sdb@uk.ac.nott.cs Fri Jul 19 16:42  16/806 "Re: X-400"
 N411 mike@uk.ac.susx.cogs Fri Jul 19 17:07  34/1390 "Re: Meeting FEES"
 N412 smf@uk.co.bt.hfnet Fri Jul 19 17:17  18/647 "Re: Text version of Input"
 N413 tam@uk.ac.lancs.comp Fri Jul 19 20:41  42/1576 "Meeting Fees"
 N414 mmdf@uk.ac.surr.ee Fri Jul 19 20:54  65/2633 "Failed mail  (msg.aa03414)"
 N415 kschmidt@dk.risoe Sat Jul 20 12:29  42/1427 "ACME accepts invitation"
 N416 kschmidt@dk.risoe Sun Jul 21 13:06  34/1346 "Convivio"
 N417 kschmidt@dk.risoe Sun Jul 21 13:17  403/12827 "Convivio instructions"
 N418 kschmidt@dk.risoe Sun Jul 21 13:22  102/3085 "Convivio minutes, 10.7.91"
 N419 colston@uk.co.gid Mon Jul 22 08:35  108/4336 "Meeting fees"
 N420 dik@uk.ac.lancs.comp Mon Jul 22 11:28  15/451 "Graham's shindig"
&
```

Fig. 1.2 A text based user agent.

The user agent is responsible for both interaction with the message system and the presentation of messages to users. A wide variety of user agents exist, each employing different techniques to interface to the underlying MHS. Traditional text-based systems (Fig. 1.2) present each user with a list of messages that have arrived in their message delivery area (or mailbox). These systems contain a command language which allows users to peruse their mail.

A traditional problem in message-based systems is *information overload* (Hiltz and Turoff 1985). It is a common experience in mature electronic message systems for users to feel flooded with large quantities of "junk" or useless information (Denning 1982; Palme 1984b), resulting in information overload. At this point the amount of information is so large and its rate of arrival sufficiently rapid that it makes it difficult for the user to utilize a large amount of the information that is directly relevant to him. Information overload has also been a central factor in the development of many cooperative message systems. To be effective systems must give message recipients the ability to discriminate easily between those messages they wish to read and those of little relevance to them.

As a direct result of their history, cooperative message systems are based upon concepts such as those identified in email systems and their associated standards. Consequently, a standard message interchange format is assumed. Cooperative message systems attempt to augment the structure of these standard message organizations to extend the amount of machine processible information available within the system.

A range of cooperative systems has emerged which exploits message-based technology. These structured message systems use either a formal model of control based on office procedures or speech act theory, or a philosophy of semi-automation, which adopts a more pragmatic model of control, providing support where appropriate.

1.1.1 Speech Act Systems

Speech act systems apply a linguistic approach to computer supported cooperation based on speech act theory (see also this volume, Chapter 8). This has developed from linguistics and considers language as a series of actions. For example statements such as "I pronounce you man and wife" are actions. Searle (1975) identifies five fundamental methods of interpreting such speech acts:

1. Assertive: commit the speaker to something being the case.
2. Directive: attempt to get the hearer to do something.
3. Commissive: commit the speaker to some future course of action.
4. Declaration: bring about the correspondence between the propositional content of the speech act (e.g. pronounce a couple married).
5. Expressive: express a psychological state about a situation.

Speech acts are elements within larger conversational structures (Flores and Ludlow 1981) which define the possible courses of action within a conversation between two actors. One class of conversational structure of direct relevance to cooperation is what Winograd and Flores (1986) term *conversations for action*. In such conversations an interplay of *directives* and *commissives* is directed towards explicit cooperative action. Winograd and Flores informally call directives and commissives *requests* and *promises*, respectively.

In a conversation for action, one party (A) makes a request to another (B). A's request has certain conditions of satisfaction, which describe a future course of actions for B. After the initial request B can:

1. Accept, and commit himself to satisfying the conditions.
2. Decline, and end the conversation.
3. Counter-offer, with alternative conditions.

Each of these in turn has its possible continuations. Winograd and Flores use graphs, similar to state transition diagrams, to plot the basic course of such a conversation (see Fig. 1.3).

Conversations for action represent only one possible form of conversation. Winograd and Flores distinguish several additional kinds of conversation which accompany conversations for action, including

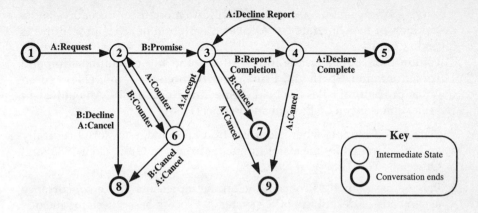

Fig. 1.3 A conversation for action.

conversations for clarification, *conversations for possibilities* and *conversations for orientation*. A further discussion of speech act theory is presented by Wastell and White in Chapter 8.

Speech act theory, as applied by Winograd and Flores, forms the basis for several computer systems and represents a fundamental area of research within cooperative working. Systems which make direct use of speech act theory include the Coordinator system developed by Winograd and Flores (Winograd 1987), XCP, a coordination system for supporting office procedures (Sluizer and Cashman 1984), and the CHAOS project (De Cindio et al. 1986), which is concerned with the use of speech act theory to support coordination within an office environment.

1.1.2 Office Procedure Systems

As Greif observes (1988), the research fields of office information systems and CSCW are similar. Both are interdisciplinary and strongly concerned with social and technical issues. As a result, office information systems have been a successful source of application for CSCW. However, as Wilson (1988) concludes, the terminology and approach used within office automation differs from that of the CSCW community. In the office automation community, the notion of group communication (as used within the messaging and CSCW communities) is replaced by the notion of *office procedures*. Office procedures describe tasks performed within an office in terms of the combined effect of a number of small subtasks or procedures and the information exchanged by them. Examples of procedures range from the well defined and understood (for example, invoicing) to less well defined tasks such as the generation and approval of an office budget. The cooperative research within office automation has concentrated on finding a unifying language that allows the specification of office procedures and a description of their interaction. A fuller description of office procedures is given in Chapter 8.

Within their paper on the interrelation of group communication and office automation, Speth and Prinz identify three main models based on how the procedural rules are held (Prinz and Speth 1987). An equivalent classification is given by Bracchi and Pernici (1984):

1. Data-based models where coordination knowledge is stored centrally and often routed by means of forms, for example, OBE (Zloof 1982) and Officetalk-Zero (Ellis and Nutt 1980).

2. Process-based models concentrate on the representation of concurrency as a means of describing office systems. Process-based systems include POISE (Croft and Lefkowitz 1984). This approach also appears as software process modelling within the software engineering community (see the IOPT project in Chapter 8).

3. Agent-based models apply artificial intelligence (AI) techniques such as goal-based planners and active agent models. Office tasks are modelled using known AI modelling techniques or systems and an inference engine is used to generate and execute task plans. Systems within this category include AMS (Tueni et al. 1988) and POLYMER (Croft and Lefkowitz 1988).

Office procedure systems rely on the use of a language to specify the office tasks, which is then used to coordinate cooperation within the office. Object-oriented languages have proven particularly amenable for this task, forming the basis of the early Officetalk-D system and the OTM system (Lochovsky et al. 1988).

Many of the systems which used procedural languages to describe office procedures found them unsatisfactory. As a result of this dissatisfaction, office automation systems have started to utilize AI technology. The POLYMER system, for example, has a task manager which uses an AI-based planner to execute actions and coordinate various interactions via an *execution monitor* to achieve the goals of the plan. This use of procedural languages to describe and control the cooperation by defining roles and activities is a common approach within cooperative message systems and has been adopted in the AMIGO (Danielson et al. 1986) and COSMOS (Gilbert, Chapter 4, this volume; Kirkwood et al., Chapter 11, this volume; Wilbur and Young 1988) projects.

1.1.3 Semi-structured Message Systems

Semi-formal or active message systems follow a philosophy of semi-automation, automating those parts of the system that are most amenable to computer support while leaving other parts manual in nature. Systems of this form provide mechanisms for automatic message handling and, more recently, support the concepts of roles and autonomous agents. The development of the Information Lens and its subsequent evolution into the Object Lens is illustrative of this class of system.

The Information Lens (Malone et al. 1986) is one of the primary examples of semi-formal cooperative message systems. The system represents a strand of research that aims at merging traditional message handling with classical AI techniques. Malone's primary concern within the Information Lens is the development of information systems that directly control the effects of information overload. As Hiltz and Turoff argue, effective systems must give message recipients the ability to discriminate between those messages they wish to read and those of little relevance to them (Hiltz and Turoff 1985). This is often achieved by imposing some structure on the set of messages a user receives, so that messages are categorized to allow the user to select those of interest.

As a result of several studies on how information is shared in organizations (Brobst et al. 1986), Malone developed the Information Lens. The Information Lens system emphasizes what Malone terms a cognitive approach to information sharing. Malone describes *cognitive filtering* as being the filtering of information based upon the topic or nature of the message. The system utilizes a number of techniques from AI, including frames, production rules and inheritance.

A number of key ideas form the basis of the system:

- Semi-structured message types (or frames) are used as the information model.

- Sets of production rules specify the automatic processing of messages.

- A consistent set of display-orientated editors are provided to the user.

- Inheritance within a frame lattice allows the specialization of message types.

In contrast to the approach adopted by either procedural systems or speech act systems, the Information Lens follows a more pragmatic semi-formal approach to group working by supporting automated distribution. Messages addressed to *anyone* as an addressee will be delivered via an automatic mail sorter (Fig. 1.4).

For each message type, the system includes a template with a number of fields for holding information. Associated with each field are several properties, including the default value, a list of possible alternative values, and a comment explaining the field. Users amend the values of fields within a template by the use of a display-orientated editor. The message templates are arranged in an inheritance hierarchy. The more general message types are at the top of the hierarchy and the more specific types at the base of the hierarchy, inheriting properties from those above them.

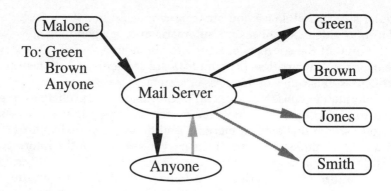

Fig. 1.4 The logical arrangement of the Information Lens. Messages that include Anyone as an addressee are automatically distributed to all receivers whose interest profiles select the messages as well as to the other explicit addressees (black arrows).

The Lens environment allows users to construct rules for finding, filtering and storing messages. Rules consist of a test (the IF part) and an action (the THEN part). If a message satisfies the test, the action specified by the rule is performed on the message. A display-orientated editor is also used for the construction of these rules.

Construction of the IF part of a rule involves filling in selection specifications for the different message fields. Specifications consist of a number of tests on the contents of a message field combined using *and*, *or* and *not* operators. If specifications appear in more than one field, then all specifications must be satisfied for the rule to succeed. The THEN part of the rule is chosen from one of a number of message handling primitives, including move, delete, save, reply etc.

Malone subsequently enhanced the work on the Information Lens to produce a more general system called the Object Lens (Malone and Lai 1988). The Object Lens has generalized the message form objects of the Information Lens to allow the construction of arbitrary objects within an *object store*. In addition to the specialization found in the Information Lens, users can construct general relationships between objects through the use of object links. Malone argues that this capability is akin to the facilities provided by current hypertext systems.

The Object Lens allows the capture of active rules as a set of *semi-autonomous agents*. Semi-autonomous agents within the Object Lens are objects which consist of a set of rules that are obeyed when an agent is *triggered*. Agents can be triggered by events such as the arrival of new mail, at a particular time or explicitly by another agent. Malone views the Object Lens as a cooperative application generator system embodying many of the principles found in hypertext, object-oriented systems and rule-based agents. The system has been used successfully to generate a range of CSCW applications including Answer Garden, a system for holding organizational

Table 1.1 Message-based systems and their form of control

Research project	Type of system	Representation
Coordinator (Winograd 1987)	Speech act	Network
Object Lens (Maloney and Lai 1988)	Semi-structured	Production rules
Chaos (De Cindio et al. 1986)	Speech act	Network
Domino (Kreifelts and Woetzel 1986)	Procedural system	Script-based
Cosmos (Wilbur and Young 1988)	Augmented procedural system	Script-based
Amigo (Danielson et al. 1986)	Augmented procedural system	Script-based
Strudel (Shepherd et al. 1990)	Semi-structured	Production rules

expertise (Ackerman and Malone 1990), and SIBYL, a system for representing design rationale (Lee 1990).

A wide range of message-based systems exist, each exhibiting different forms of support for cooperative working. A number of more prominent message-based cooperative systems are listed in Table 1.1, which lists both the type of system and the representation mechanisms used to support and control cooperation within each system.

1.2 Information Sharing

An alternative approach to developing CSCW systems has been by considering the sharing of information between users, and developing mechanisms to support this sharing. In this form of cooperative system, users interact through a shared information space, as shown in Fig. 1.5. This

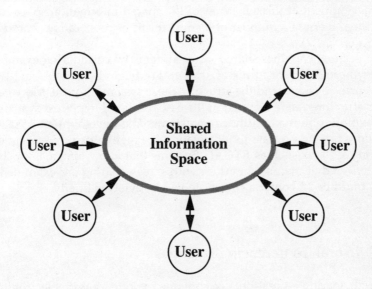

Fig. 1.5 Interaction in shared information systems.

Table 1.2 Different classes of shared cooperative system

Type of information	The form of interaction	
	Asynchronous	Synchronous
Textual	Textural conferencing and multi-user hypertext	Real-time conferencing
Multimedia		Desktop systems and multimedia systems

model of interaction is often augmented by the use of direct user-to-user communication. This communication is normally provided by either electronic message systems of the form described in the previous section or by the use of an audio or video connection such as those exploited in multimedia conferencing systems (see Section 1.2.5).

This model of cooperation has been exploited within a wide range of cooperative systems. These information sharing systems have emerged depending on two principal characteristics of the shared information space:

1. The form of interaction with the shared information space. Users can interact with the shared conference space either asynchronously over a long time period or synchronously in a real-time manner.

2. The type of information represented in the information space. Many forms of information may be represented in the shared information space. In the past this information has been textual, but with the advent of modern workstations an increasing range of media can be represented.

The development of these features of the shared information space has led to the emergence of a number of distinct forms of cooperative shared space system (Table 1.2).

This section examines shared space systems by considering examples of each of these different forms of system. We begin by considering textual conferencing systems and the structure these systems impose. More general shared structures are examined in the case of shared hypertext systems and their exploitation in co-authoring systems. The development of facilities that allow real-time access to information are highlighted by real-time conferencing systems such as RTCAL. Systems that allow information sharing to be reflected at the user interface with screen sharing are examined, and finally multimedia conferencing systems are reviewed briefly.

1.2.1 Textual Conferencing Facilities

Although sharing a great deal of common experience with electronic message systems, computer conferencing systems developed independently, and were first envisaged in the early 1970s. During the Nixon administration, the Office of Emergency Preparedness (OEP) in the USA commissioned Murray Turoff to create a computerized version of the teleconferencing facilities in use at that time. Turoff responded by developing the Emergency Management Information System and Reference Index (EMISARI).

The EMISARI system operated as an electronic network linking the ten OEP regional offices, and eliminated the constraints of time and geographic location (Hiltz and Turoff 1978). EMISARI consisted of two systems: *Party-Line*, the computerized counterpart of the telephone conference call, and *Discussion*, an on-line file cabinet of topic-specific messages stored on-line for all to see and comment on.

A typical computer conferencing system consists of a number of groups called conferences, each of which has a set of members and a sequence of messages. Conferences are usually arranged so that individual conferences address a single topic. A user subscribes to those conferences that are of interest to him. Usually the system stores information about how far every member has read in each conference. This makes it possible for the system to tell users which messages are new to them when they connect to the system.

For example, a user may subscribe to conferences on computers, information processing and music. When the user initiates a conference session, he is presented with a list of the conferences to which he belongs, and the number of messages in each, for example:

12 unseen entries in Computers

9 unseen entries in Information Processing

6 unseen entries in Music

Any replies to a message within a conference are shown to other users belonging to that conference. Each conference is controlled by a conference leader, who organizes and administers general conference book-keeping. The use of conferencing structures is analogous to participating in several simultaneous conversations, each conversation having its own pre-defined topic. The full arrangement of conference topics, entries and replies is shown schematically in Fig. 1.6.

Textual computer conferencing systems are an extension of bulletin boards, which have developed from early email systems. Bulletin board systems typically offer a fixed set of topics, which can be adjusted only by system administrators. Also, new comments are simply appended to the end of the topic, with no facility to link related comments.

Conferencing systems offer more flexibility in generating new conferences and organizing comments within a conference. The system provides a mechanism to learn about conferences, which allows people to interact with others who have common interests and experiences. Most conferencing

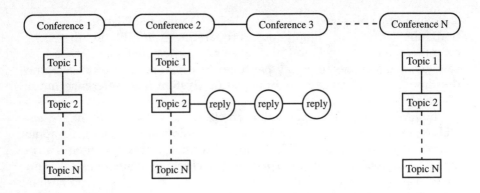

Fig. 1.6 Textual conference structures. (*Source:* Winograd and Flores (1986) The basic conversation for action. In: Understanding Computers and Cognition. Ablex, Norwood, NJ, USA, p 55. Reprinted with permission.)

systems offer facilities for monitoring changes to conferences and for searching conference comments according to criteria such as date, author and keyword.

As part of a move to improve communication and cooperation among geographically separate groups of engineers, Hewlett-Packard in 1984 investigated computer conferencing (Fanning and Raphael 1986). After consideration of the available systems (including those above) Hewlett-Packard selected and observed the use of one such system (CONFER) within its organization. The observations derived from the Hewlett-Packard experience highlight the problems associated with supporting groups using computer conferencing systems.

The most significant influences on computer conferencing were either human or environmental rather than technological. The single factor with the highest correlation with the success of an individual conference was the *activity level* of the conference's leader. Other factors that influenced a conference's success or failure included:

- *Appropriateness of discussion topics.* Choosing the remit of a conference's topics represents a considerable problem. Topics need to be sufficiently restrictive to prevent a conference wandering, but sufficiently general to include all users' comments and interests.

- *Overload and pruning.* Hewlett-Packard found their user community produced a lot of text. As a result, a new conference participant could easily spend days reading the text of some conferences. Consequently, the conference system's administrators were forced to adopt harsh pruning measures (with a subsequent loss of information) to avoid discouraging new participants. This issue is also discussed by Newman in Chapter 7 of this volume.

1.2.2 Multi-user Hypertext

Multi-user hypertext systems are a significant development from the rigid structure offered by textual conferencing systems. The term *hypertext* describes any system employing nonlinear structuring of text, graphics and other media. Hypertext systems normally form linked network structures, with data (usually text or graphics) in the nodes and occasionally typing information on the links (see Conklin, 1987 for an overview of hypertext systems). Hypertext documents resemble nets of connected nodes with each link between nodes denoting an association between the information held in the nodes.

Hypertext systems are successful in structuring information in such a manner that the user's ability to process it is enhanced (Marchionini and Schneiderman 1988). Within multi-user hypertext systems, the hypertext document (or network) is constructed by a number of users adding nodes to the network in an independent manner. However, the provision of tools which deal explicitly with the interaction arising in collaborative hypertext settings is relatively recent.

In existing hypertext systems all users make changes within a shared storage system. This situation results in numerous conflicts when several authors are collaborating on the production of a document. Current hypertext systems provide inadequate support for the resolution of these conflicts. Delisle and Schwartz (1986) enumerate these deficiencies:

- *Limited organization*: a collaborative environment should provide a means of organizing related sets of hypertext nodes and links. For example, a set may contain all the nodes and links that comprise a specific document.

- *Lack of partitioning*: there should be some mechanism that allows teams of authors to work together in independent hypertext partitions without risk of interference, and then to allow those independent partitions to be joined at carefully controlled intervals.

- *Little version and configuration control*: users should have the ability to build version trees and subsequently install specific branches as the primary version. In addition, some form of configuration management support, allowing configurations to be built and used, should be provided.

- *Lack of distribution*: the hypertext database should be distributed to support large teams collaborating on a common project.

Delisle attempted to provide a mechanism that is powerful enough to support a variety of users, resolving the above problems, while remaining conceptually simple. Called *Contexts*, this mechanism is based on the principle that users have a private view of a hypertext graph and may make modifications within this view. When alterations are completed, they can be released to other project team members by merging the user's private view (*context*) with the shared *master* view. Other systems following this line of development, each with their own individual peculiarities, include Intermedia (Garret et al. 1986) and NoteCards (Trigg et al. 1986). Many other chapters in this book discuss the issue of private versus public views of information and, in the context of collaborative writing, Chapters 4, 5 and 6 discuss some of the problems associated with merging these views. Benest and Dukić in Chapter 9 discuss this issue in some detail, and offer some example solutions.

1.2.2.1 Hypertext in Use: Co-authoring with Quilt

Many co-authoring systems apply the principles of hypertext technology in a cooperative setting. The Quilt system (Fish et al. 1988) developed at Bell Communications is representative of the general principles used by most co-authoring systems. A document in Quilt consists of a base and nodes linked to the base using hypertext techniques. The aim is that these nodes act in a similar way to paper notes, "Post-its" and marginal comments in paper documents.

The general principle of cooperation in Quilt, as in most co-authoring systems, is that the users read a publicly available document, annotating the document to reflect their comments. At any time a Quilt comment network will consist of:

1. A current base document consisting of the text and other materials the authors consider publicly available.

2. Revision suggestions, which are available in a form where users with appropriate permissions can swap existing document paragraphs.

3. Comments with an associated set of permissions which in turn distinguishes them to be one of three different types of comment:

   a. Private comment, visible only to the creator.

   b. Public comment, can be read by anyone with permission to read the parent.

   c. Directed message, whose existence is displayed only to named individuals or groups. Directed messages may make use of a notation facility to inform users of their existence.

The principles employed in Quilt as a co-authoring system are mirrored by those found in other co-authoring systems, including the Co-Author system at Passau (Hahn et al. 1991). The premise is that each node within the graph can be one of a number of types, reflecting the kind of comment being made. The process of generating comments from an original document consists of a number of authors and reviewers constructing a hypertext network for these typed nodes reflecting their comments.

1.2.3 Real-Time Conferencing Systems

Computer conferencing systems and multi-user hypertext traditionally address asynchronous interaction among users. However Sarin and Greif (1985) outline a number of areas, such as crisis management, where synchronous communication is necessary. Several of the current conferencing systems provide rudimentary real-time support by providing text-based real-time communication between users.

A prototype conferencing system that highlights the principles of real-time conferencing was developed by Greif at MIT. The prototype, RTCAL (Real Time CALender), provides computer support for the scheduling of meetings by building a shared workspace of information from participants' on-line calendars. The shared workspace is displayed in real-time to users in conjunction with their own *personal* calendar. While RTCAL provides users with information and tools for decision support, it does not automate the selection of a meeting time. RTCAL demonstrates a number of features applicable to most real-time conferencing systems:

- Shared and private views which allow information to be visible to either a single user or the whole user community.

- The alignment of related information between a user's shared and private views to be displayed appropriately.

- An on-line voting scheme lets users express their opinions on a number of proposals (see also Chapters 6 and 9, this volume, for further discussion on voting systems).

- Participant autonomy gives participants the ability to act independently of the user community.

- A number of conference distinct roles are provided, in particular a *chairperson* oversees all activity in the conference, determining who has the *floor* at any given time. Only the person given the floor has control over shared views. Similar roles are suggested in many of the other chapters in this book, although given different names (for example, "host" in Chapter 4, " director" in Chapter 5 and Diaper's "honest broker" in Chapter 6) and involving slightly different functionality.

- Status information regarding the conference topic, its participants, who the chairperson is, and who currently has control is displayed as a public view to all participants.

- Two types of command exist: those relating to conference control, for example requesting the floor, and those concerned with applications, for example the local editing of information.

Although RTCAL demonstrates some general principles of real-time conferencing it supports only a specific application area. The development of workstation technology combined with high bandwidth communications has led to the emergence of a particular class of real-time conferencing system called desktop conferencing. These systems allow both whole screens and window contents to be displayed and manipulated by more than one workstation.

1.2.4 Desktop Conferencing

The merging of workstation technology and real-time computer conferencing has had a significant impact on CSCW. This merging has been termed *desktop conferencing*, an integral part of which is the use of *multi-user interfaces*. Lauwers and Lantz (1990) outline two approaches for the development of multi-user interfaces. The first approach suggested is the development of special-purpose applications, which are *collaboration aware*.

The second approach that can be taken is to provide facilities that allow existing single-user applications to be shared between users in a *collaboration-transparent* manner. Examples of projects which take this approach include Vconf (Lantz 1986), SharedX (Gust 1988), Conference Desk (Piccardi and Tisato 1989) and MMConf (Crowley et al. 1990).

The most generally applied model of a shared window system is shown in Fig. 1.7. The role of the conference agent is to multiplex the output from the shared applications onto the users' workstations and to route the input from the users to the appropriate applications.

1.2.4.1 *Shared Windows and Protocol Splitters*

The development of *cooperation-transparent* synchronous systems relies upon exploiting the nature of network windowing systems such as X-windows (Scheifler and Gettys 1986) or NeWS (Sun Microsystems 1987).

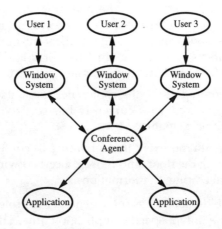

Fig. 1.7 A shared window model.

The basic technique is to insert a "protocol-splitter" between the clients (the applications) and the servers (the user display) within the window system's client–server architecture. This approach is best thought of as broadcasting the output from a client to a number of servers (Fig. 1.8a). The inputs from a range of servers are then multiplexed to drive the applications (Fig. 1.8b). The normal practice is for one of the servers to be allowed to send events to the application at any one time. This server is normally referred to as having "control of the floor".

Each display server has control of the local layout and placement of windows. As well as the I/O control necessary for the sharing of applications, the central conference agent software is also often responsible for:

- *Floor control*: controlling the input from users to allow input to come from the user who is currently authorized to input for a particular application. This is analogous to passing the pen for the board during a meeting.

- *Workspace management*: the layout, placement and grouping of shared windows is controlled within the shared workspace by the conference agent. The allows alterations and changes to the layout to be reflected in other users' workstations.

- *Dynamic reconfiguration*: the addition of new users and the early departure of existing users is the responsibility of the conference agent. Each addition or departure necessitates reconfiguration of the system.

- *Secretarial functions*: the setting up of conferences, the initialization of appropriate systems and the recording and logging of conferences are often provided by the conference agent.

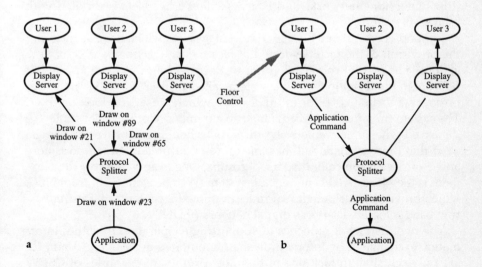

Fig. 1.8 a Broadcasting requests; b routing events from servers.

1.2.5 Multimedia Conferencing

A further trend in cooperative systems is the emergence of systems that aim to support synchronous cooperation in a manner which unifies both remote and co-located users. These systems combine the shared screen facilities provided in real-time conferencing systems with video and audio communication services.

An example is the Rapport multimedia conferencing system (Ahuja et al. 1988). Rapport is illustrative of a number of current systems that exploit multimedia and real-time facilities. These systems, like most interactive real-time conferencing facilities, are currently limited by technology to supporting locally remote groups. Locally remote groups are those which, although demonstrating many of the working practices of geographically distributed groups, exist within one organization or site.

The Rapport multimedia system was developed at AT&T Bell Laboratories in New Jersey. The current system supports interactive, real-time distributed conferences among two or more users. Rapport helps users to participate in meetings without leaving their offices by the provision of *virtual meeting rooms*. This perspective highlights important characteristics of face-to-face meetings that have been reproduced in the Rapport conference environment. Rapport also supports the conventional telephone service within its conferencing framework and allows application programs to execute within a conference.

A single cluster prototype of Rapport has been implemented using a network of Sun workstations connected by both an Ethernet and a voice network. The custom voice network provides call control and conferencing facilities similar to those provided by existing private branch exchange (PBX) telephone networks and is accessible via headsets associated with each workstation.

Rapport is typical of a number of recent systems which have as their aim the provision of the facilities found at face-to-face meetings within remote groups. The virtual room metaphor of Rapport has also been applied at Bellcore in the development of a system called Cruiser (Root 1988). Cruiser provides a virtual corridor of offices into which a user can look or enter. The system provides multimedia links to a number of offices, which may be displayed when a user enters an office. As technology improves it is envisaged that these systems will become more widespread and support more and more geographically dispersed groups. One example of this development is the MERMAID conferencing system (Watabe et al. 1990) from NEC, which provides distributed, real-time, multimedia conferencing using narrow-band integrated services digital network (ISDN).

The two distinct approaches of supporting cooperation by either information exchange or by information sharing outlined in Sections 1.1 and 1.2 are not exclusive. In fact, one of the most prominent examples of CSCW represents the merging of information sharing and informal face-to-face communication. These systems focus on providing computer support for co-located meetings and are considered within Section 1.3, on electronic meeting systems.

1.3 Electronic Meeting Systems

The support of face-to-face cooperation represents the most recent and distinct research development in CSCW. Chapter 10 of this volume provides a detailed description of one specialized multimedia face-to-face meeting system. A typical approach to this form of support is to develop a meeting room furnished with a large-screen video projector and a number of computer workstation/terminals. Often these systems include a control terminal. A typical meeting room arrangement is shown in Fig. 1.9.

Most systems that employ meeting rooms to support cooperation among local groups have developed from a class of systems know as *decision conferences*. Decision conferences are related to earlier decision support systems (Ariav and Ginzberg 1985), but focus on improving decision making by groups rather than individuals. Decision conferences emphasize the use of structured decision processes, mainly involving statistical computer models but increasingly utilizing models that embody collaborative notions.

A number of decision conferences have been developed, both in industry and in university research centres. In industry, systems include the Group Decision Aid of Perceptronics Inc. (Steeb and Johnston 1981) and the Decision Conference of Decision and Designs Inc. (Patterson et al. 1981). In universities, decision conferences include the various electronic meeting rooms at the University of Arizona (Nunamaker et al. 1991). A fundamental

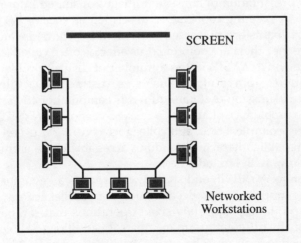

Fig. 1.9 A typical meeting room arrangement.

principle of electronic meeting systems like decision laboratories is the emphasis on models of interactions, which coordinate group activities.

A discussion of group discussion support systems (GDSS) and decision conferences is given by Kraemer and Kling (1988), who identified a number of functions that group decision systems can provide. Kraemer and Kling identify the following software elements as being important to the construction of decision conferences:

- Decision analysis software
- Modelling software
- Voting tally
- Display software

The collaborative laboratory (CoLab) (Stefik et al. 1987a) at Xerox PARC represents a move away from the reliance on quantitative models exhibited by more traditional meeting room systems. CoLab does not incorporate formal decision models and quantitative techniques. Rather it supports writing and argumentation using verbal models and qualitative techniques through the manipulation of text and graphical images.

Physically, CoLab consists of bitmapped workstations communicating over a local area network, and a shared electronic display which allows the flexible placement of text and figures.

The developers of CoLab state that "a fundamental requirement for meeting tools is that they provide a co-ordinated interface for all participants". CoLab achieves this aim by the utilization of a multi-user interface based on an abstraction they call WYSIWIS (what you see is what I see). In fact, CoLab was one of the forerunners in the development of the shared screen technology described in the previous section. The term WYSIWIS refers to the presentation of consistent images of shared information to all participants. A meeting tool can be described as *strictly WYSIWIS* if all meeting participants are presented with identical views, including indication of where the others are pointing (this effect is often called *telepointing*).

In practice, strict WYSIWIS has a number of distinct problems. The display of cursors from multiple users is distracting, while the small granularity transmission of data required is computationally expensive. To combat these problems CoLab uses a relaxed version of WYSIWIS (Stefik et al. 1987b). For example, Stefik and colleagues consider it useful to differentiate between public interactive windows accessible to the entire group and private windows with limited access.

In addition to WYSIWIS and shared workspaces, a key issue in meeting tool design is supporting parallel activities. For parallel actions, a task must be broken up into appropriately sized operations that can be performed independently by different group members. In addition to allowing parallel activities, meeting tools must be aware of conflict and provide some form of conflict resolution between parallel actions.

Previous meeting systems have tended to be developed as purpose-built meeting rooms, which have been expensive to construct and maintain. In contrast, more recent systems, such as those developed at the University of Arizona, have tended to exploit personal computers with low-cost local networking capabilities. A full examination of the various characteristics of electronic meeting systems is outside the scope of this chapter, and readers are referred to Nunamaker et al. (1991) for a complete overview of the issues surrounding electronic meeting systems.

1.4 Summary

This chapter has highlighted the different technological approaches to supporting cooperation. It began by examining the different systems derived from electronic message systems and the different forms of cooperative system which emerged from this technology. The nature and form of control within message-based systems highlights three different classes of cooperative message system: speech act systems, procedural systems and semi-structured systems.

The approach adopted by the more "formal" message systems such as speech act and procedure-based systems is to attempt to capture the cooperation taking place. In contrast, semi-structured systems aim merely to provide support for cooperating users by alleviating those tasks that inhibit effective group work. These systems do not attempt either to automate or even to represent the cooperation taking place.

An alternative technological approach to supporting cooperation has been to focus on the sharing of information and providing facilities to structure this sharing to support cooperation effectively. This approach provides a wide diversity of different classes of cooperative system, depending on the nature of the shared information and facilities provided to structure this information. Most notable examples of information sharing systems include various forms of computer conferencing and multi-user hypertext systems.

Information sharing systems assume the existence of a number of communication channels surrounding the shared information. The most striking example of this is in the case of electronic meeting rooms, where the informal exchange of information in face-to-face communication is central to the success of the system. Electronic meeting systems and the construction of purpose-built meeting rooms represent a recent trend in CSCW systems, which is likely to change many of the existing views of meetings.

CSCW, like many research areas centred on the application of computer technology, is influenced by the development of previous technologies and systems. This is reflected in the use of essentially technical classifications in the examination of CSCW systems. Successful CSCW will require the merging of these technical viewpoints with insights gained from other disciplines on the essentially human nature of cooperation.

Chapter 2

User Interfaces for CSCW Systems

J. Brooke

We are only just beginning to come to terms with the fact that users of computer systems are individuals, and that they may wish to do their jobs in ways that don't quite fit with the collections of functional services and user interface styles known as "applications" dreamt up by software developers. The potential of Computer Supported Cooperative Work (CSCW) systems to place the user into even more rigid technological straitjackets has to be viewed with considerable unease, since the whole history of the development of computer systems points to technology, rather than the needs of the user, calling the shots. Studies of early examples of CSCW systems have shown that they don't work well if they can't be adapted to fit the prevailing style of working in an organization (e.g. Carasik and Grantham 1988).

If cooperative working using computer systems is to succeed, it is important to ensure that systems support the user, rather than impose rules and ways of working on them. The type of support that such systems should provide includes:

- Allowing each individual to access shared functions and information in their own preferred fashion.

- Facilitating the exchange of information and ways of working between individuals.

- Allowing evolutionary development and dissemination of working practices and support mechanisms.

2.1 Introduction

For some considerable time, the basic model of computer usage has been of
the individual user, either with a "personal" computer or with a personal
"account" on a shared system. Paradoxically, users have typically had little
choice in this personal environment about the way in which they actually
use the system; the functions available to them and the style of interacting
with the computer has been determined by some third party, usually the
application developer. The result of this has been that there is a poor infrastructure for building systems that support cooperative working. In this
chapter I explore some of the issues that this raises, and its implications for
constructing interfaces for CSCW systems. Such implications are also discussed by Hewitt and Gilbert (Chapter 3) and Kirkwood et al. (Chapter 11).
Rosenberg and Hutchison are also preparing a book in this series on
"Design Issues in CSCW" (Rosenberg and Hutchison 1993).

2.2 The "Personal" Model of Computing

The "personal" computer or computer account has effectively built a wall
around the user. Getting information over this wall, both inwards and out-
wards, is a major (though not the only) reason why computer systems that
are currently available fail to be appropriate to the needs and requirements
of their users.

2.2.1 Mine, All Mine – But Do I Want It?

The "personal wall" has many effects. It places barriers to the free flow of
information between cooperating individuals. For instance, one need only
look at the difficulties experienced by managers and secretaries who are
trying to make the transition from a paper mail system to an electronic mail
(email) system to realize that the benefits of electronic communication are
at least counterbalanced by what is lost in the social processes that have
developed over years. In the paper mail world, the secretary acts as a first-
line filter of messages, deciding which are important, which can be dealt
with without ever going to the manager, which can be consigned straight to
the bin. In addition, the process of filtering this mail allows the secretary to
monitor what information the manager is receiving, thus allowing greater
synergy between the two as a team. (The issues of social processes are variously discussed in many of this book's other chapters. Gilbert (Chapter 4),
Sharples (Chapter 5) and Diaper (Chapter 6), in particular, discuss the
evolution and management of such processes).

Most computing environments do not support this, because they assume
that the place where mail, like any other information, "lives" is within the

bounds of the personal wall; thus the secretary cannot gain access to the messages without gaining access to the rest of the information owned by the manager. Managers have the choice of either allowing the secretary free access to all the information that they "own", or of using some other method of storing and maintaining information which is for their use only, and not to be seen by the secretary.

Add to this the bland uniformity of email messages – electronic junk mail has none of the tell-tale marks that allow you to detect paper junk mail without even opening it – and you are left with a system in which the additional speed of communication is no compensation for the increased volume of messages coupled with lesser scope for filtering. (Naturally, the technologist's response to this is to try to build yet more tools: see Rodden, Chapter 1, this volume).

2.2.2 Throwing Information Over the Wall

In more general terms, the personal wall makes it difficult for any user to share information and data with others. In a typical system, especially those where the "personal wall" also maps to the physical limit of a personal computer or workstation, which may or may not be connected to a network, sharing usually means either finding some way of transporting it to the intended recipient in some other personal domain using a medium such as email, or a physical medium such as copying a disk – but there is no guarantee that the recipient will be able to receive or to use material transported in this way. Even where several users are using a shared resource such as a timeshared system or clustered computers, where there is a reasonably predictable environment in terms of the capabilities available, facilities for granting access to data are complicated and limited, often operating at the level of granting access to people from a group, rather than to individuals on a per-need basis.

2.2.3 It's Yours; You Look After It

The "personal wall" model of computing has other consequences that act against the ability of the individual to get on and use the system for the purposes for which it was intended. For instance, every user of a personal computer is, by and large, also the system manager for that computer. The user is responsible for the integrity of data and the availability of applications on that machine. Even the user of an account on a timeshared system has to do a certain amount of looking after the information they "own" because it resides in their account and is thus assumed to be their responsibility. This means that time must be spent doing things that are peripheral to the job in hand, and not doing them well because it's not their job. Similarly, Benest and Dukić in Chapter 9 refer to people's "implied self-managing role".

2.3 Applications versus Appropriate Systems

As pointed out above, despite the fact that the "personal" model of computing persists, there is actually very little personalization of the applications available and the way in which one interacts with them once one gets within the boundaries of the wall.

2.3.1 Software as Product

The software industry is an outgrowth of the hardware industry, by and large, and sees much of software as discrete "products" or "applications". If one takes a product-orientated approach to building software, then several things arise as a consequence. One is that in order to make money from producing software, one must sell as many units of product as possible. Inevitably, this means that any product must have as broad an appeal as possible; therefore it must be used by a wide range of people, for a variety of different jobs, and in as many environments as possible. The net result of this is the generic software application, that has the potential to do many different things for many different people, but is not necessarily a good fit to any of the particular contexts in which it may be used. The typical product of the software industry, thus, is the "spreadsheet" rather than "the program for making an expense claim following the procedures of the Acme Tool Co. Ltd".

As Sharples suggests in the context of collaborative writing, "The problem with [such] programs ... is that they lead to *premature commitment...* . They require users to commit themselves to courses of action ... when they may not have a rational basis for making the decision, or may prefer to leave the options open" (Chapter 5, this volume). In consequence, in order to apply a tool to a job, the user has to modify his way of working to fit the tool, rather than being able to employ a tool tailored to his style of working.

Whereas Gilbert makes the traditional suggestion that: "it would be desirable for users to configure the system to suit their changing needs" (Chapter 4, this volume), we have argued elsewhere (Barrett and Brooke 1989; Brooke 1991) that to build appropriate systems for the end user one must move away from the model of generic applications to one where it is possible rapidly to build "virtual applications", which are tailored to a particular context – that is, a particular user, or well-defined group of users, doing a particular job in a particular environment. We have also argued that it is extremely important to recognize that the context of user, task and environment is in a state of continual change, so the virtual application must also be capable of change in order to remain appropriate to the context.

2.4 CSCW: Imposition of Common Methods of Working or Facilitation of Cooperative Working?

Let us now consider CSCW systems. It rapidly becomes apparent that the problems outlined above of the "personal wall" and of the need to build highly customized and adaptable systems that are appropriate to the context both have some bearing on ways of building CSCW systems that are likely to succeed or to fail. Both Kirkwood et al. (Chapter 11) and Wastell and White (Chapter 8) provide examples of such failures.

2.4.1 Access to Shared Information: Each to His Own

The personal wall model of computing obviously needs to be rethought when building CSCW systems. The examples given above indicate why this is important. However, once one starts to consider a computing environment in which data and information resources are shared, then one must consider that just because people have access to the same data, they may not necessarily want to access it or manipulate it in the same way. This may be because they are performing different jobs as part of the overall task; for example a secretary may set up the agenda for a meeting system, whereas participants at the meeting may only want to read the minutes and respond to action items. It may be that they have different hardware environments with different capabilities – one person has a high resolution graphics workstation while another has only a character-cell terminal. Different people may be accessing the same information from different physical environments (e.g. one person is accessing it via a workstation in the office while another needs to access it via the phone from an airport departure lounge). Alternatively, a single individual may access the shared information for different purposes from different environments at different stages in some particular cooperative task. Wastell and White (Chapter 8) provide an example of the different roles of different personnel in the context of a medical CSCW system.

2.4.2 Cooperation: My Way

The ability to allow different people to map their preferred way of working on to the underlying shared data does not necessarily square well with the approach taken by some CSCW applications, which embody particular theories of how people work together (or ought to work together), and which try to impose rational structures on the way people use the system, with the intention of improving the quality of cooperation between participants in a task. The value of using such systems is, however, not easily demonstrable. Carasik and Grantham (1988), for example, reported that attempting to apply one of the early CSCW tools (the Coordinator) to an existing organization failed, primarily because the way of working assumed by the tool did not map well on to the way that people actually worked (see also Sharples, Chapter 5 and Wastell and White, Chapter 8).

While it may be possible to use CSCW tools as agents for change, basing your design on the assumption that people will change their working practices to fit your tool seems to be building a house on sand. While it is recognized, particularly in the task analysis literature (e.g. Benyon 1992; Diaper 1987, 1989; Diaper and Addison 1992) that current work practices are partly determined by the technology associated with current tasks, there is no guaranteed means of controlling or designing how new technologies will modify existing working practices. Thus, while the waters of time and usage may turn sand to concrete, we generally cannot predict the shape of the foundations that result. This leads Gilbert to suggest that systems need to be flexible so as to accommodate changing user needs, and for Sharples to suggest that there are "good reasons for not rushing to invent or use sophisticated (CSCW) programs".

Equally, of course, one should realize that if one tries to modify organizations and the processes used within organizations, then the technology used must support the organization and its processes; all too often, the existence of a particular technology acts as a brake on organizational change. Organizations, processes and technology are all highly interdependent.

2.4.3 Piling Complexity upon Complexity

It seems reasonable to assume that, given a task of a particular level of complexity, developing an application to enable people to cooperate on that task will necessarily be more complex than developing an application for a single person to perform the task, because the application must include functions for shared access or transmission of information between individuals, and there must be some level of "social" control built into the application (e.g. locking a particular item in a code management system when an individual has reserved it). If the temptation with CSCW applications is not only to produce generic functionality that allows many different people to do many different things in different environments, but also to layer on top of that further complexity in the form of the "cooperative" functions then the likelihood is that CSCW applications will finish up as exceedingly complex applications. Such increases in the complexity of

CSCW systems compared to single-user systems are also discussed by Hewitt and Gilbert in Chapter 3 and by Kirkwood et al. in Chapter 11. Since one of the major problems perceived with the usability of systems is that they are already excessively complex (e.g. see Business Week 1991), this bodes ill for the potential usability of CSCW applications.

2.4.4 Groups Change As Well As Individuals

As we have stressed elsewhere (Barrett and Brooke 1989; Brooke 1991), the only constant thing is change. In earlier papers, we have addressed the issue of change as it affects the individual user of computer systems.

However, change affects groups of users as well. For any cooperative working system to be effective it must be capable of allowing new work practices, new organizational structures and new individuals to participate in the process. There must also be effective ways of communicating such changes to the people involved in the cooperative task: it's no good one person unilaterally deciding to change the way they are going to perform their part of the task without communicating that to others and either allowing them to modify their work practices in turn, or veto the change. (Diaper, in Chapter 6, provides an example of how roles and working practices changed over time in a group editing a paper collaboratively using email.)

It is therefore critical that CSCW systems should allow not only the modification of ways of working, but also that they should facilitate dissemination of such changes among those people affected by them.

2.5 Implications for CSCW Interfaces

The construction of successful CSCW interfaces, therefore, is likely to depend on a number of things. The first of these is open to debate, but my personal bias is that CSCW systems should facilitate cooperation between individuals, rather than impose methods of working on them. Systems are far more likely to be acceptable and accepted if they do not cause a complete dislocation of the status quo.

Secondly, designers of CSCW systems should be striving to construct many small, interrelated applications, rather than building monolithic applications which encompass the whole spectrum of tasks that go to make up cooperative work in any particular sphere. The little applications that can be "bolted together" to make up a larger task should be capable of being adapted to the specific needs of the individual who is performing them, and to the environment in which they are carrying out the task.

Thirdly, information to be used in cooperative working needs to be taken out of the limits of the "personal wall". Cooperative working means common access to information, on a needs-driven basis. CSCW systems will never be successful while they continue to make information the property and responsibility of single individuals.

Finally, CSCW systems should recognize that change is the order of the day, and that they must be capable of allowing for redefinition of procedures and processes, and of disseminating these changes to all those individuals who are working together.

These factors may make it more difficult to build CSCW systems. However, the author, for one, is certain that if they are ignored, then CSCW, like many other technologies before it such as expert systems and hypertext (e.g. see Diaper 1992), will merely be a passing fad and will not endure.

Chapter *3*

Groupware Interfaces

B. Hewitt and G.N. Gilbert

... that we view those (knowledge and skills) of the prospective users of the technology as central, and that we incorporate into the design process as sophisticated an understanding of the social world as the technology involved ..." (Suchman 1988)

To help the interface designer take account of human capacities and skills, a number of guidelines for user interface design have been formulated, and there is now a general consensus about the desirability of abiding by these guidelines. However, the guidelines were formulated with "single-user" systems in mind; that is, for systems where the user interacts *with* the computer. Recently, there have been a number of experiments with and designs for systems that are intended to support computer-mediated communication, that is, where the user interacts with other users *through* the computer (e.g. Crowley et al. 1990; Patterson et al. 1990; Watabe et al. 1990). Such systems aim to support synchronous group working (see Chapter 1), where each user is linked to others through a computer network and possibly through audio and video channels. Brooke (Chapter 2) discusses the issues concerning the design of single-users versus systems for group working in more detail.

In this chapter, we examine whether the standard guidelines for user interfaces are applicable to such "groupware" systems, and identify additional issues to which groupware interface designers need to attend. In Section 3.1, we briefly review a core set of single-user guidelines. In Section 3.2, we elaborate those guidelines for groupware interfaces, and then we discuss two further guidelines applicable primarily to groupware.

3.1 Some Standard Interface Design Guidelines

As the design of computer systems has become more user-centred, the interface has become more attuned to non-programming users (Grudin 1990a). This has led to the development of manuals and standards for application builders to use when designing interfaces. Typical examples of such guides are the Apple Macintosh Interface Guidelines (Apple 1987), the BT User Interface Style Guide (British Telecom 1989) and the basic usability guidelines of Molich and Nielson (1990). Although not all design guides mention exactly the same guidelines, there is a considerable degree of consistency. The following five guidelines are common to all three guides and to similar documents from other sources (Schneiderman 1987):

1. *Effective applications are both consistent within themselves and consistent with one another* (Apple 1987, p. 6). Both actions and their effects within an application and across different applications should be consistent. For example, the action required to delete a piece of text should be the same regardless of the application. Likewise, key combinations should be consistent: if "<command> X" means "cut" in one context, its meaning should be the same in all other contexts. The effects of similar actions should also be consistent. If deletion requires a confirmation dialogue in one context, the same should be the case in other apparently similar contexts.

2. *Provide immediate feedback* (British Telecom 1989, p. 24). Feedback is defined as sending back to the user information about what action has been done and what result has been achieved (Norman 1988). For example, in direct manipulation systems, feedback is displayed through changes in the behaviour of the objects that the user manipulates (Hutchins et al. 1986). Feedback should appear to be instantaneous (see also Gilbert, Chapter 4 and Kirkwood et al., Chapter 11).

3. *Use the user's model* (British Telecom 1989, p. 23). The conceptual model is the model the user has of the system he or she is using. The user forms this model by initially having a conception of what the system or particular application is going to do, transferring knowledge from other computer systems, transferring knowledge from comparable "real-world" situations, and learning how to interact with the system and what it is doing. This means that the model changes as the user becomes more familiar with the system.

4. *The user, not the computer, initiates and controls all actions* (Apple 1987, p. 7). For users to be in control, they must have knowledge of the current state of the application, its previous states and the ones that they can reach from their present state. The guidelines of consistency and feedback help to ensure that in most single-user direct manipulation interfaces, the present state is visible through the current configuration

of the display. This gives the user some control over his computer screen. In some systems the user is also permitted to tailor the display to suit his personal wishes.

5. *Use concrete metaphors and make them plain, so that users have a set of expectations to apply to computer environments* (Apple 1987, p. 3). Designing interfaces which allow users to trade on previous experience, whether of the "real world" or of other applications, makes learning faster and permits users to make appropriate inferences about the interface from their existing knowledge.

While there are many other widely promoted guidelines of good interface design (for example, avoid the unexpected, provide on-line help, validate data entered, be forgiving of users' mistakes), these five were chosen because they were common to all interface guidelines mentioned here, which suggests they have the highest priority.

3.2 Designing for Groups

The transition from single-user systems to systems intended for group working brings with it a subtle change of perspective (see also Brooke, Chapter 2). In the single-user case, the user is interacting with a (relatively) dumb machine, and can and should be firmly in control (see Section 3.1). The only "intelligence" in the system is likely to be a reflection of the user's own actions (as in, for example, automatic reminder programs, where the user might be reminded of an event which he or she had forgotten, but which had been programmed into the machine by the user on an earlier occasion).

In groupware systems, in contrast, there are always other intelligent agents, whether they are human or machine generated, and this has consequences at the interface. Firstly, other users may do things that may be unexpected, and possibly unwanted. No longer can one user be wholly in control. Secondly, groupware systems have to be capable of supporting communication between users as well as information processing. For example, a system providing a shared editor must support not only the collective amendment of documents, but also discussions between the participants about what is to be amended and why. Thirdly, while even in single-user systems the fact that the user is embedded in a social system is important (Malone 1987), groupware is always used within an organizational context and the interface must take account of this.

The result is that designing interfaces for groupware must be more complex than designing interfaces for single-user systems. (Brooke makes this point strongly in Chapter 2). From the user's point of view, the interface is not only to a computer system, or systems, but also to the other members of the group through the computer. Because the group is engaged in a collective task, the interface must support task level activity, but it must also, at the same time, support the maintenance of the group at the "relationship level" (Kraut et al. 1988).

3.3 Groupware Interface Issues

In groupware systems, the interface between the single user and the computer is still present, so all of the above guidelines of interface design remain relevant. However some of the guidelines have different implications and their application to groupware interface design is less straightforward. This section discusses the five interface design guidelines from the perspective of group working.

3.3.1 Be Consistent

In many CSCW systems, users have access both to applications shared among the group, and to applications used individually. For example, a shared editor may co-exist on each workstation with an individual file browser for manipulating local files. There needs to be consistency across these different types of applications.

However, interaction methods that are provided consistently for all local individual actions may have untoward consequences when provided in shared applications. A problem of this kind was observed in an experimental teleconferencing system implemented on a Macintosh. In Hewitt's (1989) pilot study of Timbuktu (Farallon Computing 1987), a teleconferencing system in which all participants' displays are the same and change on any screen is broadcast to the others, it was found that users had to be prohibited from using keyboard shortcuts. This was because if, for example, one member of the group "cut" an object using the "<command>X" key, the other group members would only see the object disappearing and not how it was done. This violated the users' conceptual models, which suggested that display changes occur only as a result of users' direct manipulation of interface objects. The effect appeared magical and incomprehensible.

Unfortunately, the principle of consistency would then dictate that such keyboard shortcuts should be eliminated from *all* the users' applications, including local programs where the cause of a change resulting from a keyboard shortcut would be obvious, because the user had made the change.

The difficulty arises from attempting to provide consistency between those applications where the user is controlling the computer and those in which the user is (also) communicating with other users.

3.3.2 Provide Feedback

Feedback in a single-user system is generated due to the action of the user. The user does something to the system, which should then provide a response. This notion of feedback is still present in a groupware situation as each participant is individually interacting with the system. However group members are also using the system to interact with other members. In this case, the feedback has to come from another group member. If no feedback is forthcoming, the originator does not know whether there is problem because the action has been not been received, or because it has not been attended to.

Lack of feedback is a common experience in asynchronous groupware systems such as those based on electronic mail (email), but it is also a problem in synchronous systems such as shared editors (Jirotka et al. 1991).

3.3.3 Use the User's Model

In a groupware situation, the user's conceptual model has to be extended to include a model of the social relations of the group. All group members will need to have the same conceptual model of what the system is capable of, but extensions to the model will be different for the different group members, depending on the role they have within the group, the task that they have to perform and the social interactions present within the group. The issue of such social interactions is discussed in many of the book's other chapters.

3.3.4 User-Centred Control

User-centred control is a much more complicated issue in groupware systems than in single-user systems because of the effect of social roles and differences in status between members. For example, what should happen if a group member wants to delete a shared file? The answer to this question may differ depending on the task and the role of the individual within the group. As this example shows, groupware systems need to provide access controls and means of negotiating access between the members. One common, although inflexible, solution is for the system, or the group, to nominate one member – the chair, the secretary or the "facilitator" (Viller 1991) – to have complete access rights, and for other members to request this person to act on behalf of the group. Most of the book's other chapters make similar suggestions about this role, although there are subtle differences in the precise nature and responsibilities associated with it.

Another issue relating to user-centred control is screen layout. The style corresponding to WYSIWYG in single-user systems is WYSIWIS (what you see is what I see) (see Rodden, Chapter 1). However, this is not sufficiently flexible for most groupware systems (Stefik et al. 1987b), as there is no provision for each group member to have private windows within the shared application, nor the opportunity to have their screens tailored to their personal preference.

3.3.5 Use Metaphors

The metaphors that have been applied widely in single-user systems – the desktop for operating system interfaces, the sheet of writing paper for word processors or the ruled accounting pad for spreadsheets – will need to be reconsidered and perhaps replaced for groupware systems. For example, most shared editor systems retain the typical word processor presentation of a single blank display area and a single cursor representing the point at which one types. But there is no "real-world" equivalent that users could use to help understand these systems: no group of authors ever attempts to write a document collectively using one sheet of paper and one pen.

New metaphors that users can employ to understand groupware systems, which borrow specifically from collaborative work situations, are needed. For example, current local area network email packages (Microsoft Mail, for instance) successfully use the metaphor of sending business letters through the post, providing electronic address books, in and out trays, and so on. The Rapport teleconferencing system (Ahuja et al. 1988) uses a virtual meeting room as a metaphor. If you wish to have a conference with anyone then you have to go into the virtual meeting room before you can share applications.

3.4 Additional Design Issues for Groupware Interfaces

Synchronous groupware systems introduce additional issues not often encountered in single-user systems. These stem from the fact that the interface has to reflect the actions, not only of the user, but also of the other participants.

3.4.1 Focus

For most of the time in single-user applications, the user's attention is focused on one interface object – a window, an icon, a menu etc. – and other objects on the screen are ignored. On those few occasions when the system needs to attract the user's attention, rather dramatic methods are usually employed, such as sound, flashing icons or dialogue boxes which appear in the centre of the screen.

In a group working environment, focus is much more difficult for the user, and the designer, to manage. Because each participant can be doing something different and all participants' actions can be affecting the user's screen at the same time, monitoring the activity can be very confusing. One solution often proposed is to impose "floor control" (see Chapter 1), that is, to regulate whom among the participants has the right and ability to make changes. Often, the mode of control ensures that only one user "has the floor" at a time. However, this can greatly reduce the value of group working, because it has the effect of serializing members' activities. Furthermore, it is very difficult to design floor control strategies that are sufficiently flexible to support ordinary group activities; they have the same kind of stultifying effect as formal rules of procedure do on committees.

3.4.2 Concurrency

Concurrency is a well understood issue in computer science, but this view of concurrency is from a technical standpoint, for example as described by Rodden in Chapter 1. When designing groupware interfaces, the interest is in how to support the concurrent activities of group members rather than how the system is designed for concurrency. What is needed is support for multiple simultaneous inputs to a shared application (Olson et al. 1990). Without this, the amount of time that each group member can spend accessing the shared application is determined, in part, by the number of members in the group. The larger the group, the less time a group member potentially has for accessing the shared application.

3.5 Conclusion

A substantial body of design knowledge has accumulated through thirty years of human–computer interface research and development. This body of knowledge is, however, almost entirely concerned with helping to design interfaces that allow individual users to act on their own, individual computers (or, in the case of time-sharing computers, on a virtual single-user machine). Nevertheless, the same guidelines of user interface design also apply to the design of interfaces for groupware applications.

However, groupware also introduces new interface design problems. These arise from characteristics that are unique to groupware applications. Three fundamental points are mentioned here. They are: communication among the group members, managing input from several users, and support for social interactions.

Firstly, the user of a groupware program is involved not only in the kind of task related activity that is familiar from single-user applications, but also in computer-mediated communication with other participants. The latter consists of working *through* the computer to interact with other group members.

Secondly, the activities of other group members are not, and cannot be, placed under the control of the user. Thus, no matter how well the interface is designed, it is impossible to eliminate "interruptions" from other participants or to insist that other users provide immediate feedback. It is not a matter of designing these problems out of the system, as in the case of single-user systems. Rather, the interface must help the user to manage them.

Thirdly, groupware involves an additional level of complexity, for the designer has to be concerned with social interaction, including issues such as status and role, with mechanisms for adjudicating between participants' actions, and with providing new, group-orientated metaphors to help make the interface usable.

Acknowledgement This work was supported by British Telecom Laboratories as part of the project "Theories of Multi-Party Interaction".

Chapter 4

CSCW For Real: Reflections on Experience

G.N. Gilbert

"Groupware" or, more formally, Computer Supported Cooperative Work (CSCW), is currently enjoying a vogue as an area of research and as a topic for new software applications. But like most new things, it is firmly based on old ideas mixed up and set into a new mould. This chapter explores some experiences of collaboration through the medium of the computer which took place without the benefit of any special software and, in one case, without the participants being aware that they were actually engaged in CSCW at all. The purpose of the chapter is twofold: to show that cooperative work using computers is possible now using existing facilities, and to explore, through some tales of good and bad experiences, some of the requirements that useful groupware must have.

This chapter does not, therefore, have ambitious theoretical objectives. It is merely an account of some of my own experiences of using CSCW, or "proto-CSCW", systems. For all that, since practical experience of using CSCW for "real" tasks, rather than in artificial laboratory scenarios, is still quite rare, my observations may be helpful to designers. It must be remembered, however, that I am not the average user: for the last ten years I have been involved in the specification and implementation of a variety of demonstration systems built for research in artificial intelligence and Human – Computer Interaction (HCI). Although in this chapter I am placed in the unusual position, for me, of being the user asked to evaluate and express opinions, my reactions are, of course, much influenced by my knowledge of the field. Nevertheless, it may be that such reflexive evaluations can be helpful.

One reason that it is important to reflect on present day CSCW systems arises from the observation, documented in the rest of the chapter, that computer supported collaboration has been possible for the last ten years using existing facilities. Yet it is obvious that computer supported collaboration is, in fact, rarely practised. It is worth asking why this is so, and whether systems currently being developed will avoid the problems that at present stand in the way of wider use. In this chapter, therefore, I will examine three examples of computer supported collaboration with which I have been involved over a period since 1982. In each case, I will look at the factors that were helpful to the success of the venture and those that might have had negative effects. Consideration of these factors might provide clues about the kinds of circumstances where CSCW systems could be used effectively and those where they would be doomed to failure. In addition, I shall indicate the lessons which, with hindsight, might be drawn from these experiences of CSCW. These can be compared with Brooke's discussion in Chapter 2 of why CSCW systems may fail and Kirkwood et al.'s (Chapter 11) description of a system which did fail.

The three examples of CSCW I shall discuss are: the collaborative writing of a conference paper by authors distributed throughout England using a centralized bulletin board system; the use of international electronic mail (email) links to write a lengthy specification document jointly between the participants in a European project; and the design and implementation of a multiuser game, derived from the commercial board game, *Diplomacy*.

4.1 BLEND: The Pioneering Spirit

BLEND (the Birmingham and Loughborough Electronic Network Development) was an experimental electronic journal system funded by the British Library (Shackel 1982). Articles, reviews and other material about HCI could be submitted to BLEND just as to an ordinary journal. The text was stored on a mainframe computer at Birmingham University and readers could access it through modems and the public telephone network. One topic of interest in the experiment was whether readers would be prepared to comment on the articles for the benefit of later readers. To assist this, a teleconferencing system was provided on the computer (Chapters 1 and 7 define and describe teleconferencing). The software allowed readers to step through an article, a "page" at a time, and to link commentary to the article. Experiments with refereeing articles on-line were also carried out. The main thrust of this work was establishing the software requirements for supporting electronic journals, and discovering whether readers and referees could navigate through texts reasonably efficiently (Shackel et al. 1983).

Members of the HCI community were invited to participate in the experiment and had some of their telephone expenses defrayed by the British

Library. A few of them became interested in the possibilities of email and began to use the teleconferencing software as a medium for discussion. They developed the idea of an "active mailbox", a mail agent which took an active role in sorting mail, extracting mail from a number of different mailers, possibly on different hosts, and also which acted as a personal calendar and reminder. During 1983, a paper was written by those involved in this discussion and was submitted to an IFIP conference (Wilson et al. 1984). This paper was written entirely on-line, without any meetings between the authors. The messages which passed between the authors were automatically recorded and retained by the BLEND system, and after the paper had been written, the authors and myself (I was a latecomer to BLEND) decided that it would be interesting to analyse these messages for what they revealed about collaborative working over a wide area network. The results of this analysis were reported in a paper presented at the 1984 INTERACT conference (Maude et al. 1984). Naturally, this paper was also written using BLEND and it was not until I arrived at INTERACT that I got to see what my fellow authors looked like; I had not previously met any of them face-to-face.

The preparation of the second paper was thus truly an example of CSCW, although it was not until two years later that the term was coined. The authors were located in North London, Manchester, Guildford and Birmingham. Some worked on the writing as part of their jobs as researchers. Others were involved only as an extracurricular activity, phoning the Birmingham computer from home.

The venture undoubtedly benefited from the enthusiasm and the pioneering spirit engendered among the participants, for the technical obstacles in the way of collaboration were substantial. The modems communicated at a maximum speed of 1200 baud (about 120 characters per second). The display was a 24×80 character terminal. The software running on the mainframe provided a hierarchical system to message areas within which it was easy to lose one's way. The editors were difficult to use. Nevertheless, there was a strong commitment to the concept of collaborative working among the group, which overcame these difficulties. Another factor in favour of the project was that it was clear that there was an interesting paper to be written, and no other way of getting it done. It had to be BLEND or nothing. Diaper describes similar goals and constraints in Chapter 6.

As well as the technical problems, there were also problems about how to get five people (and sometimes more: although the five authors were the core participants, there were three others who contributed to the discussions) to work efficiently together. Multi-authored papers are difficult to organize when all the authors are in the same location and known to each other, and the problems were obviously even greater in this case. The solution we adopted was to impose a quite elaborate structure and set of roles on the participants. This helped everyone know what the others' expectations were. The writing was divided into phases, with each phase having a "director" to ensure that the task for the phase was completed on time. A "time-scale watcher" monitored the project schedule and an "absence coordinator" kept a record of when participants were going to be away for more than a day or two (e.g. on holiday or at a conference) to ensure that their absence did not hold up the others. After the paper had been planned, it was broken down into sections and a writing team, consisting of a writer and commentators, was established for each section.

This elaborate organization evolved because the available mechanisms for applying sanctions on reluctant group members seemed to be much weaker than in a face-to-face collaboration (compare the less formal and more flexible approach described in Chapter 6). The allocation of roles and the construction of agreed timetables for the work were a partly successful attempt to impose moral pressure on participants to continue to fulfil their obligations. Many of these ideas about roles and structure were later to form the basis of the Alvey COSMOS project, and the idea of allocating roles to participants is now quite a common one. For example, Chapters in this volume by Hewitt and Gilbert; Sharples; Diaper; Newman; and Benest and Dukić, all propose such roles with various titles and more or less the same responsibilities, depending in part on the group's task and the technology used for communication.

One of the most frustrating aspects of the system was the recurrent absence of feedback to reassure the sender that messages were being received and understood. The importance of feedback is also noted by Hewitt and Gilbert in Chapter 3 and by Kirkwood et al. in Chapter 11. There were many occasions, especially in the early phases, when participants "disappeared" from the discussion for long periods of time – days or weeks. The others did not know whether the failure to contribute was due to a lack of interest, absence from home or work, technical problems, or what. A protocol developed by which whenever one logged in, some message was contributed, no matter how trivial, just to maintain a presence. The need for "speakers" (in this case, senders of messages) to be able to monitor the continued presence and interest of "hearers" is, as we shall see, common to all computer-mediated communication systems.

The protocol that one always contributed a message every time one entered the system is one example of the norms that gradually evolved during the preparation of the two papers. These norms ranged from the way that messages were titled, to conventions about how to refer to previous messages. Generally, these norms were not explicit and not sanctioned; they just became the "right way" to do things.

One of the reasons for the development of these norms was that the software was in many respects rather crude and unsupportive. A particular problem resulted from the fact that new messages were always added to the end of the existing sequence of messages, and when a user logged in, he or she was taken straight to the first unread message. Old messages therefore became invisible unless one made special efforts to search them out. The consequence was that discussions tended to focus on current topics and ignore what came before. There was little sense of the accumulation of knowledge and, in several instances, old issues were re-introduced, the participants having forgotten about the earlier discussion.

Despite these weaknesses, and others documented in Maude et al. (1984), a paper was written by the deadline and was accepted for presentation at the INTERACT conference. The authors had managed to work their way around the problems, primarily by inventing social practices, such as the norms of communication mentioned above, which partially compensated for some of the difficulties in operating the system. Provided that there is sufficient motivation, users will find a way to overcome usability problems. As Sharples in Chapter 5 also suggests, a system does not have to be perfect to be usable, although this is, of course, no excuse for bad design.

4.2 European Collaboration

The next example of collaboration I shall draw on for lessons to help with the design of better CSCW systems is, like the BLEND example, one that used asynchronous communications, that is, all participants did not have to use the system at the same time. But the scale of the collaboration was in almost all respects much larger. An ESPRIT project, Sundial, was set up in 1989 to develop a prototype computer-based telephone information service. By the end of the five-year project, the intention is to have a speech understanding system that can answer simple enquiries by telephone from the public, on matters such as the flight times of aeroplanes or train connections. The project, which is still continuing, is a collaboration between twelve partners in five European countries: Logica and the University of Surrey in Great Britain, CNET, CAP Gemini Innovation and IRISA in France, Siemens, Daimler-Benz and the University of Erlangen in Germany, CSELT, the Polytechnic of Torino and Saritel in Italy, and Infovox in Sweden.

The work of the project is divided into eight "work packages", one of which is concerned with building a module, the Dialogue Manager, which controls the telephone conversation with the user. Only a subset of the partners are involved with this work package (the Universities of Surrey and Erlangen, Logica, CNET, CAP and Daimler-Benz), but this still means a collaboration between a dozen researchers in three countries and six organizations.

The first product of this group was scheduled for eighteen months after the project started and was to consist of a functional specification of the Dialogue Manager. This was completed in July 1990 (Bilange et al. 1990) and consisted of 160 pages of complex material, in English. All participants spoke English to a greater or lesser extent. Meetings of the collaborators were expensive to hold (travel and subsistence costs for the ten people who usually came to a meeting would normally amount to about £4000) and time consuming, because of the distances involved. Thus, most of the work was done at each participant's local site, with communication by email, occasional telephone calls and meetings held every two to three months. Because the partners each had somewhat different hardware and software, although all were running UNIX, the text processing package, LaTeX, was adopted as a project standard. Fortunately, LaTeX files are simple text files with embedded formatting commands and so could be sent over email networks. Diaper discusses this in Chapter 6, and compares examples of LaTeX and plain text with respect to their suitability for email transmission.

Once again, this collaboration had to struggle against technical and organizational obstacles. Email links between European countries are still far from reliable, although the coming of X.400 services should improve matters over the next few years. In practice, one never knew whether a message sent to another partner would actually arrive and, just as with the BLEND case, a recurrent anxiety among participants was whether the messages they were sending were arriving and whether all the messages the others were broadcasting were being received. These email difficulties were not always the fault of the wide area networks: on numerous occasions, the fault lay in the links between computers within the organizations or in mail machines which mysteriously stopped working or stopped forwarding mail to users.

Some compensation for this was the generally high level of technical competence among the participants, together with a degree of patience and understanding for technical faults, learnt over the course of previous projects. Technical prowess also came in useful in dealing with LaTeX, which does not compare well in ease of use with the WYSIWYG word processors that we used for day-to-day writing. An unexpected problem, which was not solved satisfactorily, is how to deal with "version control". When there are many authors and commentators all making changes to a document, one has to ensure that everyone is working on the latest version of the document and that one person's changes do not interfere with those of another. This is a difficult problem even in tightly controlled projects when everyone is using the same computer; when the participants are distributed about Europe with unreliable communication links, it is nearly impossible to solve. A formal protocol, perhaps involving the passing around of a "baton" to indicate permission to make changes, so that only one person is altering the document at any one time, might have been one solution. In fact, the project overcame the problem by splitting the work into many relatively independent chunks and then relying on one editor to put these parts together. This is not an entirely satisfactory solution, because it is not possible to remove all the interdependencies between parts of a long and complex document, but we made it work in this instance.

Some solutions to the version control problem are considered in Chapters 4 and 6.

A similar, but more serious, problem of version control arose later in the project when the Dialogue Manager was being implemented. Fortunately, the architecture of the software was such that it could be divided into several independent modules with fairly well defined interfaces between them, but even so, integration of the modules proved to be impossible without everybody being together on one site, and even then, it took several week long meetings. Distributed version control appears to be a CSCW topic that urgently requires further study.

While these were factors tending to make collaboration difficult, there were also factors on the other side of the equation. The goal of the work – the specification – was clearly defined and the contents of the document established at a meeting early in the life of the project. The meetings helped a great deal because they allowed the participants to get to know one another as individuals. On the other hand, the meetings also revealed the considerable differences between the participants about the theoretical approach that should lie behind the design of the Dialogue Manager. Neither the discussions at the meetings nor the correspondence by email did much to reduce these differences. The divergent theoretical positions stemmed partly from the very different backgrounds and experiences of the researchers and partly from the inevitable language and cultural differences, which made communication of complex ideas particularly difficult. In the end, one side of the theoretical debate simply withdrew and concerned themselves with other issues in the project, leaving the others a free hand in defining some aspects of the Dialogue Manager. It is difficult to say whether the outcome would have been different if the participants had all been in the same locality, speaking the same native language and able to spend more time discussing the issues. The social pressures to arrive at a compromise would probably have been greater, so perhaps this is one example of where communicating using a CSCW system is likely to yield a different result than face-to-face interaction.

4.3 Diplomacy

The third and final example of my personal experiences of CSCW that I shall describe differs in many ways from the previous two. Perhaps the most significant difference was that it was an experiment that was explicitly set up to test some ideas about CSCW, rather than a collaboration which happened to be supported by computer. The experiment was intended to help understand how computers could support work where there was an element of competition as well as of collaboration. In most real settings, it is clear that while the participants may have a common goal, they also have their own individual goals and that these may conflict. Thus most collaboration can be regarded as a mixture of cooperation and competition. Nevertheless, few of the existing designs for CSCW systems recognize this or permit users to do anything but pursue the (often predefined) group goal.

In order to investigate the effects of having participants involved in both collaboration and competition, we needed to set up an appropriate "laboratory" situation. Eventually we hit upon the idea of using an existing game, *Diplomacy*, which is normally played around a table on a special board. The board shows a map of Europe in 1901 and the players take the part of the countries. The ultimate objective is to conquer the whole of Europe, but the rules of the game are such that it is more or less impossible to win without forming coalitions with other partners. Cheating on promises and agreed plans is a characteristic of the game, as players attempt to compete with the other countries, yet collaborate with their allies to win new territory. This mixture of collaboration and conflict is, of course, just what we were looking for.

The project team built a version of *Diplomacy* that ran on Apple Macintosh II computers connected on an Appletalk local area network. Up to five people could play the game together, each in a different room with their own Macintosh. The program provided a picture of the board on each screen and a number of "windows", one for textual communication between players, one for a "trial map" where allies could plot their strategies, and one for specifying army and navy movements to the player who was chosen to be "campaign manager". The program organized the synchronous exchange of data from one computer to another during play to keep the screens up to date. The players were able to communicate using headsets and microphones, set up so that everyone could hear what everyone else was saying. Players could also send messages to subgroups of players by typing messages into the communication window.

Writing a multi-user game of this kind could have required a major software implementation effort, had it been done without tools. To help with setting up synchronous CSCW systems, a number of research groups have written "shells" or "desktop conferencing" systems – the terminology is not yet generally agreed. These systems typically provide a multi-user editor, often integrate video and audio facilities and sometimes offer drawing and file exchange tools (e.g. Ahuja et al. 1988; Crowley et al. 1990; Lantz 1986; Patterson et al. 1990). However, although these complex systems would have given us the communication services we needed, they would not have allowed us to duplicate the board game on the screen as we wished. Instead, we chose to use a standard, single-user prototyping tool augmented by some simple communication routines. The program was implemented using the Supercard package (an enhancement of Hypercard, with multiple, colour windows) and some procedures written by Apple for client server communications on an Appletalk network which could be plugged into Supercard. This provided a cheap (£125 per copy), object-oriented programming environment which makes the creation of complex user interfaces exceedingly easy, but which can also be used to prototype CSCW applications.

Trials of the program were carried out by recruiting groups of five people to play on Sundays. The board game can last for days and even with the teams playing for about four hours, none of the trials got near to ending a game. Nevertheless, the activity between the team members provided fascinating insights into how people are likely to manage with synchronous CSCW systems (see, for example, Jirotka et al. 1991). In order to assist analysis, all messages typed by players into their communication windows were time-stamped and logged, and the audio communication was recorded on tape.

Overall, the teams seemed to enjoy the experience, despite some disasters. While a direct comparison with playing on the conventional board was not part of the research, it did not seem to be more difficult to play the game using the computer than using the board. However, it was easier to form alliances with subsets of players because the communication window provided a private channel not apparent to other players. This contrasts with the situation in the board game, where to obtain privacy, an alliance has to leave the room, making the existence of the group obvious to all.

One of the main reasons why the trials were enjoyed by the participants was that the teams were chosen so that the members all knew each other as friends or work colleagues beforehand. A second reason is that the game is, of course, enjoyable to play. Thirdly, there were no distractions; the players were able to devote their whole attention to playing the game. None of these factors are as likely to be present in other, more realistic, situations where CSCW might be employed. Participants would usually not all know each other well. The task in an organizational setting may not be intrinsically enjoyable. And unless special precautions are taken, participants are likely to have many external distractions from telephone calls, visitors and other tasks which need to be completed urgently.

A number of general lessons were learnt from the experience of implementing and carrying out trials of this system. As in the previous examples of CSCW systems that I have described, feedback was important. The hearer (or reader) needed to be able to reassure the speaker (or writer) that they were still present and were still understanding what was being said. In ordinary face-to-face conversation this type of feedback is maintained by body posture, gaze and occasional vocalizations. The audio channel in *Diplomacy* permitted some backchannelling spoken feedback, but this was made more difficult by the fact that the speaker did not always know exactly which of the other four players was producing the feedback. This was not a problem with the text communication window, because the authors of all messages were automatically identified by means of a prefix to the message. The problem with the text window was that feedback had to wait until the writer had completed his or her turn and often was not forthcoming at all. Occasionally, the lack of feedback that a message had been received and understood had the consequence that the author wrote another message to try to obtain a response. If meanwhile the recipient was composing a reply, the messages got out of synchronization, resulting in considerable confusion.

We observed that some of this confusion was the outcome of the fact that the text communication window had some of the characteristics of textual communication (the composition of the message was usually slow and deliberate, and the recipient got the message only when it had been completed) and some of the characteristics of conversation (the interaction was a dialogue in which each message was intended as a response to the previous one). While, in conversation, speech is usually acknowledged by immediate feedback, with textual communication, such as letters and email, one only gets feedback after the message has been despatched. It would have been better to have chosen either the textual or the conversational mode and supported that mode exclusively at the interface. For the conversational mode, this could be done, for example, by providing a video link showing a picture of the hearer's or reader's expression to provide a parallel feedback channel. For the textual mode, automatic acknowledgement of receipt of messages back to the sender, and a means of knowing whether a message has been read (a facility offered by some email systems that run on local area networks) would provide helpful feedback.

4.4 Some Reflections

In the previous sections, I have outlined some of the features of three CSCW systems and identified some of the aspects which seem to me, with hindsight, to be significant in determining their usability. Although none of the three systems is particularly outstanding, reflecting on general lessons that could be drawn from the examples is worth while because there are very few accounts of CSCW systems being used – even in laboratory settings. This is partly because the research literature is at present much more concerned with technical issues than with questions of usability (see Rodden, Chapter 1). This is understandable while basic questions about the human interface to multi-user systems remain unanswered. What, then, are the lessons one might tentatively draw from the three case studies?

The first point that can be made is that using any of the systems I have described was hard work, involving learning to use difficult software, being patient with system failure and having to overcome frustration at the system's inadequacies. Despite the efforts of designers, this is likely to continue to be the case for the indefinite future. Single-user software, for example, has undergone continuous research and development for twenty years, yet is still often difficult to use. The consequence of this point is that CSCW systems will only be used when there are no easier alternatives available. For example, it is now, and probably for a long time will be, easier to pop next door to talk to a colleague than to set up a computer conference with him or her. On the other hand, if the participants are dispersed geographically and travel is time consuming and expensive, people will be much more willing to use CSCW facilities. This suggests that small-scale systems based on local area networks will have a harder time to get established than those geographically distributed systems constructed on top of wide area networks (although Diaper in Chapter 6 describes a case where he and a colleague regularly work together using local email even though their offices are adjacent).

Second, the first two examples pointed to the need to make not just technical innovations to support communication, but also social innovations to organize the collective effort and to manage scheduling. This was less necessary in the third example, because roles and time keeping were dictated by the rules and structure of the game of *Diplomacy*. The need for CSCW systems to support social roles was also recognized by the COSMOS project (see COSMOS 1989; Rodden, Chapter 1, and in particular, Kirkwood et al., Chapter 11), but the COSMOS implementation allowed only predefined roles, established before the communication system was set up. This would be unduly restrictive, especially since roles will change as the task in which the participants are engaged develops. Further studies are needed to identify the roles that are involved in typical activities such as collaborative report writing and collaborative design, and to suggest what kind of support these roles require.

Third, in all three examples, the way that the technology was used evolved during the lifetime of the collaboration, as participants discovered new facilities, and new ways of carrying out tasks, and as they became more accustomed to the system. Moreover, in all three cases, norms about the "accepted" way to do things gradually developed, often one suspects for no better reason than because doing something in the same way as it has been done before saves the effort of making choices anew. There are two implications of this for design. One is that it would be helpful if the system were able to accumulate knowledge about how to use it. This need not be anything more ambitious than preserving the history of the interactions (as the BLEND system did), together with facilities for searching through and, perhaps, analysing those interactions, although more "intelligent" help could also be useful. A second implication is that it would be desirable for users to be able to configure the system to suit their changing needs.

Fourth, the importance of providing feedback has been a recurrent theme in the description of these case studies. Feedback is an accepted requirement for single-user systems, where it is a basic design principle that the effects of user actions need always to be acknowledged by the system, but CSCW system designers have not yet taken this principle as seriously as it warrants (see Hewitt and Gilbert, Chapter 3 and Kirkwood et al., Chapter 11).

4.5 Conclusion

If one reads the research literature on CSCW, such as the proceedings of the biennial CSCW conferences, it is easy to get the impression that a variety of difficult technical problems must be solved before such systems could possibly be used. As the examples I have discussed in this chapter indicate, this is far from the truth. With a little ingenuity, CSCW systems can be constructed relatively easily from existing systems and tools. The resulting systems may be far from perfect, but are nevertheless still useful. In particular, such "string and sealing wax" systems can help to advance knowledge by indicating the circumstances in which computer supported collaboration is effective, and by identifying ways in which CSCW systems are likely to be used in real situations.

The examination of "real-life" use, through field studies and accounts from users, is particularly important for research on CSCW because the design of useful systems depends not only on technical advances, but also on social innovations (although sometimes the boundary between the technical and the social is hard to determine). It is only through such studies that we will be able to pinpoint the most important design issues. In this chapter I have made a first attempt along these lines, and have shown the importance of feedback, of social roles, and of the group learning and changing its behaviour during the collaboration, but these observations based merely on personal experience are only a small contribution to what could be learnt from detailed studies of CSCW "for real".

Acknowledgements The research reported in this chapter has been supported by the British Library, the Commission of the European Communities as part of project P2218: Sundial, and British Telecom Laboratories. I am grateful to these bodies and also to my colleagues, especially my co-authors of the BLEND paper, the members of Sundial Work Package 6, and my fellow researchers on the BT "Theories of Multi-Party Interaction" project: Marina Jirotka, Betty Hewitt and Sylvia Wilbur of Queen Mary and Westfield College.

Diplomacy is a registered trademark of H.P. Gibson & Sons Limited.

Chapter 5

Adding a Little Structure to Collaborative Writing

M. Sharples

At first sight distributed collaborative writing seems a prime candidate for new types of Computer Supported Cooperative Work (CSCW) system. Writing with others at a distance is a relatively new form of working, the task is complex with many conflicting requirements, there is a need for synchronous and asynchronous communication, and the participants must keep track of the emerging document and their own responsibilities. But I want to argue that these are all good reasons for *not* rushing to invent or use sophisticated programs to assist collaborative writing. Until the process of collaborative writing is better understood, writers should use existing media such as telephone, fax and electronic mail (email), and develop their own conventions to manage and coordinate the work.

In this chapter I shall describe some basic collaborative writing strategies and suggest some simple techniques for structuring and coordinating collaborative writing using existing media. These will be illustrated by a case study of the collaborative writing of an academic paper. Seven people (including myself) from the Sussex Collaborative Writing Research Group wrote a position paper over two-and-a-half months, using only media commonly available to academics. The basic tools were a computer with word processing software and a terminal for each partner, shared access to computer files, an email system allowing easy transfer of ASCII text to and from the word processor, telephones and a meeting room. I shall discuss the writing project and suggest some guidelines for other groups using these media for collaborative writing.

5.1 CSCW and Premature Commitment

Collaborative writing is a growing practice, pushed by a demand for jointly-authored documents and pulled by the availability of new information technology such as fax and email. There are no set rules of collaborative writing, nor a recognized training method. Instead, the participants in a newly-formed writing group will piece together parts of their existing work practices: techniques for writing alone, for communicating by telephone and letter, and for working with small groups of colleagues. Merging the different practices can be a haphazard process since there is very little in the way of a vocabulary and conceptual framework to talk about the process of collaborative writing. The writers reach a method of working mainly through tacit agreement and mutual accommodation.

It is possible to envisage a CSCW system that would assist with the entire process of collaborative writing, including planning a document, scheduling meetings, reminding the partners of commitments, merging their contributions and maintaining the drafts. Some components of such a system already exist. The Coordinator (Winograd 1988) follows the thread of requests and commitments in sequences of email messages. It groups messages into categories such as "new", "ongoing" and "completed" and prompts the sender to specify a category for each message such as "question", "offer" or "request". Quilt (Leland et al. 1988) provides annotation, messaging, computer conferencing and notification facilities to support communication and information sharing among collaborators on a document. It prompts a user to select a style of collaboration, which determines the social roles played by the collaborators and the type of action (such as "co-write" and "comment") which a role may perform on each type of object.

The problem with programs such as the Coordinator and Quilt is that they can lead to *premature commitment* (Green 1991). They require users to commit themselves to courses of action (such as selecting a social role or a type of message) when they may not have a rational basis for making the decision, or may prefer to leave the options open. Until the partners have gained the experience of working together they cannot make informed choices about which options offered by the CSCW system to choose, nor even whether the range of options fits their style of working. As Neuwirth et al. (1990) point out, roles such as "co-author" and "commenter" may alter or evolve during the task, so taking a pre-defined role may inhibit activities. Some commenters, for example, may decide they want to modify a version of the text rather than just attach comments to it (Diaper's case study in Chapter 6 provides just such an example).

Other types of computer support for writers include multi-user text editors, such as ShrEdit (University of Michigan 1990) and annotation programs such as ForComment (Opper 1988) and PREP (Neuwirth et al. 1990), which separate the document text from the comments of reviewers and co-authors. These types of support-giving CSCW system may well be appropriate where the strategies for collaboration have been understood and agreed, but for informal or newly-formed groups then the most appropriate tools may be "blank slate" ones based on familiar media, that allow the partners to impose structure gradually to suit their needs as they arise.

5.2 The Process of Collaborative Writing

Writing is an open ended design task. Unlike playing chess or solving equations, there is no fixed goal. It is under-constrained in that there are infinitely many possible texts that could fit a writer's goals, and an infinite (or uncountably large) number of actions that a writer might take at any stage. It is creative, and the act of writing sparks off the creation of new ideas that need to be incorporated in the text. There is no clear division of time between writing and not-writing (ideas gained by taking notes in the library, browsing through a book or talking to colleagues may be incorporated in the text), nor between the document text and meta-text such as plans and annotations.

For collaborative writing, the problems of constraint satisfaction, communication of new ideas, time management and annotation are all exaggerated. The writers need to make explicit their intentions and to agree on the basic dimensions of the document, they need to communicate any ideas or changes of plan that affect the other contributors, they need to agree responsibilities and schedule subtasks, and they need to maintain a distinction between the text to go in a draft and any comments and asides. They must also manage the dynamics of distributed writing, which may include reconciling different approaches to writing, arranging meetings, merging drafts and maintaining versions of the document. Lastly, whenever people work together there are conventions to be followed, statuses to be respected, conflicts to be resolved and partnerships to be forged, some of which can be managed at a distance, and others which require face-to-face meetings.

One general way of categorizing collaborative writing is in terms of closeness of collaboration. At one extreme is the *shared mind* where the partners meet together for the entire writing episode and the text is developed around group discussion. At the other is *division of labour* where parts of the task are allocated to each partner, working alone. In practice, a collaborative writing episode will usually involve sessions of solitary writing interspersed with bursts of close collaboration between some or all of the partners. Even when a writer works alone, the collaborators are *in mind* in the sense that their ideas contribute to the writer's text, and their intentions must be accommodated so that the writer's contribution can blend into a complete draft document.

5.3 Strategies for Collaborative Writing

Thompson (1967; cited in Bass 1980, pp. 475–479) describes three types of coordination in teamwork: pooled, sequential and reciprocal. These appear to be similar to the strategies for managing collaborative writing identified from empirical studies of writing groups, variously described as *parallel partitioning, longitudinal partitioning* and *working together* (Sharples et al. 1991), or *meeting needs and circumstances, exchanging drafts* and *writing together* (Rimmershaw 1992). Since there is no agreed set of terms to describe the strategies, I shall call them *parallel, sequential* and *reciprocal*. They are shown as diagrams in Fig. 5.1. The strategies are not mutually incompatible, and a writing group may move from one strategy to another as circumstances demand.

5.3.1 Parallel

Parallel working divides the writing into subtasks, either corresponding to parts of the document or jobs that can be accomplished in parallel such as

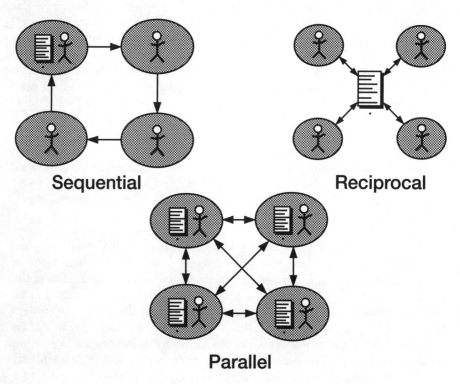

Sequential

Reciprocal

Parallel

Fig. 5.1 Strategies for distributed collaborative writing.

checking spelling and tidying references. The collaborators all work simultaneously and send their products to each other or to an editor. It is an
effective use of time, but the problem lies in setting constraints and in merging the products. Diaper in Chapter 6 shows some of the difficulties that an
editor may have in reconciling different versions and comments. To avoid
the writers getting out of step with each other, either they must be in regular communication, or it must be possible to partition the work into largely
independent subtasks. Parallel working is particularly appropriate for
loosely coupled writing tasks requiring little interaction. For closer working, such as writing jointly authored academic papers or collaborative grant
proposals or multi-site company reports, parallel working may need to be
supplemented by group meetings.

5.3.2 Sequential

With a sequential strategy the writers divide up the task into stages such
that the output from one stage is handed on to the next writer in line. If the
product of each stage is a complete draft, or a part draft in document
sequence, then the text written so far acts as a constraint and each writer is
guided by the results of the previous stages. But a draft document does not
reveal all the writer's intentions. It does not say *why* the writer included any
given piece of text, nor what was left out. Like a game of Chinese whispers,
the further the draft is passed round, the more it may depart from the intentions of the first in line, and coordination is needed to ensure an easy
transfer of material from one person to another. Sequential working is slow,
since each writer must wait in turn for a chance to work on the draft, and
the product is particularly sensitive to poor performance by any one person
(Bass 1980, p. 477).

5.3.3 Reciprocal

For a reciprocal strategy the group members work together to create the
material, mutually adjusting their activities to fit the evolving document.
One practical means of reciprocal working is for the writers to set up a
central file containing the draft text, to which all the writers contribute sections or revisions as they please. When they want to revise a part of the
draft text they copy that part to their own text editor, edit it and then write
the revised version back to the file. Rimmershaw (1992) gives a quotation
from one writer who used this method:

> We developed a technique where nobody quite knew who we were writing with
> because we used to leave things on the machine and people would just add in
> and take out. Nobody really knew who'd done what. I mean we used to let it

emerge, particularly as the working hours of the project were twenty-four ... so that was quite intriguing seeing things change.

The strategy need not be so free-wheeling – the collaborators may choose to work on prescribed sections of the text, or they may have scheduled hours of working – but self-scheduling can be an advantage, allowing each writer to choose a piece of the draft that fits her needs and the resources of the time. Problems with this strategy are that two or more writers may choose to work on the same text at the same time, duplicating effort, and that the need to coordinate the work and communicate intentions is even greater than with the sequential strategy, since a writer can make changes at any point and can leave the text in any state of partial completion.

5.4 Adding Structure to Collaborative Writing

This section suggests how four aspects of distributed collaborative writing – scheduling, coordination, constraints and intentions – can be assisted by adding some structure to the task. Scheduling is the dividing of the writing task among the partners. Coordination is the means whereby the partners ensure that the work is on track and incorporate any changes of plan. Constraints are the plans, boundaries, resources, knowledge and existing material which focus and guide the task. Intentions are the ideas and issues which motivate the writing. Table 5.1 shows in summary for each writing strategy how the task can be scheduled, the general level of coordination needed, the types of constraints that can be imposed, and how intentions can be communicated.

5.4.1 Scheduling

Scheduling for parallel working is a matter of allocating tasks to the partners, setting a time for completion and merging the results. It works best when each partner has an independent and well defined subtask. The difficulties arise if, when all the sections are brought together, there are found to be overlaps and omissions. One solution is for the group to appoint a "host" whose role is to monitor the parallel activities, by communicating with the partners and inspecting work in progress, to ensure that the pieces of the document will fit together and that the partners will be able to complete their work on schedule (for examples, see the "director" role in Gilbert, Chapter 4 and the "co-ordinator" role in Diaper, Chapter 6).

For simple sequential working there may be no need to make out a schedule of work; each writer completes a section and then passes it onwards. It might be necessary to decide the sequence of movement and to

Table 5.1. Characteristics of strategies for collaborative writing

	Scheduling	Coordination	Constraints	Intentions
Parallel working	Parallel partitioning	Low	Prior plans and instructions	Communication between partners
Sequential working	Sequential partitioning	Medium	Plans and instructions *plus* draft text in document sequence	Communication between partners *plus* annotations of text
Reciprocal working	Self-scheduling	High	Plans and instructions *plus* draft text	Communication *plus* annotations of text

set time limits, but with no parallel working this method avoids any problems of synchronization.

Reciprocal working does demand some management, of concurrency and version control. The problems of concurrency, where two or more people attempt to amend the same piece of text simultaneously, are well known to designers of databases. The normal solutions offered by database designers, such as locking and transaction mechanisms (grouping a number of actions performed by the user into a single transaction) assume that each person should have the illusion of being the only user of the system and that the computer should manage the concurrency, hiding its effects, wherever possible, from the users (Ellis et al. 1991). But in groupwork it may be better to allow the participants to see the effects of simultaneous working and let them manage concurrency through social convention. Experiments with the GROVE shared editor suggest that removing all technological constraints and allowing everyone to see and edit any part of the text can be surprisingly useful, because the users soon develop their own appropriate social protocol (Ellis et al. 1991, p. 47).

The simplest social management technique is to agree that only one person should work on the shared product at a time (i.e. enforcing a "sequential" strategy). This can be done by the person annotating the file with a note that it has been "captured" for work. A more flexible convention is for each partner to either delete any section of text that has been taken for revision (with the analogy of removing pages from a ring binder) or to copy the text and leave a mark to notify the other writers at the beginning and end of it. When the revision is complete the new text can be put in place of the old. The most successful social conventions are those that are in the direct interests of the participants; in this case a writer can override the convention and decide not to leave a mark to inform others, but then runs the risk of spending effort on revising the same section as someone else.

If only one person is working on the file at a time then version control is straightforward: the partners can either work with a single file, or can write each revised version to a new file and give it a new version number. (As Gilbert points out in Chapter 4, there still remains the problem of interdependencies between the different contributions.) If the collaborators are working on more than one section simultaneously then they can either create a new version whenever a section is written back to the shared text, or they can finished the simultaneous working at an agreed time and create a new version with all the revisions.

5.4.2 Coordination

Coordination is needed to cope with conflicts between partners, changes of circumstance (such as a partner being unable to work to schedule) and changes of intention (when a partner has a change of plan or develops new ideas that might affect the others). People working in the same space and time may be able to coordinate through mutual adjustments and non-verbal communication, but coordination in distributed working requires verbal or textual communication. The strategies needing tighter coordination also need more frequent and more elaborate messages.

Speech act theory (see Rodden, Chapter 1 and Wastell and White, Chapter 8) addresses the way in which messages with very different surface appearances, such as "I request you to accompany me to the station" and "how about taking in a movie?" perform similar acts (in this case a *request*) and require similar types of response. An initial request from partner A to B leaves B the option of *promising* to do what is requested, *declining* the request or *counter-offering* (suggesting an alternative). The Coordinator (Winograd 1988) is a CSCW messaging system based on speech act theory. It adds structure to email by prompting the user to specify a category of message (for example, the categories for an opening message are *request*,

---

From: mike

To: charles, eevi

Subject: HCI book

Category: request

Do you have a copy of Harold Thimbleby's HCI book?

Fig. 5.2 An email message with a field for speech act category.

Table 5.2. Categories of purpose and action

Purpose (type of impasse)	Action		
	Expect response	Hope for response	Notify / no action
Opportunity	"Please make use of this"	"Could you make use of this"	"Here is..."
Need	"Please give me..."	"Could you give me..."	"I don't have..."
Choice	"Please choose between"	"Could you choose between..."	"Here are some possibilities..."
Help	"Please do it for me"	"Could you do it for me"	"I haven't done..."

offer, promise, what if, inform, question and *note*) and then constrains the recipient of the message to a set of appropriate responses.

The Coordinator could be partially simulated on an ordinary email system by providing each user with a map of the allowable openings and responses and adding an additional header field to the message, which the user must fill in to indicate the message category (see Fig. 5.2).

A somewhat simpler scheme for structuring email is outlined in Table 5.2. Its categories are less comprehensive than those of the Coordinator, but it is intended for focused tasks where there is less opportunity for protracted negotiation and so the initial message can contain information (such as expected response) that might otherwise be negotiated. The scheme has the advantage of allowing grades of imperative: *expect action, hope for action* and *notify/no action*. It does not provide the Coordinator's support for negotiation but there are no long chains of conversation to be tracked.

The scheme is based on the notion (adapted from the Soar model of problem solving; Laird et al. 1987) that in focused tasks, where the partners are working with shared resources to solve a common problem, so long as the work is progressing smoothly there is no need for task-related conversation. Conversation normally arises from an *impasse*, where one of the partners cannot determine what to do next. An impasse can be caused by a *lack* of resources (such as a writer missing a reference source), a *surfeit* (such as a choice of ways to write the next section), a need for *help* (to solve a problem or take over a task) or an *opportunity* (such as a writer coming up with an idea that a partner could use). Each impasse can be *repaired* by the receiver of the message carrying out an appropriate action: providing the missing resource, choosing between options, providing help or accepting the opportunity.

Table 5.2 shows the interaction between the purpose of the message, arising from the type of impasse and the expected action. Each entry shows an example of the form of language that might be used in an unstructured message.

There is no need for any new technology to implement this scheme: it can be done simply by the sender adding three fields to an email message,

From: mike

To: lydia, james

Subject: limitations section

Purpose: choice

Action: expect response

Respond by: 1st May

Should we put the limitations section at the front of the paper or at the back?

Fig. 5.3 An email message indicating impasse and expected action

indicating "purpose" and "action" (with categories from Table 5.2) and the date to "respond by" (see Fig. 5.3). (In the case of "notify/no action" then there is no onus to respond, so "expiry date" may be more appropriate as the third field.) The last two fields could be omitted, and this would indicate the impasse that led to the message, but leave the choice of action to the receiver.

5.4.3 Constraints

Constraints perform a number of functions. They ensure uniformity of style and content, they restrict the coordination needed in creating a text, and they guide the process of writing by providing an agreed framework within which to create text. Constraints arise from four sources:

- The task set by the writers: its theme, intended audience and purpose, and more specific boundaries such as the maximum number of words or the readability level.
- The external resources such as books, papers, notes and written plans and intentions.
- The linguistic knowledge of the writers, and their stock of ideas, mental schemas and remembered text.
- The material that has already been created in draft form.

It is not possible to specify all the constraints in advance, and the constraints tighten as more text is created, because the task becomes clearer and the text itself acts as a constraint on the writers. If the work is progressing in parallel then as constraints arise they need to be communicated among the writers. This not only requires frequent communication of drafts, it also means that some constraints may be left implicit, to be inferred from the content, style and structure of each writer's text. But the more that constraints can be made explicit and imposed at the start of writing, the more this reduces the mental strain of inferring them from the other writers' texts, or the labour of imposing them late in the writing process through major revisions of style and structure.

Building up an agreed set of constraints from scratch is a tedious process since a reasonably comprehensive set might include: the intended content (topic areas, existing material, means of creating material, reference sources); structure (outline of sections, dependencies between sections, maximum or minimum length); terminology (abbreviations, spellings, definitions); grammar and style (readability, usage such as active/passive forms and non-sexist language); formatting (layout of text, tables, equations, footnotes, references). It could save considerable time to "buy in" a set of ready-made constraints that can then be adapted.

Formatting, terminology and style constraints are the easiest, since they are covered by formatting guides such as publishers' notes for preparation of typescripts, style manuals like the *MLA Style Manual* (Achtert and Gibaldi 1985), and programs for spelling, grammar and style checking such as Writer's Workbench (AT&T), Grammatik (Reference Software) and Correct Grammar (Writing Tools Inc.). Guidance can be extended to cover the intended structure of the document (e.g. by agreeing on an outline of headings and subheadings) and suggested topics for inclusion. For the less well defined constraints a writing group may decide to follow exemplars of *text types* (Pemberton and Sharples 1988); these are everyday classifications of documents, such as "research report" or "newspaper feature", which evoke a bundle of conventions about structure, topic, function and audience. The constraints governing a text type are implicit, but the writers are able to refer to archetypal, successful examples (such as a published research paper or a printed newspaper feature) in advance of writing.

5.4.4 Intentions

Every piece of text is a partial reflection of the writer's intentions. A writer, however erudite, cannot express every idea as a piece of prose, and because the text must fit into the larger document it cannot express everything a writer might want to say if there were space and freedom of context. So, as each piece of text is written it is shadowed by a, normally implicit, *meta-text* of intentions and unexpressed ideas. The intentions drive the writing forward by providing a motivation for the writing and a stream of unresolved issues that may appear, in some form, in later parts of the document. In collaborative writing there is more need to make the intentions apparent, for issues that are not resolved, or are inadequately expressed, by one writer could be taken up by another.

All the writing strategies described earlier can be helped by the writers' annotating chunks of text in the draft to indicate the aims, background ideas and sources from which the text was formed, the status of the text (such as "needs to be revised", "I'm happy with this version"), and plans for its development (such as "I want to flesh this out with an example"). The merging of drafts from parallel working can be helped by an understanding of the intentions of each author and whether any intentions have not been expressed in that author's text. With a sequential strategy, the text is passed from writer to writer but, unless there is explicit meta-text, the intentions are lost at each handover. A reciprocal strategy can suffer from duplication of effort by two writers each unaware of the other's intentions, or a battle between two authors each changing the same piece of text to make it conform to their own intentions.

Meta-text might be associated with text of any length from a single word to a section, but paragraphs are a convenient unit. PREP (Neuwirth et al. 1990) is a text editor designed for just such paragraph-level annotation and the meta-text can be created by the original writer or by a co-writer or reader. But by using some basic conventions, collaborating writers can create meta-text with conventional editors. Programming languages already offer notations for meta-text, in the form of comments that are ignored by a compiler, and writers can use similar conventions, at sentence level by including the meta-text in brackets {this is a piece of meta-text}, at paragraph level by separating out lines of annotation:

```
---------------------------------------------------------------------

    Meta-text at paragraph level
---------------------------------------------------------------------
```

and at section level by providing header text, possibly as a form to be filled in with the author, sources, status, and plans for development. In Chapter 6 Diaper suggests some general conventions for annotating ASCII text and indicates some of the problems of including annotation within a document.

5.5 A Case Study in Collaborative Writing

There is structure in the dynamics of collaborative writing, from each person's rhythm of writing and reflection, to the larger scale patterns of interaction between the partners. There have been few studies of the process of collaborative writing (for a bibliography see Lay and Karis 1991) and even fewer of the process of computer-mediated collaborative writing (Diaper, this volume; Gilbert, this volume; Posner et al. 1991; Rimmershaw 1992). In order to gain an insight into a complete episode of collaborative writing, the seven members of the Collaborative Writing Research Group at

Sussex wrote a jointly authored academic paper and monitored the work from its inception to the submission of the completed article for publication. At that time the group consisted of two tenured faculty members, two research fellows, two postgraduate students, and an undergraduate on secondment as a research assistant to the project. A third research fellow contributed to early drafts of the paper. The completed paper is available as Sharples et al. 1991. We used only tools for writing and communication that are available to many academics – a variety of text editors including Word and Emacs, the UNIX mail system, and the telephone – and held meetings of the whole group and smaller working groups. All the written communication was kept, as were each person's notes, plans, drafts and annotations. An audio recording was made of each meeting of the full group and notes were made of the activities and decisions of the smaller meetings. The group worked to a deadline for submission of papers to a conference and the writing episode lasted two-and-a-half months. During this time all the members of the group carried on their normal academic work; the writing was a part-time activity.

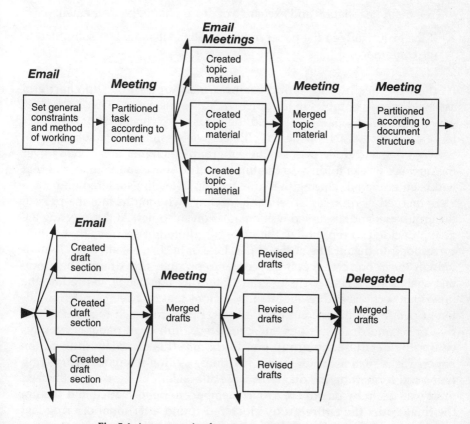

Fig. 5.4 A structure for the process of collaborative writing.

The general structure of the writing episode, omitting many subtasks and smaller meetings, is shown in Fig. 5.4. This organization was not set in advance but unfolded with the needs of the group.

The writing episode began with an email message from myself to the other members of the group suggesting that we "put our ideas about collaboration into practice by working together on a first position paper". The email message set out some global constraints including the proposed audience, deadline, general style and length, and some possible topics. It also suggested "ground rules" for collaboration:

- Anyone in the group could join the group of collaborating authors or not. Anyone who decided to join would be a named author of the paper. Anyone not joining would be welcome to add material, use any of the data and observe the sessions (in the event everyone joined).

- As initiator of the project, I would act as "host" for the paper, undertaking to coordinate the discussion and the writing, and would take final responsibility for pulling it all together.

- The main negotiation and exchange of drafts should be over email.

- If the group judged the paper to be acceptable it should be submitted to the conference.

At the first meeting the group brainstormed topics to a flip chart and assigned groups of topics to headings. At a meeting a week later, each topic was written on a separate card and the cards were clustered spatially on a large pin board. Each of the ten clusters was assigned to a subgroup of between one and three people. The subgroups then met occasionally over the next six weeks to discuss the topics and to share source material that had been gathered. During this time the topic headings altered and some were merged or dropped. Then, at a meeting two months into the project, the group met and discussed written notes on six topics. At this meeting the group decided to reorganize the material into eight sections that would correspond to the outline of the paper. Five of these were allocated to individuals (or in one case a pair of people) to produce first drafts. The group met again a week later to discuss the drafts, delegate people to produce the unwritten sections and re-allocate the sections that had been written to different people for the second partial draft. I then collected together all the first or second draft sections and produced a full draft paper. Two days before the deadline the group met to discuss this complete draft of the paper. Tasks such as making final revisions, writing references, correcting typos and formatting the diagrams were allocated. The next day a finished draft was taken by one of the group members to be formatted and then in the final hours the entire group clustered round a terminal offering last minute corrections and amendments.

5.5.1 Guidelines

Although this is presented as a relatively systematic and efficient process it did not appear so at the time. There was much argument about the structure and content of the paper and only a frenetic burst of activity in the final week ensured that the paper was finished for the deadline. Some tentative conclusions can be drawn from the experience of the case study as guidelines to other groups using conventional media for collaborative writing:

1. *Appoint a "host" for the writing task.* There is research evidence that covert leaders have a negative effect on performance (Lane et al. 1982), and a good host can coordinate the activity, arbitrate in discussions and take on responsibility for pulling the paper through the final stages of revision. Similar roles are discussed by Gilbert in Chapter 4 and Diaper in Chapter 6.

2. *Set clear constraints on content, style and structure.* The constraints should guide but not impede the writing and they should be open for revision throughout the task. It may seem unnecessary to add that all the participants should be aware of the constraints and should agree to follow them but in our writing project the initial list of constraints was included at the end of a longer email message and one group member did not read them until after the paper had been finished!

3. *If possible hold a meeting to resolve any major topic requiring negotiation.* Although we had intended that email should be used for negotiation, we needed to make quick decisions to solve problems and reschedule the task. Face-to-face meetings, with everyone present were often the only convenient way to uncover disagreements or misunderstandings. A general finding from our collaboration was that face-to-face meetings are useful for generating ideas prior to writing and for discussing how the drafts should be merged. Diaper (Chapter 6) also indicates the value of face-to-face meetings for the initial planning of a document, but Gilbert (Chapter 4) shows that it is possible (given time, good organization, and goodwill) to write an entire document without the collaborators meeting each other.

4. *Plan a writing sequence but be prepared to modify it.* We constructed an initial sequence of activities, but when people were unable to meet deadlines, or discovered new topics to pursue, we were able to alter the activities to fit. A more structured writing task, such as the production of software documentation, can be more clearly specified in advance. But if the work is rigidly partitioned and allocated to people working in parallel, then each subtask becomes a critical path. If one person fails to deliver, or moves outside the constraints, then unanticipated effort may need to be spent on reorganization or repair. Wherever there is reciprocal or closely coupled parallel working, it is important to have good communication

between the collaborators, to be able to revise the plans and constraints, and to spend time on merging the results.

5. *Suit the medium to the activity.* The different parts of the collaborative writing process are suited to different media. *Topic organizing* is suited to face-to-face meetings or real time audio and computer conferencing, where the participants can exchange ideas and develop a collective understanding of the task and topic. *Generation of material* can be done in small groups or individually, using fax to exchange topic diagrams and plans and telephone for negotiation. *Drafting* is best carried out alone or in small groups since it is difficult to debate and write simultaneously, transferring between the informal dialogues of conversation and the well structured monologues of written drafts. Email or fax is needed for resolving impasses and exchanging drafts. *Merging* of drafts is likely to require meetings, unless a person or subgroup is given sole responsibility for resolving mismatches of style and content. Revising can either be delegated to a person or group or (as in our case study) carried out in parallel, in which case a further stage of merging may be needed.

6. *Keep a clear record of versions and alterations.* Especially in parallel working it is very easy to lose track of the revisions and for the partners to be working with different drafts. If possible, the sessions of parallel working should all end at one time and the results merged into a new version of the draft.

7. *Distinguish the document text from the intentions and constraints.* There need to be clear conventions for separating the drafts from notes, plans and annotations.

8. *Annotate the document text with intentions.* Just as computer code should carry extensive comments, to indicate its purpose and to ease revision and maintenance, so draft documents should be annotated with comments to indicate the writer's aims, the background ideas, sources from which the text was formed, the status of the text and plans for its development.

9. *Structure the communication to indicate purpose, expected action, and deadline.* In the pressure of writing to deadlines it is easy to forget a request or miss a deadline, especially if it is left implicit or is buried in a lengthy message.

10. *Be prepared for rapid changes in individual and collective mood.* The experience of our case study, and anecdotal evidence from other collaborative sessions, is that there are occasions where the group experiences collective shifts of mood. These can be quite sudden and may not be articulated, but if one occurs near an important deadline it can cause severe disruptions. In the case study disillusion set in when the parts of the second partial draft had been collected, but had not been merged and filled out into a complete draft paper. Three of the partners kept private diaries and at that time their entries included "I am worried about the work still

needing to be done", "Lot of hostility to section 3", "I lost hope almost entirely". Four days later the same people were commenting "Mighty relieved" and "Paper coming together quite nicely". If the group can recognize that there are likely to be collective shifts of mood and can anticipate the most likely times for problems then they can take steps to relieve the problems (for example by planning to assemble the parts into a complete draft at an earlier stage) or to ride out the anxiety. More research is needed into these affective aspects of collaborative writing.

11. *Leave formatting till late*. If the collaborators are using a variety of text editors then it is wise to exchange the drafts in ASCII form so that they can easily be annotated and merged with other material (Diaper discusses this in detail in Chapter 6).

5.6 Conclusion

The aim of this chapter has not been to prescribe a structure for collaborative writing, but to offer a set of techniques and guidelines that might allow collaborating authors to apply enough structure to manage and coordinate the task of writing at a distance. If the collaborators initially work with their existing tools for writing and communication then there is no new software to be learned or modified nor any investment in expensive CSCW systems. The collaborators can experiment until they find a way of writing that fits their needs and approaches and they can generate requirements for a CSCW system to support their practice of collaborative writing.

Acknowledgements My thanks go to the other members of the Collaborative Writing Research Group – Eevi Beck, Steve Easterbrook, James Goodlet, Lydia Plowman and Charles Wood – for sharing their ideas and their understanding of collaborative writing, for providing the raw material for the case study, and for giving me copious annotations on earlier drafts of this chapter. This work is supported by a grant from the Joint Council Initiative in Cognitive Science and Human–Computer Interaction, Award No. 8919574.

Chapter 6

Small-Scale Collaborative Writing Using Electronic Mail

D. Diaper

This chapter describes one experience with using electronic mail (email) to support the editing of documents by a small group (three people) and is contrasted with similar experiences with larger groups. My own experience of collaborative authoring in these contexts spans about a dozen instances and generally has involved geographically disparate, often international, groups using a heterogeneous set of hardware and software platforms. Indeed, one reason why email was used was because the groups were international. In many cases the collaborative authoring enterprises were far from satisfactory, although in virtually all cases the documents were finally produced. The advantages of the speed of email and its machine readable status were more than offset at times by the disadvantages associated with version control, formatting and managing suggested changes, particularly of a detailed nature.

After reporting a case study, the chapter concludes with a proposal on how authoring at the later stages of the editing cycle can be managed with current technology using a mixture of media. Overall, we need many more detailed case studies before we will be in a position to understand the wide variety of ways in which people collaborate for the purposes of writing documents. Such an understanding is essential for the production of the high quality requirements specifications that are needed for the design of Computer Supported Cooperative Work (CSCW) authoring environments.

6.1 Electronic Mail

In the UK the Joint Academic Network (JANET; see Newman, Chapter 7) is provided as a service to academic institutions and to commercial companies involved in government-funded collaborative research projects with academia. Access to international email systems via JANET is usually possible.

The advantages of email are that it is possible to distribute a document to one or more people directly from a user's own computer system with relatively little effort, although some people with limited resources may have to use a computing environment different from their normal and/or preferred one. The use of the "copy to" or "cc" facility and aliased lists of recipients allows an email sender to distribute a document to many people via a single operation, rather than having to re-send the same document to each group member. Email is generally reliable, although delivery failure messages, particularly internationally, are far from reliable, or even comprehensible when available. It is also fast: in general one expects mail to arrive anywhere in the world within half a day and it is occasionally possible for transatlantic mail, for example, to take only minutes from sending to delivery at fortuitous times of the day.

The only comparable technology that is widely available to people for document transmission is fax. The advantages with fax lie in its analogue nature so that formatted documents, figures and handwriting can be transmitted. Its disadvantages compared to email lie in:

- The time it takes to transmit a document of more than a few pages to one person, never mind to many people.

- The general unreliability of fax transmissions, both in making a real-time connection and its frequent within page errors, which are not immediately detected at unattended fax machines (particularly common when crossing time zones).

- That fax, being a paper-based technology, does not allow its receivers to use their own computer systems for document processing.

The limitations of email arise because of the variety of hardware and software platforms used by different people, ranging from PCs or Macintoshs to large workstations and even mainframe computers. In practice this means that text needs to be standard ASCII with no more than 80 characters per line. While word processor or text formatting commands can be transmitted via email, these are often a hindrance to those who do not possess the software to interpret such embedded formatting commands. As will be exposed later in this chapter, this places a large constraint on collaborative authoring in cases where a standard software environment (see also Gilbert, Chapter 4) is not available to all. Furthermore, even in groups where the same hardware and software is available to everyone, this does not eliminate all of the problems of collaborative authoring and editing via email.

6.2 Authoring and Editing

This chapter makes a distinction between two aspects of the collaborative writing of documents using email:

1. Authoring, which involves generating part or all of the first draft of a document.

2. Editing, which involves modifications to a draft document.

While no claim is made for the quantitative validity of this distinction, it is intended that the authoring function is restricted to those cases where very considerable amounts of new material are produced by one person: one person, because this chapter is not concerned with real-time collaborative authoring environments which may have facilities such as WYSIWIS (What You See Is What I See; see Rodden, Chapter 1). New material would generally be several paragraphs, at least, if not the complete document, and explicitly excludes rewriting existing paragraphs, sections, etc. Authoring is thus restricted, in general, to the early stages of document generation, but may not be restricted to one individual, for example, where different members of the group prepare different sections of the document (see, for example, Sharples, Chapter 5).

Editing, both in individual and collaborative writing, often takes much more time and effort than the first draft authoring, and it is assumed in this chapter that it is the major area of group collaboration since most documents are subjected to many cycles of editing. There are many different ways of organizing the editing cycles and these depend on the size, social and managerial structure of the group, and also on its goals and the pressure to meet deadlines. While there are many ways of organizing the editing cycle, there are probably two factors that most clearly distinguish the different styles:

1. Responsibility for making editing changes.

2. How suggested changes are communicated via email.

It is at least possible to suggest examples of these two factors operating in different styles (Table 6.1). The way suggested changes are made (the "change mechanism") is characterized by just two means:

1. Notes, which are comments about the document and, excluding general comments, require a mechanism for identifying the location in the document to which the comment applies (e.g. Section 2.3, paragraph 2, line 4–5).

Table 6.1

Responsibility	Change mechanism
(a) Single manager who makes decisions about suggested editing changes	Notes sent about the document
(b) Single manager who makes decisions about suggested editing changes	Document changed by each group member separately
(c) One manager who makes decisions about suggested editing changes, but this function rotates around the group	Notes sent about the document
(d) One manager who makes decisions about suggested editing changes, but this function rotates around the group	Document changed by each group member separately
(e) Decisions about suggested editing changes are made by the group	Notes sent about the document
(f) Decisions about suggested editing changes are made by the group	Document changed by each group member separately

2. Document changes, which involve the actual editing of the document and, if changes are to be detectable by other group members, need to be marked in some way (how this may be done via email is discussed later; see also Diaper 1989).

Since with email the source document is available on each group member's computer, these two change mechanisms are not mutually exclusive. A mixture may be used so that notes may be mixed with quoted sections from the document which, by using cut and paste type operations, do not require retyping.

The responsibility factor is illustrated in Table 6.1 by contrasting a managerial role for one person (a – d) with a group decision making process (e and f). Group decision making is complex, poorly understood, diverse and slow. Option (f) is almost certainly unworkable with a document of even modest size where real-world constraints and deadlines operate. Furthermore, voting about proposed changes (see also Chapter 9), even if the proposed set is clear to all group members, will often be an unreliable mechanism in that it is likely to lead to stylistic inconsistencies. The style of a manager can, of course, vary from the dictatorial to the passive, although for collaboration, as opposed to merely group working, some intermediate style is generally suitable. Usually the manager will also be responsible for document version management.

In general, there is a gradual transition in the type of editing as the editing cycle is repeated. Early in the process the comments and suggested changes will tend to be general (e.g. reorganize the sections, tighten up the grammar, use the third person singular, etc.) and group members may rewrite paragraphs or even sections. In later cycles the comments will be more detailed and finally will concern the phrasing of sentences and even word selection. Such changes in the nature of the editing cycles over time will necessitate a transition from a notes style of change mechanism to one of editing the document itself.

The other area not covered above, which is critical to collaborative writing, is the agreement on the document's structure. Generally this will be some sort of outline of greater or lesser detail. This agreed structure and how it is achieved is beyond the scope of this chapter. The social processes for such agreement are extremely complex and diverse, and if done only via email (e.g. Gilbert, Chapter 4), which is probably unusual, are more akin to how other types of decisions are made via email. As such, this area of collaborative authoring is distinct and different from the actual authoring and editing of a document.

6.2.1 Small Groups

Small groups in the context of this chapter refer to groups of two to four people. Even in groups of this size, there is a critical social effect, which has a major impact on the style of interaction, the roles of the group members, and the management of the group. Social parameters of particular concern here include:

1. The equality of status, or otherwise, of the group members.
2. How well the group members know each other.
3. The differing personalities of group members.

In general, small groups can work successfully with low managerial and social overheads because differences of opinion and style can usually be resolved without there having to be an explicit or formal conflict resolution mechanism. This is not to say that there are not, occasionally, explosive exchanges even between friends, but that these are resolved by the group members using their own social skills. Virtually all people are considerable experts at small group interaction as this is the standard social environment that we all inhabit everyday. While the communication medium does cause differences in how such social skills are deployed, they are modified by the medium, rather than being novel or unusual to the group members.

6.2.2 Larger Groups

While a specific example is not provided in this chapter, the working of small groups collaboratively writing can usefully be contrasted with that of medium sized groups. A case study is *not* included because, while I have some experience of working in larger sized groups, I do not have sufficient access to quality data after moving between various computer systems over the years.

Medium sized groups in the context of this chapter might consist of ten or so people. Unlike small groups, it is inevitable that groups of this size will have within them a considerable diversity with respect to all the social parameters listed in Section 6.2.1 (i.e. it would be rare for all group members to be of equal status, to all know each other equally well, and for there not to be very different personalities within the group).

Medium sized groups need to possess, either by design or evolution, a whole set of procedures and mechanisms for group and work management. Some of these may be general to all the activities of the group, but some will be fairly specific to the authoring and editing task of the group, although some will arise by modifying the more general ones. The politics of medium sized groups can be complicated, and can lead to major problems within them because they are small enough for each person to have a significant impact on the work and on decision making, but are large enough for there to be possible factions, subgroups, etc. The temptation is for medium sized groups to start with little or no management structure, organization, procedures and so forth and to solve problems and conflicts as they arise. Generally, these arise very quickly and what at first are *ad hoc* solutions to problems soon become a set of precedents and standard practices.

Unless a medium sized group is in the unusual and fortunate position that nearly all its members are working almost full time on the group's writing activities, then there will also be version management problems. Group members will tend to put in different amounts of effort and time, depending on their resources, status and enthusiasm, and it is often difficult for the group manager, or the group as a whole, to know if all members of a group have contributed all they intend, which may be nothing, to a particular document version. In contrast, small groups can overcome this problem because it is often possible for group members to know the general and specific limitations on the other members (e.g. X is away for most of this week, Y can only spend a few hours on this version, Z's computer system is down today, etc.). Large groups have to have formal deadlines, version control and management mechanisms and, since most of its members' contributions are proportionally smaller, the effects of one or two members missing a deadline is less serious to the project (although this may be very frustrating to the individuals).

Thus, the difficulties of collaborative writing in medium sized groups are potentially more problematic, at least initially, than either with small or large groups.

6.2.3 Comparing Writing Technologies

This subsection is concerned with the facilities available to group members for the editing of documents. It is not concerned with the actual editors used by group members, but rather with the style of document the technology causes. A comparison is made between sending a document electronically either as an ASCII string or with embedded format commands. These two document styles are compared with using a paper-based technology, which might be distributed to group members physically or by fax. The disadvantages of these latter technologies, concerning speed, effort, reliability, etc. are not considered further in this section.

6.2.3.1 Making Notes on a Document

This section looks at the main problem of group members making notes on a document (see Section 6.2). The problem is adequately to identify to other group members the location in the document to which each note or comment applies. This is a problem for the person making the notes because unless these are easy for the other group members to use, their content is likely to be lost or ignored because of the effort required by the recipients. It is difficult enough being constructive with criticism, without causing additional offence by the style of the notes. Such emotive aspects in collaborative work are ignored at our peril. A comparison is offered between paper and electronic versions of documents.

To anticipate the conclusion of this section, there are advantages to ASCII versions of the document being prepared as ASCII from the beginning: if embedded text format commands are included in a file, then the automatic section and subsection referencing, the indexing and the bibliography facilities, for example, make referencing a part of the document to which a comment applies more difficult because the appropriate numbers, citations, etc. are not available unless each recipient has access to the appropriate text formatting software.

The disadvantages of ASCII, compared to a paper-based version of a document, however, are considerable. Whereas with paper, it is relatively easy to simply highlight some portion of text by several means (e.g. underlining, circling, placing a vertical line in the margin, etc.; see Diaper 1989 for an analysis of annotation styles with paper-based documents), this is not a facility easily available with an ASCII string file and email. Furthermore, it is quite easy to identify a portion of text in a paper-based document for the purposes of creating a set of commentary notes; it is not so easy with either

Table 6.2

Referencing Style	Paper	ASCII	Format
Sections	Yes	Yes	?
Pages	Yes	No	No
Paragraphs	?	?	?
Lines	Yes	?	?

an ASCII file or a file to be formatted. Table 6.2 shows which of these referencing facilities are principally available in the three document types.

The question marks in Table 6.2 indicate that, while it is possible to use these means of referencing a part of a document, they are not particularly easy. Easy or not, however, at least some of these mechanisms must be used. To send notes, for example, each note needs to use some subset of the levels listed in the table above, along with, perhaps, words. To give some real examples generated by the author as comments on a draft research project report:

1. **General** – The introduction needs to be ... (*2 more lines*)

2. **1. Introduction, para 1, line 3** – The principles, ... (*2 more lines*)

3. **section 1.1 bullets** – Where are principles?

4. **section 2.2.3** See LPU document ... (*1 more line*)

5. **QD2a – Draft 2, section 2.2, page 4, first bullet** – I think ... (*3 more lines*)

6. **final page** – Replace ... (*1 more line*)

The second is a typical example of how a small part of a document can be located for a comment to be made about it. The fifth, however, illustrates that the interaction of the reference styles/levels can be complex. If we consider this example, reproduced in full below, so as to compare our three technologies, then a useful description of this example might be:

- 5. **QD2a – Draft 2, section 2.2, page 4, first bullet** – I think that this bullet needs changing, for example, you might add before the ";" – "(in conjunction with the TOMUsr to perform work in the application domain (as modelled by the TOMDom))" – or something similar.

Table 6.3

Section Level	ID style	Example
Major part	Title	QD2a – Draft 2
Subsection	Number	section 2.2
Page	Number	page 4
Paragraph	–	–
Detail	Text	first bullet
Word	Text	";"

If we now imagine that these entirely paper-based comments were to be used on an electronic version of the research report and that both report and comments were to be distributed by email either as an ASCII file or as a LaTeX.tex file then it is possible to see some of the problems of working with the electronic version. In this example, it is assumed that at least some group members do not have easy access to the LaTeX software.

The main difficulty is that pages cannot be referenced at all and hard copy print-out will split pages differently on different printers. Thus it is likely that paragraphs will be counted. Identifying specific paragraphs presents a problem, however, as there is not a standard convention. For example, does a quotation of several lines, which is separated in the text, count as a paragraph, and does a set of bullet points count as a paragraph? With paper-based documents where page numbers are available, then there is still a difficulty as it is unclear if paragraph 1 is the first new paragraph, or the continuation of the final one on the previous page. Furthermore, paragraphs have to be counted manually and this leads to errors, particularly if done on-line as many scrolling mechanisms are not well suited to the task. The usual solution here is to identify the paragraph by quotation, e.g.

- Para. 6 "The main difficulty ...", ...

Paragraphs are also more likely to have to be counted because while there can be few sets of bullet points on each page, it is more probable that there will more than one set in a section. The "Detail" level is included as there are a number of different, context sensitive methods here: bullet points are particularly convenient, whereas the alternative is either to count lines or to use a quotation from the paragraph. The latter is dealt with separately in the table as it allows a precise location of the comment at the word level.

Line counting at first seems an ideal mechanism for referencing a part of an electronic document. One critical constraint generally is to ensure that line lengths do not exceed 80 characters, but even here care is required unless a line length convention is established for the whole group (80 characters is simply the most common default, for technical reasons, most often attributed to IBM). If we assume that lines are split at the same point for all group members, for the sake of the example, then an obvious technique is to automatically number the lines (a common facility that can be applied on most systems to a file prepared on a word processor as well as on program editors). Line counting manually, of course, is both tedious and liable to error. Automatic line numbering, while an obvious solution, is not without its own difficulties. Primarily, these concern version management: line numbers will inevitably change between versions, so it is critical that all group members work on the correct version.

Quoting a part of the document allows a reasonable identification of a note's location. With paper documents a commentator tends to keep the quotations as short as possible, for example, the ";" above. Where an electronic version is available, longer quotes have the utility that a section can be found using a global string search facility. However, cut and paste operations are often tedious for the commentator, particularly as they are likely to involve some file transfer operations, and often the quote is retyped rather than copied. This can prevent the use of a search technique if the quote is not identical to the text. Thus, while the use of quotation is an accurate means of locating part of a document, it is often clumsy and time consuming.

Preparing text using only ASCII from the beginning has some advantages over using a formatting language such as troff or LaTeX and then running such files through a "stripping" program to prepare them for transmission. Even bullet points become confused after the removal of LaTeX format commands by such a program, because the points become indistinguishable from paragraphs of text. No doubt more sophisticated stripping programs could be built that would, for example, replace LaTeX commands such as

\begin{itemize}

\item ...

\item ...

\end{itemize}

with asterisks or similar symbols to denote the bullet points starting with backslash item. Such programs are not generally available of sufficient power to do this adequately, particularly as they need to be highly context sensitive and would thus be difficult to write. Tables present particular problems, which are probably insurmountable for automatic format command stripping so as to produce something easily readable. To illustrate this a previous, very simple, table is reproduced below in three ways:

1. As if produced originally in ASCII by the author.

2. As actually produced in LaTeX for this chapter.

3. As produced in LaTeX after running the author's LaTeX stripping program on it.

Obviously, only the first is at all easy to read, although a knowledge of LaTeX does allow the second to be understood. The stripped version is just about manageable in what is a very simple example, but would be impossible with more complex tables.

Of course, logical and mathematical notation and figures present problems that are particularly difficult. It is possible to draw crude figures using the ASCII character set, and this was done in the case study described in this chapter. In general, however, one is forced to use analogue transmission media such as fax or physical post for these, which present problems of coordination and version management between group members. I have found this to be a particular problem with mathematical formulae where group members have wished to discuss and modify these.

To return to the main point, to produce notes on a version of a document, group members must be able to locate accurately a part of the document. This is non-trivial with any technology, and is tedious when there are tens, if not hundreds, of comments. A solution possible with paper, and particularly if postal services are used, is to mark up a copy of the document with numbers and then reference these numbers in the notes.

Table 6.4

1. ASCII

```
Referencing Style    Paper    ASCII    Format
-------------------------------------------
Sections             Yes      Yes      ?
Pages                Yes      No       No
Paragraphs           ?        ?        ?
Lines                Yes      ?        ?
```

2. LaTeX

```
\begin{center}

\begin{tabular}{lccc}
 Referencing Style & Paper & ASCII & Format \\
\hline
 Sections & Yes & Yes & ? \\
 Pages & Yes & No & No \\
 Paragraphs & ? & ? & ? \\
 Lines & Yes & ? & ? \\
\end{tabular}

\end{center}
```

3. LaTeX after command stripping

```
center

tabular  lccc
Referencing Style   Paper    ASCII    Format

Sections   Yes    Yes    ?
Pages   Yes    No    No
Paragraphs    ?    ?    ?
Lines   Yes    ?    ?
tabular

center
```

This tends to be costly with fax because of the sheer number of additional pages that need to be transmitted, and requires a style with email that resembles the mechanisms used to indicate edited changes to the document itself. This latter is covered in Section 6.2.3.2.

6.2.3.2 Editing a Document Version

Particularly for minor points, what is required for a natural style of working is for a group member to be able to suggest a modification to the document. In Diaper (1989) I described my experiences of doing this over email. Briefly, one selects a word, phrase, line, or set of lines or line-parts; this section has its beginning and end marked with a distinctive ASCII character (an asterisk for example); either the whole line, or lines, or just the marked section are then copied below the marked section; the copied section is then edited and a comment may be made below it.

To illustrate this using part of an early version of this chapter:

```
> Particularly for minor points * *, what is required for a natural

  Particularly for minor points * which, as suggested previously, are,
  at least proportionally, more common in the later editing cycles,
  * what is required for a natural

---  This phrasing clumsy but point needs to be made somehow.

> style of working is for * a * group member to be able

  style of working is for * each * group member to be able


> to suggest a modification to the document. I, (Diaper, 1989) have
> already described my experiences of * doing *
> this * over * electronic mail.  Briefly: one selects a word, phrase,

  already described my experiences of
  this * using * electronic mail.  Briefly: one selects a word, phrase,


>                               Briefly: * one selects * a word, phrase,
> line, or set of lines or line-parts; this section has its
> beginning and end marked with a distinctive ASCII character
> (an asterisk * for example *); either the whole line, or lines, or
> just the marked section are then copied below the marked
> section; the copied section is then edited and a comment
> may be made below it.

                        Briefly:
  1. a section of text is selected (e.g. a word, phrase,
  line, or set of lines or line-parts);
```

```
2. this section has its
beginning and end marked with a distinctive ASCII character
(e.g. an asterisk);

3. either the whole line, or lines, or
just the marked section are then copied below the marked
section;

4. the copied section is then edited and a comment
may be made below it.
```

This minor example illustrates that the electronic equivalent of marking a paper document version results in the production of comments that are difficult to read and time consuming to produce. The commented version is also considerably longer. With paper documents one merely highlights a section of text and makes a comment on the paper, or numbers it for written comments produced on separate sheets. In the above example the actual production of the comments took an order of magnitude longer than deciding on them. Furthermore, the process is not simply mechanical: there is a considerable problem solving element associated with the production of comments.

Looking at the example more closely, the ">" symbol is generated automatically in many mailing systems when using a reply facility. It conveniently marks the original. New text doesn't have this symbol, although it can be spuriously generated if cut and paste operations are used, and a meta-commentary can be seen if versions are circulated in a "sequential" manner (see Sharples, Chapter 5) by there being multiple symbols (i.e. >, >>). Care was taken in the example given, although this meant that the ">" had to be manually deleted from some lines.

The marking symbol * is obviously confusing as it fails to mark differently the beginning and end of text sections and therefore fails to allow embedding. In the example, the final suggestion concerning bullet points was not marked with *s because such a potential confusion occurs on the first line:

```
>                    * Briefly: * one selects * a word, phrase
```

Square ([]) or curly ({}) braces are not, however, as visible as *s and may be used in the text, as round braces almost inevitably are. Personally, I am loath to use curly braces as LaTeX uses these to mark its command parameters or command scope.

While the example above uses my own style and notation, it does illustrate the problems that have to be solved by some means. Diaper (1989) describes an analysis of annotating paper versions of documents as part of real refereeing processes. The range of annotation styles was found to be large, but varied systematically with the size and type of annotation. Importantly, the analysis, using the TAKD task analysis method, proposed that all annotations can be thought of as potentially possessing three components:

1. The source, which is the section of text that is relevant in the document.

2. The destination, which is the annotation, but is not so called because sometimes the annotation is only a direct reference to another annotation.

3. The link, which shows how the source and destination are related.

While many annotations possess all three, for example, a few words are underlined (the source), a line is drawn out to the margin (the link) and a comment is made (the destination), a considerable proportion possess only two of the three and in the extreme case of using printer's marks (e.g. the wavy line between letters to mark a letter transposition) then one pen stroke serves all three (i.e. the source is marked in a way that indicates by the mark itself the meaning of the annotation, and since source and destination are the same the link is implicit, although the reader must possess knowledge of the mark's meaning).

6.3 Small Group Case Study

So far this chapter has attempted to discuss small and medium sized group writing in general. This section provides an example of writing a document in a small group and the problems faced by the group. While it is important to understand the details of the example, the purpose in presenting it is first to identify where email was and was not successful at supporting the writing process. Second, it is intended that the experiences gained from the example can be generalized to other groups involved in writing, albeit with different goals, personnel and management structures.

The example involved the preparation of what is a small document, yet it presented the group members with considerable difficulties, which can only be amplified with increases in the size of documents and groups. Notwithstanding the problems encountered, a document that was of journal publication standard was successfully produced.

6.3.1 The Case Study

This example involves the production of a brief paper (Barlow et al. 1989), in fact a "commentary" paper of three pages plus references for publication in the journal *Interacting with Computers*. This journal was, at the time of writing the paper, in the process of being launched and one reason for writing the paper was to provide an example in the first issue of this paper type.

The three people involved in writing the paper were:

1. Dr Judith Barlow, who at the time held a number of academic and industrial posts in the USA but who was in Liverpool at the time of planning the paper.

2. Professor Roy Rada, of the Department of Computer Science at the University of Liverpool.

3. Myself, Dr Dan Diaper, the author of this chapter, and the general editor of *Interacting with Computers*. At the time I had only recently been appointed a lecturer in the same department as Roy.

Judith and Roy had been involved with the refereeing of the paper that the commentary addresses (Bench-Capon and McEnery 1989). Judith had been in Liverpool at the time the commentary paper was planned, which was done by several face-to-face meetings. The paper was written while she was in the USA and all three members of the group communicated by email. While Roy and I have adjacent offices in our department, we work very different hours and communicate a great deal of the time via email. The submitted draft of the paper was refereed/reviewed by the members of the journal's General Editorial and Management Board because of my role in the journal and the pressure on the journal to go to press.

Having agreed on the basic criticisms we had of the Bench-Capon and McEnery paper, which we also thought was worth publishing, I then wrote a first draft of the commentary paper. While I acted informally as the group manager, there were no agreed social or organizational mechanisms within the group, and all of us perceived ourselves as being equal status group members. We had not known each other long, but had met both socially and at work. As can be seen from Fig. 6.1, which shows the social and personal relationships between the group members reduced to arrows, it was Roy who had the stronger relationships between us all. All three of us, for many reasons, not least academic and social friendship, were committed to the collaborative writing enterprise and everyone responded promptly to each version of the paper. In contrast to the experience of Gilbert (Chapter 4) in using email, we had no problems. Indeed, for us, email was so reliable that we were confident that if a message was sent, then it would arrive. To quote this book's co-editor a couple of years later (Sanger, personal communication 1991) "this is email, not bleedin' post-it notes".

The paper went through eight versions before it was submitted to the journal and each version corresponds to an editing cycle as described in Section 6.2. The paper was written from the beginning using only ASCII because of the different hardware and software platforms used by each group member:

1. Judith Barlow: SUN workstation, UNIX and MicroSoft Word.
2. Roy Rada: Hewlett-Packard workstation, UNIX and EMACS.
3. Dan Diaper: BBC B microcomputer and the VIEW word processor.

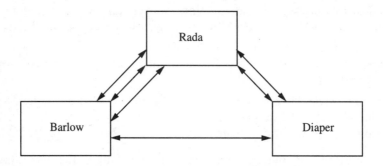

Fig. 6.1 The relationships between the group members.

My first draft was commented on by both Judith and Roy. Judith sent what was in effect a revised draft of the paper by substituting or adding parts to the first draft. She also suggested a considerable number of deletions. Her contributions presented no great problems with respect to their location as she was offering paragraphs, or substantial portions of paragraphs. She also made comments between paragraphs. Roy also made a substantial contribution to the first version. He generated quite lengthy comments addressing the theoretical issues concerning the paper. Again, the part of the paper his comments addressed was not difficult to spot because they were inserted at paragraph boundaries. Both also provided some general comments at the beginning of their files and were supportive overall of the first draft. Turnaround was a matter of a few days.

My role at this point was to coordinate Judith's and Roy's contributions. It is irrelevant how I came to have this role initially, but what is relevant was my perception of this role as an "honest broker" between the three of us. I was not, however, merely a passive coordinator. Taking hard copy print-outs of the first draft and of Judith's and Roy's contributions, I worked with Judith's revised version, noting on the hard copy where Roy's comments applied. In addition, I also considered my own opinions and did not choose to accept all of either of the other two's views, although it must be stressed that as an honest broker, I employed the heuristic that unless I had a strong opinion I would default to the others. Some may think this an attempt at a "fair" strategy since I wrote the first draft. It was not intended to be: rather, I saw it as an essential part of the necessary social engineering that is essential for genuine collaboration. The heuristic is probably a useful one for others in a non-passive coordinator's role, and indeed to other group types, such as the chairs of electronic committees, but it is probably less useful to attempt a social analysis of such a heuristic and its costs and benefits, because there are many others, and with small groups there is a very wide variability because each member usually makes a considerable impact on the group.

My task at this point was actually more complex than it first appears. I had basically two versions of the document and a set of comments from Roy about my first version, but not about Judith's version. The following list, which is not intended to be exhaustive, illustrates the range of contingencies that I had to cope with. The list ignores the content of the examples, but this is, of course, a crucial aspect and required me, as coordinator, to have not only a social model of Judith and Roy, but also a technical one and, of course, a model of the group interaction. I was under many other constraints, not least that the paper, as an example commentary, had to fulfil the requirements of *Interacting with Computer*'s General Editorial and Management Board, who had discussed the nature of such papers in detail over a considerable period of time. The following examples are offered:

1. My text is left unchanged and uncommented on – I may leave it or change it slightly.

2. Judith substitutes her block of text and Roy has not commented on my version – unless I have strong opinions I leave Judith's text, but I may rewrite partially or re-add some deleted text from my version.

3. Judith substitutes her block of text and Roy has commented on my version – here I have to consider whether Roy's comments are still relevant. If they are, does Judith's substitution cover Roy's comment, in which case I will probably, but not necessarily, bow to the majority. If Judith's substitution still does not cover Roy's point then does new text need to be written and some of my text re-inserted, or should Judith's text be edited to cover Roy's point?

4. Both Judith and Roy have commented on the same portion of my version. However, they may agree, disagree or make different points. Assuming I agree with at least one of the others then it is likely that I will edit Judith's version to accommodate the point. However, where Roy and Judith make different points then I need to check if Judith has already covered Roy's point elsewhere in her version.

5. Judith and Roy may disagree with each other where Roy supports my version and implicitly disagrees with Judith. If I agree with Roy I may re-insert my version and delete Judith's, although I am likely to edit my version to accommodate Judith if at all possible. However, I may agree with Judith (i.e. I change my opinion) and thus may judge Roy's support irrelevant and leave Judith's version, but again I may edit Judith's version to accommodate Roy's, and my own, earlier position.

The list above is constructed by the interaction of two basic factors:

1. The views of the three group members who may agree or disagree with each other, or have different opinions, both technical and stylistic.
2. Whether the text is present in Judith's version, my version, or both.

I then concatenated my version to Judith's and edited hers, cutting and pasting from my version where appropriate. I then did a lower level editorial job on the paper, amending style, grammar and so forth. Within a week of the first version being sent by email, I produced and distributed the second version. Problems of version control were handled by having the version number written at the top of the file. I also supplied a covering note explaining what I had done, and why.

Given the complexity of the circumstances and options open to me, it is difficult to see how one could easily arrive at an adequate specification of this task for the purposes of designing a CSCW support tool for the document coordinator's role. One too obvious suggestion is that what is needed is a multi-window editing facility with an inter-window cut and paste facility. However, before we race off to design such toys (see also Sharples, Chapter 5), it is worth asking if such a facility would actually be better than using hard copy print-outs, marking one up and then using one's preferred editor to make up the next version. Paper is a very flexible medium, which the coordinator can use in a wide variety of ways, including physically cutting it up if necessary.

No doubt one of the reasons for the complexity of my own coordinator role lies in the fact that the group made no agreements about how comments, changes and so forth should be presented. We used our own preferred style. The design of a set of procedures or software tools, however, is non-trivial if group members are not to be so constrained as to make their tasks more difficult.

After several versions, with the changes becoming less global and the overall structure of the paper becoming fixed, there was a change in the way we worked. Judith generated the fourth version of the paper and distributed it to Roy and myself. I had problems spotting the difference between the versions, although Judith used the UNIX utility "diff" to find where changes had occurred. She described the use of this utility as "definitely sub-optimal, but the best choice I had". Since I had no such utility I had to take a position of trust. Judith and I worked in a cycle where each directly modified a version, did not indicate where the modifications were and, until an issue was spotted by Roy, I accepted the version. Roy's comments on a version and Judith's and my modifications (and occasional comments) were sufficiently sparse in the later versions that the complex interactions of the early drafts between us did not recur. Modifications in the final versions were more syntactical than anything else. Overall, the paper took about three weeks to produce.

The change in how the group worked was not explicitly negotiated, but evolved from what appeared natural and convenient at the time. All three authors were interested in the topic of the paper and motivated to produce it within a tight time constraint. We also possessed somewhat different areas of expertise, in that Judith had a background in programming and artificial intelligence (AI), Roy in AI and CSCW, and myself in Human–Computer Interaction (HCI). Thus, conflicts between us also tended to get resolved in favour of the person with the most relevant expertise, although all three of us were eclectically knowledgeable about all the areas touched on in the paper. One wonders however, whether other small groups would be as successful as we were at collaborative authoring/editing. One has to have a belief in the improvement of quality that results from collaborative authoring, as it certainly requires greater effort to write papers collaboratively than to write them alone. It would have probably taken about a third of the time for me to have knocked my first draft into an acceptable form for publication, but I am sure it would not have been the paper that result-ed from the collaborative enterprise.

Almost as a footnote, one interesting consequence of our use of email did have a major presentational consequence to the figure in the published paper. I had drawn the figure using ASCII characters (e.g. using | - > < and particularly the blank space character).

The figure was redrawn by the publisher's artist but it remains easy to see its origins. While not major for the paper, the figure's format is certainly odd, with arrows having to be broken into horizontal and vertical steps. We should at least be aware of the possibility of such technology push leading to poorer representations than is necessary. While all technology constrains, we should not be blinkered by our tools, particularly not by those of such supposed flexibility as computers. (Personally, I question whether we will even get the flexibility from a graphics package that we get from analogue drawing tools.) An example of this is with the formal specification language Z. Some people object to Z's graphic layout, which is difficult to produce on some smaller computers. There are good reasons for Z's layout (e.g. Sommerville 1989) and a non-graphical version of Z does exist (Johnson 1987). Using Z's graphical layout being a difficulty for some computers (and the problems are not really very great) as a reason against Z is a good example of unacceptable technology push. The figure in the Barlow et al. paper is a small example, but is a warning about our relationship to our tools.

6.3.2 Learning from the Example

Section 6.2 anticipates many of the experiences commented on in the case study described above, particularly with respect to the problems associated with the style, location and nature of comments. My job on the early drafts

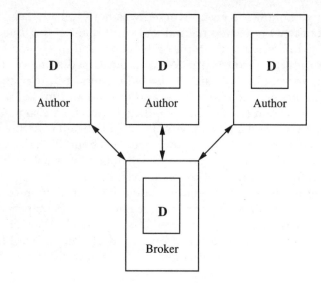

Fig. 6.2 Parallel working – single product.

of combining the comments and alternative texts from Judith and Roy was, on analysis, one of very considerable complexity and involved much effort. In fact the style adopted for this collaboration appears as a mixture of the strategies that Sharples (Chapter 5) described as "parallel working" and, perhaps, "reciprocal": *parallel* as each group member worked in parallel and their output was sent to all the other group members; *reciprocal* because my honest broker editor's role on the early drafts in effect meant that "the product" (the current version of the paper plus the comments) consisted of these plus my processing of them. Fig. 6.2 represents the situation, using a similar style to Sharples, which might be called "parallel working–single product" so as not to confuse it with synchronous working (e.g. see Rodden, Chapter 1), where group members all access a single version of the document.

It is also worth noting that the later style, where Judith and I simply edited the paper, and Roy produced comments on a version, is also a mix of Sharples' strategies. Between Judith and I there is a "sequential" sort of strategy but it still resembles the parallel working strategy in that each person has a copy of the document. Fig. 6.3 suggests an extension to Sharples representation in two ways. First, it separates the document (D) from comments about the document (C). Second, it freezes the editing cycle, in the case of Fig. 6.3 with Judith generating the current version of the document, and identifies who will generate the next version ("Dan" in Fig. 6.3). This latter is represented by the use of dashed lines and more accurately represents the sequential strategy. While Judith will receive Roy's comments on her current version, she is unlikely to deal with them herself

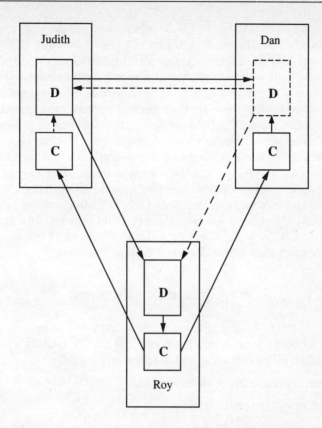

Fig. 6.3 Sequential–parallel, showing two different collaborator styles and the current (–––) and next (– – –) document (D) and comment (C) versions.

but will expect me to incorporate them in my next version, which is why I've represented her comment (C) to document (D) arrow with a dashed line, as the situation will be reversed when she receives the version subsequent to her current one. Such a figure is not very satisfactory as its syntax is poorly specified and potentially ambiguous, a common problem with graphical representations and one best solved by using a formal representation language such as Z.

There is absolutely no intention here to criticize Sharples' modelling of CSCW writing strategies. What Sharples usefully does is to identify different basic types of strategy. What the analysis of my example does is to show that these basic strategies may be mixed together and that to represent such mixtures we do need a better representation, whether graphical or otherwise. It should also be borne in mind that Judith, Roy and I did not have an agreed style of working and that we used a very basic technology which may, at times, have been clumsy but which did not greatly constrain us to a particular style of working.

With respect to the design of CSCW systems to support just the collaborative editing of documents, it could be suggested that any CSCW system be capable not only of supporting Sharples' basic strategies, but also different mixtures of these strategies for different group members and where these mixtures of strategies may change over time. This suggestion therefore supports Sharples' view that we should be reluctant to rush into the design of sophisticated CSCW systems in the absence of a good understanding of how people wish to work collaboratively. What is required are more case studies, ideally at a level of detail similar to that provided in this chapter. From the resulting data, the complete range of collaborative strategies and how they may be mixed together may be identified and ultimately expressed in an unambiguous notation. Only after this will we be in a position to design with some confidence this aspect of distributed, asynchronous CSCW writing systems. This, of course, is not sufficient for the design of such systems, as Section 6.3.3 suggests.

6.3.3　CSCW Authoring System Requirements

There are two separate and necessary parts that need to be considered for the design, perhaps some years from now, of CSCW writing systems that support collaborative authoring and, particularly, editing:

1. The authoring and editing environment.

2. The communication environment.

The problem of editing a document, where the document is to be marked with proposed changes, is discussed in Section 6.2.3.2. The problem is that the use of virtually any current computer system requires considerably more effort than the use of paper document versions. As an expert and frequent referee of papers for many purposes, I expect the production of typed comments on a document to take me at least five times as long as annotating the document itself, which is obviously a very inefficient use of my time. Diaper (1989) looked at this issue by analysing how people annotated paper documents. The proposed solution was to develop a hypertext annotating system which would allow portions of text to be highlighted and then selected as "hot spots" which would show the annotations (and meta-annotations) associated with that portion of the document. That not all such comments were local means that the design of such a hypertext system is itself non-trivial. Furthermore, it would be necessary for every member in the group to possess the same software system, a situation which will not often be possible.

With respect to the communication environment, there is a technocentric portion of the CSCW community (e.g. Brooks 1991) that concentrates on communication protocols (see Rodden, Chapter 1 and Newman, Chapter 7). While such work is essential, it is not itself sufficient. What is required in addition are mechanisms that support the different styles of CSCW strategy discussed in Section 6.3.2. Just how this can be done, particularly for the support of groups larger than the example reported in this chapter, is not at all clear. One option may be to extend Sharples' proposal concerning the use of "opening messages" so that the status of each contribution is explicit and that there is, in addition, software behind some of these fields that supports automatic distribution, relative recipient status (i.e. what each recipient is expected to do, if anything, with the document sent), automatic version tracking and management, and so forth. As suggested above, we are not yet in a position to design these facilities because we simply lack a sufficient corpus of data derived from case studies.

6.3.3.1 A Mixed Media Solution

This chapter, like much CSCW work, has concentrated on the exclusive use of computer technology. If it were not for the physical limitations of fax, in that it is slow and unreliable (Section 6.1), then there would be a good argument for using a mixture of fax and email. The analogue nature of fax is ideal for the writing of annotations, which supports a quick, easy and natural style of commenting on a document. Its disadvantage is that it does not allow recipients to use their own computer system. Furthermore, fax transmission is generally expensive and doesn't support multiple recipient transmission because it uses telephone technology, so there is an argument for a system where transmission is still via email. These problems with fax as a technology could be overcome if a scanner were used as an alternative to fax. In such a system users could print and mark up a document version, scan it and then transmit it via email to other group members. They could also edit versions of the document, as at present, and send these. Scanners are now becoming cheap and available for most computer systems, although they remain relatively slow, until compared to sending multiple copies of a document by fax. This solution also assumes that users can laser print a transmitted, scanned file, which currently still presents an equipment compatibility problem. This problem is entirely technological and may be readily overcome if there is user-driven pressure for such standardized capabilities. In the longer term, a combination graphical scanner and Optical Character Recognition (OCR) reader would be preferable, ideally with compatible paper- and screen-based outputs.

6.4 Conclusion

In conclusion, the collaborative writing of papers via email for small groups is possible and can lead to a successful outcome. However, it does not necessarily follow that this will always be the case. The collaboration described in the case study required a considerable amount of confidence and trust in the other group members. I have had the unfortunate experience of participating in groups where such trust and confidence has not been shared by all group members. The results were disastrous and the documents were never adequately produced to any of the group members' satisfaction.

At present there are just not enough well documented case studies of collaborative writing to provide a sufficient corpus of data for adequate requirement specifications for future systems. In this, this chapter agrees with Sharples (Chapter 5), and further suggests that case studies using existing technology, including fax as an expensive emulation of the scanner type solution proposed above (Section 6.3.3.1), would be highly desirable. What we need are models of the complex ways in which people wish to collaborate and these models should be derived from data where people are as unconstrained as possible by the technology they use. Thus we will learn more from using simple technologies such as fax and email than by designing sophisticated CSCW writing systems, because the latter will force on users the model of collaboration embodied in such software. Such models at present are theoretically derived where what is needed is empirically derived models from case studies.

Acknowledgement My thanks are due to Dr Judith Barlow, Professor Roy Rada and Dr Mike Sharples for their considerable help with this chapter, and to my co-editor, Colston Sanger.

Chapter 7

HICOM as a CSCW Environment

J. Newman

This chapter presents a computer supported cooperative work (CSCW) perspective of HICOM, the communications and information service of the Human–Computer Interaction (HCI) community in the UK. It outlines the perceived needs of the professions, industry practitioners and researchers which gave rise to the establishment of HICOM, situates these needs in relation to the processes of knowledge production and distribution and the strategies and institutions of professionalism, describes the current and developing uses of HICOM, and outlines some of the lessons that have been learned over the past three years and some issues that are currently being researched within the HICOM context.

7.1 Research, Collaboration and Professional Practice

The development and application of scientific and technological knowledge is a collaborative activity. The mythology of innovation tends to attribute discovery to individual genius; but the scientist and the practitioner alike need collaborators to share tasks, colleagues with whom to discuss ideas and an audience to validate them. This is generally recognized in the funding arrangements for basic research, where the existence of a "well funded laboratory" and of an active and productive research group may be as important as the specific quality of a proposal in determining the funding of a project. It is also recognized in the career decisions of individual scientists, who may even trade off material rewards, status and security against the opportunity to work with a particular research group.

The collaborative aspect of knowledge production is only in part catered for by the local groupings found within research laboratories and institutes, R&D departments etc. An equally important role is played by formal and informal organizations that cross the boundaries of universities and firms, such as learned societies, professional bodies, special interest groups (often formed under the aegis of the latter) and "invisible colleges" of researchers in related areas who keep in touch through meetings and correspondence. Communication across boundaries is not only important for basic research, but for the transfer of scientific knowledge into technological application. Freeman (1974) and Robertson et al. (1972) showed that close contact between industry and the relevant scientific community was one of the main prerequisites of successful innovation.

Professional bodies address several needs (Burrage and Torstendahl 1990; Johnson 1972), some of which are conducive to collaboration (e.g. the functions of a learned society) but others tend towards exclusion (e.g. the function of a qualifying association, controlling occupational entry, restricting the right to practise in the interests of standards, and exercising disciplinary sanctions for infraction of a professional code) (see Pullinger 1989, for a discussion of the problems of professional codes related to HCI). Where, as in the case of HCI, innovation crosses the boundaries of existing professions, a single professional body may not fully embrace an interdisciplinary research community. Since "invisible colleges" often depend on contacts initially formed at professional meetings, this fragmentation at professional boundaries can also affect the development of informal and semi-formal contacts. This can be a particular problem for those working in smaller groups and organizations. Thus, Reynolds sees the emergence of an "information gap" between "favoured" and "disadvantaged" scientists (Newman et al. 1990; Reynolds 1990) (as both computer science and human factors are arguably applied technologies rather than sciences, here and subsequently the term "scientist" may be taken as short for "scientist or engineer"):

> The "favoured" scientist will be engaged in full-time research, as part of a research centre working in a well regarded and well funded specialism. There will be good technical facilities, and access to a specialist library with ready access to online indexes, etc. Social interaction with experts in the same specialism will occur almost every day, and much useful news will be gleaned from common room chats and the notice board. Experts from elsewhere will be invited to give seminars. The opportunities to visit conferences and other research centres will be good, and this will be supplemented by contacts with colleagues who have attended other conferences or centres.

At the other extreme there is the "disadvantaged" scientist who is applying knowledge in a small organization, perhaps lecturing or perhaps in industry. Social contact with other experts in the particular specialism will be rare: there may be no-one else knowledgeable in that field within the organization. The only specialist library will be a couple of personally-subscribed journals and a few books. Specialist technical facilities, online services, conference attendance etc. will all need to be cost-justified, and there will be far less opportunity to share such costs than in the "favoured" scientist's research centre. (Newman et al. 1990)

Such considerations have underlain several approaches to the computer support of collaborative work. For example, in March 1989 the US National Science Foundation organized a workshop relating to a possible "research centre without walls", entitled the National US Collaboratory, in which information and communications technology would be employed to support geographically dispersed communities of researchers so that they could interact, exchange ideas and share data and instruments as easily as if they were located together. Wulf (1989) identified five significant advantages of such a collaboratory:

1. Improved productivity of individual researchers through access to better resources.

2. Removing the geographical restriction on access to stimulating colleagues.

3. Facilitation of interdisciplinary research.

4. Increasing the number of active researchers and the quality of education by helping academics at smaller institutions to take part in active research.

5. Increasing the relevance of research to social and economic goals, and improving the transformation of ideas into products, by bringing together academics and industrial practitioners.

The conference identified possible features that such a collaboratory might support as including: remote meetings; electronic mail (email); a scientific reference service; electronic journals with peer review (as described by Gilbert in Chapter 4); an on-line library (including multimedia and hypertext documents); and intelligent tools to help in the planning, scheduling, coordination and design of proposed experiments (Lederberg and Uncapher 1989; Rosenberg 1991).

Although the term "collaboratory" was not used at the time, HICOM's founders similarly envisaged the computer conferencing system on which it was based as the first step in building a support system for collaborative work in HCI within the UK, with goals very similar to those outlined by Wulf (HICOM Executive 1988).

7.2 Computer Support for the HCI Community

HICOM provides an electronic environment for researchers and practitioners interested in HCI to exchange information and ideas, and as such can be considered a simple collaboratory. It is at present hosted on a single central computer, donated by DEC under a sponsorship agreement. Other sponsorship, in the form of software, services or small cash sums, has been given by ACE Microsystems, CSC Europe, Loughborough University (which houses and operates the HICOM computer), the British Computer Society, the British Psychological Society, the Ergonomics Society and the Institution of Electrical Engineers. HICOM is at present entirely text-based; as Rosenberg (1991) notes, the "paradigm shift" from text-based to image-based remote collaboration may require networks operating with data rates of one gigabit per second.

The HICOM service which commenced operations in 1988 (Shuttleworth 1988) built on experience of computer conferencing going back over a decade, in particular on the BLEND electronic journal experiment (see Gilbert, Chapter 4; also Dodd et al. 1985; Pullinger 1985; Shackel 1986; Shackel and Pullinger 1984; Shackel et al. 1983). The initiative which led to the establishment of HICOM came from a Working Group on Electronic Mail set up by the IT Special Interest Group of the Ergonomics Society (ITSIG) in February 1986, "with the objective of providing electronic communications for ITSIG which could subsequently be extended to link ITSIG members with other HCI people and organizations" (HICOM Executive 1988). Identifying requirements and options, obtaining sponsorship, and planning and installing the system took two full years from the initial establishment of the ITSIG working group to the opening of a live HICOM service in February 1988. The development of HICOM has continued over the four years of its operation, as a voluntary effort on the part of many of its members, guided by the overall goal of establishing and maintaining an environment for collaborative work in HCI within the UK.

HCI has now a much higher profile than in the early 1980s; in the UK there are important concentrations of HCI specialists at several universities and there is a flourishing British HCI Group; and the Department of Trade and Industry's "Usability Now" campaign has made useful case studies and reference materials available to industry. Nevertheless, it appears that in the UK as elsewhere, many HCI engineers in software houses and development teams have little communication with the HCI research community. In the view of the rapporteurs of the INTERACT '90 workshop on HCI education, "The professional in HCI applies the knowledge about science and the solutions from science but does not interpret the science or adapt new methods and theories from science. Such an individual works with existing standards ... the professional is given the guidelines and works at applying them" (Mantei et al. 1991). If this opinion is correct, the

HCI engineer in many software development groups still tends to be in the category of Reynolds' "disadvantaged scientist", in comparative isolation from other HCI practitioners, rather than the "favoured scientists" working in a large and well funded laboratory. There is also a widespread but ill founded belief in the industry at large that with the advent of graphical user interfaces such as MS-Windows and X-Windows all HCI problems have been solved, which exacerbates the difficulty of cost-justification for the "disadvantaged scientist".

The HCI community is also dispersed, both geographically and between disciplines. Four major UK professional bodies have HCI special interest groups: these are the British Computer Society, the British Psychological Society, the Ergonomics Society and the Institution of Electrical Engineers, each of which organizes HCI-related meetings.

This fragmentation also affects the professional literature. Although British HCI now has its own well established journals, *Interacting with Computers* and *Behaviour and Information Technology*, much of the literature of HCI is still dispersed among many other journals, which concentrate on their respective professions and disciplines, with HCI as just one interest among many. Moreover, many up-to-date developments are often to be found not in the formal published journals but in the "grey literature": photocopied reports and working papers available on request from the author, papers presented at conferences or scientific meetings but not yet published in journal or book form, etc. Refereed publication is an important guarantee of quality and standards, but its requirements inevitably introduce delay in the dissemination of information and ideas. Garvey and Griffith (cited in Hiltz and Turoff 1978) estimated that original journal publication represents results that were available in preliminary form two years before the journal appeared, describing work that was planned three years before the journal appeared; and that by the time the results are first cited in literature reviews they may be over three-and-a-half years old. While *Interacting with Computers* has a specific goal of rapid publication comparable to conference proceedings, even conventional conferences operate on a time-scale that is considered long by industrial standards (Page 1992).

The importance of industry/academic links in promoting innovation has already been noted. Within the HCI community, the problem of bridging the gap between industry practitioners and academic researchers and teachers is acute, because practitioners and researchers develop different skills and different frames of reference, and are subject to different reward contingencies:

- Practitioners will often criticize academics for presenting as "innovative research findings" what the practitioner regards as "established standard industrial good practice", while academics will criticize practitioners for naive and inappropriate application of scientific models and research findings.

- For the practitioner, funding for HCI work is contingent on a demonstrated contribution to profits via product or process innovation, while for the academic it is contingent on being seen to make fundamental contributions to knowledge.

- Large-scale projects intended to foster industry–academic collaboration often disintegrate into several separate mini-projects within the individual partner organizations, leaving each side with the view that the other has little to offer.

The HCI community is also in a state of flux, at the level of personnel and at the level of technology. Given its marginal position between four professions, it will inevitably acquire new members from each of them from time to time. In view of the difficulty of funding HCI work, many of these members will inevitably migrate to other specialisms within information technology, either returning to their original discipline, or using HCI as a bridge to cross from one professional discipline to another. Technological changes affecting HCI only partly arise within the specialism itself. HCI specialists, like others in IT, must devote considerable effort merely to keeping up to date with changes in the underlying available technology.

To the extent that a significant part of the HCI community is dispersed, fragmented and in personal and technological flux, and that many of its members are in Reynolds' category of "disadvantaged scientist", there is an identifiable need for technological and human support for collaboration across spatial and organizational boundaries. The dispersed nature of the community indicates the importance of basing this on a communications service, orientated to helping members to maintain contacts and to undertake collaborative activities despite distance separation:

- Technological flux makes it important that the system should give access to the "grey literature" and to accounts and demonstrations of new techniques.

- The flux of active personal membership in the HCI community indicates the need for help in identifying new contacts, both in helping newcomers to find their way around the world of HCI, and in helping existing HCI practitioners and researchers to become rapidly acquainted with new members and what they have to offer: this could be a passive database or an active contact-broking service.

- The multidisciplinary and multiprofessional nature of the HCI community makes it essential to support:
  - The exchange of perspectives through "common-room" type discussions, where the approach of one discipline can be explained to another.
  - Mutual exchange of information about activities sponsored by different professional bodies.

- Keeping members informed of relevant additions to the HCI literature which might be missed because they appear in the journals of "other" professions.

• The need to overcome the industry/academic division indicates the desirability of a system that would help to promote collaborative ventures and facilitate technology transfer.

7.3 Basic HICOM Concept and Technology

HICOM provides an electronic environment for practitioners and researchers interested in HCI to exchange information and ideas. It is hosted on a MicroVAX computer: the main software products used are VAXNotes, LEX, Kermit, VMS, VMSSERV and one or other of the editors EVE, MG-EMACS and EDT. The HICOM computer can be accessed for interactive sessions via dial-up lines or via the public packet switched network PSS, or via the UK academic network JANET. Non-interactive HICOM services are now available via JANET or PSS.

HICOM has initially been based on VAXNotes "conferences", a computer text conferencing system; VAXNotes has been found more suitable for some HICOM services than others, and those services which would be better built on different software are being migrated from VAXNotes over time. For example, details about members and their interests are now held on a LEX database.

By contrast with email, which provides relatively little structuring of information, VAXNotes allows for messages to be organized into named "conferences", and within each conference messages ("notes") are grouped into "topics". The term "topic" is used both to describe the headnote that introduces the group, and to refer to the whole group of associated notes, i.e. the "topic" and its "replies". A conference has at least one moderator, a member who has privileges to rearrange or delete material submitted by others, and also (if the conference is private) to add new members.

The structure of headnote and associated notes is versatile and adaptable: for example, HICOM members quickly set up a calendar of HCI events by creating a "topic" for each month and entering each event as a "reply" to the appropriate month. On the other hand, where VAXNotes is used to support discussions, the two-level structure of "topic" and "reply" does not reflect the complex threads of topic and comment that appear in an actual conversation: unlike some other conferencing systems, VAXNotes does not allow one reply to be nested under another (compare the discussion of message-type fields by Sharples in Chapter 5).

As well as the structure note–topic-conference, VAXNotes provides for two other ways of structuring information: "keywords" and "notebook". Within a particular conference, the conference moderator can define a number of keywords that can be used to index entries. Any member can then associate one or more existing keywords with a topic or reply. Other members can then use a keyword or keywords to identify notes they may find of interest. (This is in addition to the facility to locate notes by a fast full-text search of a whole conference.) The notebook, on the other hand, is a personal information structure for the individual user; it is an index of conferences and conference entries, jointly maintained by the user and the system. The user can add existing conferences to the notebook or delete conferences from it, and can divide the notebook into classes to represent different categories of work and to avoid screen clutter and information overload. Classes exist only in the member's notebook, and not in the directory or file structure of the conferencing system, thus the user can tailor the environment to personal requirements, by adding or deleting conferences and by organizing them into classes. The system keeps each user's notebook up to date with an indication of the number of read and unread messages in each conference. In HICOM, a subset of the available HICOM conferences is entered in the member's notebook when it is first created. Thereafter it is up to the member to add or delete conferences at will.

In developing a CSCW system using this technology, the executive faced constraints from the fact that HICOM was initially based on a centralized system, but had to deliver the service into multiple, heterogeneous environments across organizational contexts. HICOM is currently based on a single central computer because of resource constraints: VAXNotes is in fact designed to operate in a distributed environment (see Rodden, Chapter 1), and given a wide area network of VAX processors running VMS it is possible for a user's notebook to contain entries for conferences on many different machines; but in the case of HICOM only one VAX machine is available. Also, since VAXNotes runs under VMS, the number of hosts which could act as conference servers is in any event limited by the proprietary nature of that operating system.

HICOM's menu interface enables the user to select the main interactive HICOM services (e.g. conferencing, database of members) or to call up HICOM utilities (e.g. to personalize HICOM, initiate file transfer between HICOM and local machine, etc). VAXNotes, Mail and the database each have their own application interface which is not part of the HICOM menu interface. When accessed from a terminal or from a terminal emulator on a personal computer, VAXNotes is controlled by a command interface. While running VAXNotes, the user can switch context to and fro between the VAXNotes command interface and the HICOM menu interface, while keeping his/her place in VAXNotes to return to.

WIMP interfaces for VAXNotes are available, both from DECWindows (X-Windows), and from an Apple Macintosh (Alisa), but at the time of writing these are not compatible with the networks for accessing the HICOM host machine; it is hoped that this situation will be remedied shortly, but this depends upon the network administrators and is outside HICOM's

control. Members can build their own WIMP solutions if they have a
terminal emulator such as Crosstalk for Windows, which exploits a windowing environment and has a good scripting language. To ensure graceful
handling of exception conditions, the design of such an interface must be
based on modelling the network link and the remote application as well as
the user dialogue. HICOM is developing a library of models and emulator
scripts for members to use or adapt.

If VMS can recognize the user's terminal emulator as a VT100 or VT102,
remote editing is provided using a screen editor, EVE. Otherwise either
MG-EMACS or a line editor, EDT, is invoked, depending on users' prior
options. When running EVE with Crosstalk for Windows the cursor can be
positioned directly using the mouse; this makes screen editing on the
HICOM machine relatively easy despite the round-trip delay. For many
users, however, it is more satisfactory to edit files locally and upload them
using Kermit. Integration of local editing and uploading into the HICOM
environment may require some advice and help from the member's local
support service; this exemplifies the problems of the trans-organizational
context, which show that providing for remote collaboration requires a
combination of technological and human solutions.

7.4 What HICOM Provides with Existing Technology

HICOM provides members with information services, which are collaboratively maintained; with formal and informal discussions; and with support
for collaborative development and collaborative writing.

HICOM information services include the official public conferences,
Reviews, Abstracts and Journal Watch, the Calendar of Events, News and
Situations Vacant bulletin-boards and the LEX database of members and
interests. Thanks to the collaboration of publishers, abstracts of articles in
the main HCI journals generally appear in the HICOM abstracts conference
while the journal is still being printed. Reviews gives members' views of
recent HCI book-form publications (at least one formal review, plus comments) together with excerpts from published reviews. Authors are
encouraged to respond to reviewers where appropriate. Journal Watch
helps draw members' attention to HCI articles appearing in journals other
than the specialist HCI ones.

News provides an instant HCI "cuttings service". Calendar of Events
gives advance notice of forthcoming events in HCI world-wide, calls for
participation, reminders about submission deadlines, etc. Situations Vacant
advertises current vacancies in HCI, cognitive science, CSCW and related
fields. Some vacancies are excerpted from the press, some are entered by
HICOM members who have positions to offer and some are mailed to the
moderator by employers, using email, fax or surface mail.

Discussion conferences fall into several categories: there are public discussion conferences, private conferences for discussion within a closed user group, private administrative conferences, etc. Open Forum is a public conference for general discussion of any pertinent HCI topic. Exchanges there often lead to members setting up a specialist unofficial conference such as interface design, psychology of programming or CSCW.

HICOM can support a variety of collaborative development activities: any development activity that can make use of structured text as a communication design tool can benefit from the structuring facilities of VAXNotes, for example planning a conference, coordinating a software project, etc. As an environment for collaborative design, HICOM's main current limitation is the lack of a graphics or video capability: thus it is advisable that any dispersed group planning to use HICOM as a collaborative system for a design project should ensure that the text links can be supplemented by ready access to fax.

Members engaged in collaborative writing will typically set up a private conference in which to communicate and exchange drafts and supporting material. There are advantages in using the HICOM interactive services for this, even though extensive text will normally be written using a local word processor before being transferred to HICOM. In particular, although the shared structuring facilities of VAXNotes are limited to topic-reply and keywords, these can be a great assistance to multiple remote collaborative authors, provided they are used in an imaginative and constructive way. In this respect, VAXNotes is more supportive than the software used in BLEND (Gilbert, Chapter 4, gives an account of the problems of collaborative writing in BLEND).

The email-based remote services recently added to HICOM include:

- Remote text conferencing: registered members can send to and receive from public conferences without logging in to HICOM for an interactive session.

- Closed user groups (CUGs) may use HICOM as a mailing list server, each mailing list having an associated private conference which serves both for archiving purposes and to give CUG members the capability to access the CUG mail within an interactive HICOM session if required.

- The HICOM document server is now in operation, and a library of relevant HCI documents and programs is being built up, for access via the server. This service is not restricted to registered HICOM members.

7.5 What HICOM Has Taught Us about CSCW

HICOM has contributed to our understanding of CSCW in two main ways: by the experience of the HICOM executive, whose work is largely coordinated through private HICOM conferences, and which thus itself constitutes an example of CSCW; and by observation, participant observation and experience of groups using HICOM to support remote collaboration (Newman and Newman 1992; Newman and Newman 1993; Newman et al. 1990; Reynolds 1990).

One clear lesson has been that group members, particularly conference moderators, need to keep in mind a clear distinction between general discussion and directed decision making, and currently need to recognize that such a distinction is not clearly marked by VAXNotes. (See Rodden, Chapter 1, and Sharples, Chapter 5, for further discussion of conference types.) The variety of leadership roles in CSCW may be traced as a theme through many of the other chapters of this book (cf. Chapters 3, 5, 6 and 9). Terms used include chair, secretary, facilitator, host, honest broker, coordinator and team-leader. There are more or less subtle differences in the purposes and responsibilities of these roles, which are a function both of the group's aims or rationale and of the technology. One must also distinguish between roles built in to the technology (e.g. the HICOM moderator is defined in terms of privileges) and the socially-constructed role which emerges as a result of group processes (which of course may include the interpretation members put on the technically-defined role).

The HICOM experience may be usefully summarized in terms of the two different aspects of leadership in groups, commonly known as "task leadership" and "group maintenance" (or "socio-emotional support") (Bass 1981, pp. 17–25, 420–423); the former is concerned with structuring the groups' activities towards the achievement of goals, the latter is concerned with maintaining group cohesion and motivation.

In a decision-orientated conference:

- The moderator should exercise task leadership.

- Topics should be used to identify issues, and replies should be used to formulate the arguments for and against alternative resolutions of the issue to which they relate.

- A cut-off date and time should be stated for each specific issue, and a definite decision making procedure should be established and implemented.

- After each decision has been made, the moderator should remove all discussion to an archive conference or note, replacing it with a statement of the decision that has been made, so that any new participant in the conference is presented with a clear structure of decisions made as opposed to decisions outstanding.

In a discussion conference, on the other hand:

- The moderator should exercise leadership through group maintenance.

- The opportunity to participate in a discussion that has taken place some time previously should be recognized as one of the advantages of computer conferencing compared to other teleconferencing methods. Therefore the moderator generally should not alter or manipulate members' input to the discussion.

• In the interests of group maintenance, the moderator should be aware of the problems that members may have in transferring their established communication skills to the text conferencing context (Kiesler et al. 1984), and should stand ready to take remedial action, whether to encourage the retiring, repair damaged self-esteem, console wounded pride, etc.

Another lesson is that the conferencing dialogue provided by VAXNotes may be adequate for information browsing, but may not be suitable for information capture. In the Calendar or Situations Vacant, for example, a more constrained input dialogue is needed to ensure that information providers give all the information wanted, in the required or preferred format. Moreover, some constraint may be needed to ensure that providers of information divide long notes into parts of usable size: this is a problem that often arises in information conferences, but seldom in discussions.

Further lessons have been learned about the problems of integration specific to a CSCW system for a distributed professional community. Steps have been taken to improve the integration of HICOM's interactive services with one another, in particular by supporting context switching and context preservation, through calling the menu system from the VAXNotes command interface. The problems of integrating remote or interactive services into the member's local working environment are also being actively researched.

Full integration of interactive HICOM services into the member's local "desktop" may await the definition and widespread adoption of standards for open distributed processing (Hutchison and Walpole 1991). However, by providing an alternative access to the service via email and server programs, the user can, if desired, remain in the familiar local environment while accessing HICOM, albeit at the cost of some service degradation. (For example, in an interactive session it is easy to browse through conference material already seen, while remote users will have to make their own arrangements for storing and retrieving any incoming material; by contrast, documents on HICOM's document server can be accessed repeatedly by email.)

The original centralized HICOM service was the first step towards the provision of a CSCW environment for the HCI community. The recent addition of remote services has opened the service up, and it is hoped this will encourage the participation of many HCI researchers and practitioners who were reluctant to use a centralized system. This will not only improve the quality of information and discussions on HICOM, but lead to the identification of further needs, further demands and further opportunities, drawing on and feeding into our understanding of CSCW.

Chapter 8

Using Process Technology to Support Cooperative Work: Prospects and Design Issues

D.G. Wastell and P. White

This chapter describes a form of technology known as Process Support System (PSS). PSS provides a set of techniques for modelling cooperative work and a flexible generic technology for building office information systems. This chapter introduces a number of related office technologies to set the scene for a description of PSS. The approach to process modelling in PSS is introduced using a medical case study, which is also used to give a flavour of the experience of process supported office work. Epistemological and methodological issues in process modelling are explored. Several lines of work are highlighted, including the development of a design methodology for PSS and language–action approaches to process modelling. A major implementation of PSS is described in outline. Issues arising from field studies are discussed, e.g. the question of the routineness of so-called routine work.

8.1 Introduction

Computer Supported Cooperative Work (CSCW) is a diverse and eclectic field. The theme that unifies CSCW is the question of group coordination, how it is achieved as a social phenomenon and how it may be actively assisted by computer-based support. The nature of these social processes is variously discussed in many of this book's other chapters.

The question of what is "true" CSCW and what is not is a contentious academic issue. Support for non-routine "professional" work such as collaborative writing would be widely accepted as a paradigm of CSCW (see, in particular, Sharples, Chapter 5, Gilbert, Chapter 4, and Diaper, Chapter 6). Electronic mail (email), however, does not count for some as CSCW, because it is "not really tuned (or tunable) to the needs of the work group" (Greif 1988). Technologies that support routine work would appear to fall into a particularly controversial category. Traditional office automation (OA) systems come under this heading. Data processing applications, in which computer systems simply "drive" short-cycle repetitive clerical work (e.g. payroll systems): are they to be described as CSCW? Some would contemptuously say not. The authors' view is more moderate and less elitist. CSCW provides a fresh perspective, an antidote to the traditional view of systems which emphasizes information processing and the internal design of the computer system. CSCW brings people and their tasks into focus. Any area of organizational work in which people use computers can be helpfully illuminated from a CSCW perspective, even payroll! All work has a social dimension. CSCW brings it into the foreground.

This chapter describes a form of technology known as PSS, which developed out of an Alvey project involving STL, Manchester University and others. PSS was originally known as IPSE 2.5 in its Alvey days (IPSE: Integrated Process Support Environment).

PSS provides both a powerful set of modelling tools for describing organizational work and a flexible generic technology for building systems to support cooperative work. The technology was originally orientated at supporting software production, but it has much wider applicability than this domain. PSS provides a technology ideally suited for coordinating and supporting routine work in offices. It should be noted, however, that PSS is a fundamentally different type of system to traditional OA systems, which focus on automating a particular task or function. PSS focuses on the provision of coordination across functions, which may be performed by many different people and machines. In this chapter, we focus on the use of PSS as a means of supporting cooperative work in offices, i.e. as a technology for constructing Office Information Systems (OISs). The chapter describes PSS, its origins, modelling conventions and the technology itself. Current developments and new research surrounding PSS are also discussed.

8.2 Office Automation

The definitions of an office, of office-work and of OA are themselves troublesome. The interested reader is referred to Hirschheim (1985) for an extended, if rather inconclusive, discussion. Hirschheim offers the following as a general purpose working definition: "Offices can be thought of as centres of organisational information handling and processing". The idea of rules and procedures is central to the popular view of office work, leading Olson and Lucas (1982) to define OA as "the use of integrated computer and communication systems to support administrative procedures in an office environment". The design of PSS reflects this view of OA, although as we shall see the bureaucratic idea that office work is simple "procedure following" is naive and misleading.

PSS is not the first system to attempt to provide task coordination across the office environment. In order to put PSS into context, we will briefly discuss some previous attempts in the OA/OIS field which are notable either for their general importance or their specific relevance to PSS.

Ellis and Nutt (1988) give details of several automated office information systems. Officetalk, for instance, was developed by Xerox PARC during 1976–1977. Interestingly, it grew out of a study of languages for expressing office procedures. Officetalk is intended to be used to aid in document management, preparation and communication. It is based on the idea of substituting electronic forms for the paper ones commonly used in offices. Thus, the user has an electronic desktop with in-tray, out-tray, a set of blank forms, and a file for forms being worked on. Tools for tailoring blank forms are an important feature. An email system allows documents to move from one user to another.

Another system similar to Officetalk is XCP, developed by Sluizer and Cashman (1984) at DEC. They describe XCP as "an experimental coordinator tool which assists an office in implementing its procedures". Like Officetalk, XCP is very much a document-driven system. There are four basic concepts in XCP, those of person, role, actor and document. A person may perform several roles. Documents of pre-defined types may be created by certain roles, and they then move down pre-defined paths. Thus, someone in role type A will perform certain actions relating to the document, and then pass the document either to a specific person performing role B, or back to the system to assign to someone in role type B. The system tracks the progress of the document, and keeps a history of it.

Ellis and Nutt draw a distinction between document-orientated and process-orientated models of OA systems. Documents are a way of organizing information, and secondarily of organizing activities. Both Officetalk and XCP are rather unsophisticated, largely document-orientated systems. Zisman's SCOOP (System for Computerization Of Office Processing) is based on Petri nets augmented by production rules as a means for modelling offices as asynchronous concurrent processes (see Ellis and Nutt for details). In contrast to Officetalk and XCP it is process-orientated. SCOOP is run by an *execution monitor*, driven by an internal representation of a set of augmented Petri nets. The firing of a Petri net transition causes an updating of the available productions. Processes may be either automatic or interactive. There is also the idea (a key feature of the design of PSS, as we shall see) of using external tools such as document generators and mail services.

Ellis and Nutt devote a major part of their review to describing a diagramming convention dubbed the Information Control Net (ICN), developed by themselves and others at Xerox PARC. An ICN is a diagrammatic method of representing office procedures as a set of activities, a set of repositories and a set of functional mappings between these elements, backed by a formal definition. ICNs are intended to be "used both to describe offices to managers and to analyse the office". An ICN defines an office as a set of related procedures. Each procedure consists of a set of activities connected by precedence constraints.

Another interesting system is the Activity Model Environment (AME) of Smith, Hennessy and Lunt (Smith et al. 1991). They describe AME as "a framework for modelling organizational processes and a prototype execution environment". AME is an object-oriented tool to explore models of organizations. It has a conceptual framework formed of eight components: activities (goal-orientated cooperative tasks); people; roles (groups of logically related duties/responsibilities); workspaces ("conceptual work areas" containing resources for particular roles, e.g an in-tray); messages ("persistent" objects such as documents, memos etc. which convey task relevant information); information units (atomic units of information, e.g. a name, account number etc.); rules (if/then productions defining and constraining the behaviour of roles, messages etc.); and functions (atomic operations carried out by roles and messages as part of an activity).

Winograd has written several influential articles on CSCW, in which he develops what he calls a language/action perspective on the design of computer-based systems, as a counterpoise to the traditional information processing perspective (see Winograd 1988 and Rodden, Chapter 1, this volume). It is interesting that similar ideas have recently become topical in the information systems field, apparently independently (see Auramaki et al. 1988; Lyytinen 1987). Winograd makes use of the division in linguistics of language into syntax, semantics and pragmatics in order to lay the basis for his perspective. He is primarily concerned with pragmatics and draws considerably on Austin's speech act theory. The language/action perspective emphasizes that "people act through language". This has two aspects: firstly, that when people have a conversation they are *doing* something, often many things interleaved, such as giving information, helping someone with their work, establishing personal ties etc.; secondly, that speech acts can only be seen as having meaning with regard to the social context in which they are performed, in that they fulfil obligations or set up new commitments.

The main focus of Winograd's work is on what he terms the "conversation for action" (CfA). He has taken the idea that most coordination in organizations occurs through conversations (either oral or *written*) that follow certain set patterns. CfAs are chiefly composed of two types of speech acts: directives (orders) and commissives (promises). The Coordinator (see Brooke, Chapter 2 and Sharples, Chapter 5) is a software tool for setting up and managing CfAs. It offers two main advantages over conventional media. First, clarity: conversations in organizations are often mixed as to subject matter, and it may be unclear, in the case of requests, for instance, exactly what the request is for, its importance, its due date etc. The second important feature of computer-mediation is that it allows people, managers in particular, to "keep track of the action", i.e. to keep track of commitments, in particular to monitor their fulfilment. Auramaki et al. (1988) advance a similar line of reasoning for their speech act approach to modelling office activity.

8.3 PSS: Process Support System

8.3.1 Background and Overview

As has been said, PSS was developed out of the IPSE 2.5 project – a part of the UK Government's Alvey initiative. The IPSE 2.5 project involved a consortium of industry and academe: STL plc, Plessey, British Gas, Dowty Defence Systems and the University of Manchester. The original purpose of IPSE 2.5 was to provide the means by which the process of developing, maintaining, supporting and enhancing information systems could be made more efficient. Traditionally in software engineering, support environments have been considered as tools to assist the software engineer. The IPSE 2.5 project stood back from this traditional perspective and took a wider view of the problem. It was recognized that the key to better software development was not increasingly sophisticated tools, but better coordination among the many people who are necessarily involved in developing software, i.e. that support for software development as a complex sociotechnical process was required. Although the partners in IPSE 2.5 were primarily interested in supporting software development, there has always been awareness that the technology had a much wider scope. The technology produced, PSS, provides a generic platform for supporting cooperative work across many domains. Its application to general office work is of particular interest.

At the heart of PSS is the concept of a process control engine (PCE). The PCE is a computer system that provides an "active work environment" for its users, i.e. a medium which actively supports and coordinates their activities. If a PCE is to provide active support for a process, then of course it must be supplied with comprehensive knowledge of the activities to be supported. An important part of the IPSE 2.5 project was thus the development of a process modelling language (PML), which allows a PCE to be programmed, and *dynamically reprogrammed*, in order to support a given process. Using PML, a process (e.g. software production) is modelled as a network of asynchronous sub-processes that are loosely coupled and need from time to time to communicate with each other. These exchanges occur using an asynchronous rendezvous-like mechanism; the overall pattern of these exchanges reflects the cooperative structure of the modelled process.

The choice of terminology in PML reflects its work-orientated concern with support for human agents engaged in cooperative activities. Sub-processes are referred to as roles and cooperative work is thus conceived of as a network of interacting roles. Broadly speaking, developing a PML model involves breaking down cooperative work into actions and roles, and defining the dependencies between roles. Actions refer to primitive activities, which may be carried out either by people or, indeed, automatically by software tools embedded in the support environment. A role refers to a logically coherent collection of actions related to the achievement of a defined goal, often (but not necessarily) to be carried out in a fixed tempo-ral sequence. Holding a role confers upon some agent the entitlement and obligation to perform certain tasks and the necessary resources for this purpose. The dependencies between roles are referred to as interactions. Such dependencies normally reflect the need of two roles to exchange infor-mation, e.g. that person A needs to transmit such-and-such a document to person B etc.

The original implementation of PML was written in SMALLTALK (Goldberg 1984) and the language has a distinctive object-oriented flavour. The main constructs are all conceptualized as objects (roles, actions etc.). It is important to distinguish between the class definition of an object (a role-class, action-class etc.) and particular instantiations of that class (role-instances, action-instances etc.).

8.3.2 Process Modelling in PML: A Hospital Example

To illustrate the main features of process modelling in PSS and to give an impression of the experience of PSS-supported work, a case study of med-ical office work will be described. This example draws on a independent project, known as the Clinical Information Systems Project (CISP), which was set up in 1988 (for background see Wastell et al. 1987) to investigate computer support for hospital work. The fieldwork for the project was car-ried out in the cardiology department of the Manchester Royal Infirmary (a large teaching hospital adjacent to the university) and the focus of the investigation was the medical office. The reader should picture the cardiol-ogy office as a large untidy room in which five secretaries and two clerks, surrounded by piles of hospital records and using mechanical typewriters, endeavour valiantly to service the clinical work of the three consultants and their registrars. The project in its early days was a rather conventional exer-cise in systems analysis; the investigators did not initially have a CSCW outlook, nor was PSS of specific interest.

Medical office work embraces a wide range of activities: typing, liaison, coordination, communication and record keeping, all of which serve the purpose of supporting, indeed enabling, the clinical work of the medical and paramedical staff. The early work in CISP followed traditional practices: documenting data flows, constructing data models etc. It soon became clear that the orthodox design and modelling techniques were limited in their perspective on office work. They conjure up an impersonal and mechanistic image of offices as information processing systems. What was needed was a more human view of office work, reflecting its nature as cooperative social activity and doing justice to its social and technical complexity. Pava (1983) refers to the nonlinear and concurrent character of office work. Office work consists of many overlapping tasks. Moreover, these tasks are not exact replicas of an idealized template; they comprise many steps which are not simply performed in a strict sequence. Modelling tools for describing office work must thus reflect its cooperative character, its parallelism and its indeterminacy. The analytical techniques of PSS appeared to provide such a richer language and the research effort in CISP turned to develop formal models of medical office work using PML, on which some working prototypes could be developed (Maresh and Wastell 1990).

Process models for various areas of the work of the cardiology office were developed. The example here draws on a large process model which was developed to express the administrative work supporting the organization of the department's outpatient clinics. This process characteristically begins with a referral letter from a patient's general practitioner (GP) to the department, which is assessed for urgency (by, for instance, a consultant's secretary). An appointment is then made to see a doctor at an outpatient clinic. The process proceeds after the visit through a number of possible stages (e.g. laboratory investigations), culminating in a letter from the consultant to the GP reporting his expert assessment. A large number of people are involved in this process: patients, secretaries, clerks, records staff, porters, doctors, nurses etc. Frequently the process fails in various ways, e.g. notes cannot be traced, patients wait interminably, communication with GPs takes much longer than it ought. The work is complex and highly interdependent. There is, however, much that is routine and repetitive, and therefore formalizable and amenable to computer support, with the anticipation of tangible benefits.

8.3.3 A Process Model of Medical Office Work

A simple diagramming convention called the role activity diagram (RAD) has been adopted to help construct PML models and reason about processes. RADs are inadequate to express the full complexity embodied in a PML model, but are useful to give some idea of the modelling concepts and an overall view of the process under examination. Fig. 8.1 shows an RAD for the whole outpatient process. The RAD notation is simple: individual actions are indicated by boxes; interactions by horizontal bars (transects). The clustering of actions into logically related groups i.e. roles, is reflected

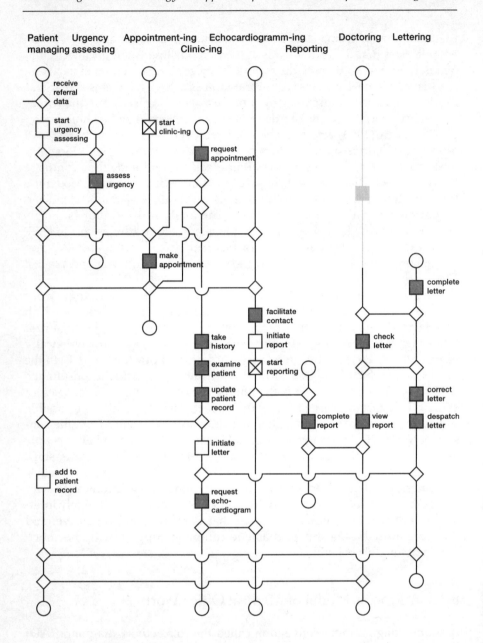

Fig. 8.1 This role activity diagram shows some aspects of the outpatient process model. Labelling has been restricted to actions to avoid cluttering the diagram. Control information is not presented in the diagram (start conditions etc.), nor are details of resources passed during interactions. Note that the vertical structure does not necessarily imply temporal sequence.

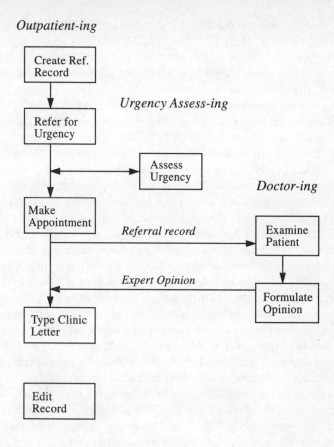

Fig. 8.2 A simplified view of the outpatient process, showing three roles.

in the columnar organization of the RAD. Several roles have been defined in Fig. 8.1, including an overarching *patient managing* role, which reflects the idea of some agent taking overall responsibility for orchestrating the whole progress of a single outpatient episode. Fig. 8.1 serves to give a high level view of the full outpatient process, but is rather cumbersome for didactic purposes. An abbreviated version of the outpatient process is shown in Fig. 8.2. This simplified version will be used for the remainder of the discussion.

Fig. 8.2 shows three roles only, with overall management of the outpatient episode for each patient in the care of an *outpatient-ing* role. The diagram should be understood as follows. In the real world, when a referral letter is received, this initiates a new patient episode; we may speak of a new instance of the outpatient process as being instantiated. Fig. 8.2 simply defines this process to involve the instantiation of three conceptually distinct activities, three roles. The first of these is *outpatient-ing*. The first action in *outpatient-ing* is to create a referral record for the new patient. Next, the urgency of the case must be assessed before an appointment can be made.

The RAD in Fig. 8.2 introduces a second role for this purpose, *urgency assessing*. This role is, as it were, triggered by *outpatient-ing*, which subsequently receives the results of the assessment via an interaction. The reason for splitting off a separate role is to allow the assessment to be carried out by an agent different from the agent associated with *outpatient-ing*, e.g the consultant rather than the secretary.

The relationship between agents and roles needs to be clarified at this point. Roles are abstract collections of logically coherent activities. To carry out these activities, an agent is required. There is an important distinction between actions (which are carried out automatically by the PSS) and UserActions, which require a human agent. At any time a role-instance "points at" a particular user, who is thereby responsible for carrying out the UserActions (if any) associated with the role. Each PSS user is represented in the PSS by a piece of software known as a User Agent which manages the user interface for the user and mediates between the user and their set of role instances. Role-User assignments may be varied dynamically, allowing considerable latitude in the division of labour, e.g. when an employee reports in sick, their work can be simply redistributed by changing role assignments. The reader should also note that as new software becomes available, more and more of the process can be transferred to the PSS (i.e. UserActions become internal actions). By such means, PSS (in principle) allows the man–machine boundary to be drawn and redrawn with considerable flexibility and without the need for radical intervention.

UserActions, as we have said, require a human agent. For *assess urgency*, this real participant might be the consultant to whom the patient is referred, or it might be a junior doctor, or even a secretary to whom the task has been delegated, via the appropriate role assignment. Once urgency has been assessed, the RAD shows control (conceptually) to return to *outpatient-ing* with the next step being to make an appointment. Patient details are then passed (via an interaction) to the third role, that of *doctor-ing*. The patient subsequently attends the clinic; *doctor-ing* carries out its two actions, culminating in the transmission of the doctor's expert opinion back to *outpatient-ing*, which in turn uses this information to produce a clinic letter to send to the GP. One further action is shown in Fig. 8.2, i.e. edit record. It is shown separately because it may be performed at any time, i.e. not at a fixed position in the *outpatient-ing* sequence.

RADs are simple high level pictorial tools for representing and reasoning about processes. The basic constructs of the RAD (roles, actions and interactions) correspond directly to the principal constructs of PML, and the RAD could be used as the basis of a graphical interface to PML. It should be noted that, while RADs provide a natural and convenient way of expressing temporal order, PML uses a much more general and versatile mechanism for handling the coordination of actions within roles. Actions in PML are simply embedded in production rule-like schemata: for each act, its preconditions are specified (e.g. the existence of an urgency assessment

as the precondition for making an appointment); whenever the preconditions are satisfied, the action is said to be *enabled*, i.e. it may be performed. It
is important to recognize that the enabling of an action does not force its
performance; discretion remains with the user.

8.3.4 Work in a PSS: The Electronic Medical Office

Process modelling with PSS is not simply a conceptual exercise. Process
models can be "executed" to create an "active work environment" for a
community of users. They are blueprints which can be used to create a
working PSS supporting the process described in the model. At the heart of
a working PSS, as we have said, is a process control engine, or PCE. The
PCE is able to "bring to life" process descriptions couched in PML.
Working PSSs can be built on a range of hardware/software platforms; a
UNIX version of the PCE, for instance, is available as well as a version for
ICL's VME mainframe operating system. PSS has been designed exclusively
with WIMP user interfaces in mind; SUN workstations and IBM compatible
PCs (Windows3) are currently supported.

We can gain an impression of work in a PSS by considering the user's
view of process supported work. As part of CISP we have used the outpatient process model to create a prototype of "the medical office of the

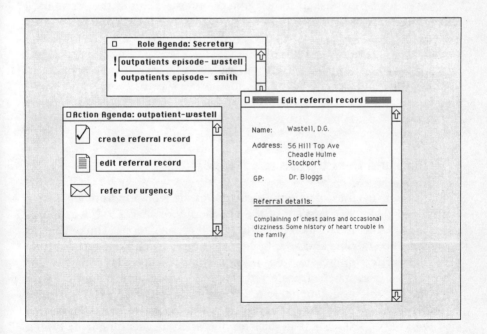

Fig. 8.3 The medical secretary's view of the outpatient process.

future" on a network of SUN workstations. To avoid gender bias, it is assumed in the following narrative that all the actors are female. Fig. 8.3 shows an imaginary scenario derived from the outpatient model of Fig. 8.2 which illustrates how the simplified outpatient process would look to the medical secretary. Having switched on her SUN workstation and logged on to the PSS, several windows have been projected onto the workstation display. Work with PSS, we have said, is structured as actions within roles. Correspondingly, we have two generic types of window in Fig. 8.3: the role agenda and the action agenda. The role agenda simply lists those roles containing actions that are currently enabled (triggered). For each active role, its action agenda lists these enabled actions and, optionally, those actions that have been completed (indicated by a tick).

Thus in Fig. 8.3, we see a role agenda for the secretary which lists two currently active roles, both instances of *outpatient-ing*, one for a patient called Wastell, the other for Smith. Apparently, the secretary has chosen to work on Wastell; the appropriate action agenda is shown in centre screen. Two actions are portrayed, i.e. the two actions whose preconditions are currently satisfied. The secretary has apparently chosen "edit record"; the appropriate icon has been clicked and a window has been projected onto the screen displaying the patient's details. As work within a role proceeds, new actions become relevant and old ones redundant. This progression will be reflected in the appearance and disappearance of icons from the action agenda.

The reader is now asked to imagine the workstation of the secretary's consultant, who is working in her own office down the corridor. Let us assume the secretary requires advice about the case's urgency, and she clicks refer for urgency. At the consultant's end (we assume the consultant is holding this role), this action will cause an "assess urgency" icon to appear in the appropriate action agenda on her screen. To enter her opinion, the consultant clicks this icon, and so on.

8.3.5 PSS and the Problem of Change

The inevitable need to change the structure of the work environment was a central and distinctive precept of the philosophy of IPSE 2.5. It was recognized that change is an inherent feature of all organizations. Thus, PSS was designed to be flexible and adaptable. One simple example is the ability to make dynamic changes to role assignments. If a doctor is absent, for example, her work can be transferred to another staff member simply by redirecting her role assignments to another user agent. If an extra secretary starts work, a new user agent and new instances of the various roles associated with secretarial work (e.g. roles for outpatienting, sending mail, typing papers etc.) are simply instantiated.

More generally, the need to support change led directly to the incorporation within PML of a number of basic mechanisms which allow active processes to be changed "on the fly": for example, PML primitives have been developed to allow new roles to be defined and extant roles to change their behaviour. These PML facilities provide the basic mechanisms enabling the dynamic change of working PSSs. They allow, for instance, evolutionary changes to be made to established processes or entirely new processes to be introduced without stopping the "model"; they allow different staff members or work groups to modify their own processes to support preferred ways of working (i.e. different specializations of a generic role-class). For further technical details of these mechanisms, the reader is referred to Warboys (1990).

Higher level constructs have also been developed to support management and change. Process model for management support (PMMS), for instance, is a generic process model of management. Management is defined as the "indirect work" of coordinating people and technology to achieve organizational goals. PMMS is a process model of management based around the idea of hierarchical delegation in which projects are instantiated (recursively), objectives defined, people assigned, and logistical and technical support identified. PMMS is dynamic and evolutionary: new projects can be defined as they arise, and the role interaction topology changed, again from within the running "model", as the organization develops. Again, for more details the reader is referred to Warboys (1990).

8.4 Current Directions: The IOPT Project

PSS provides both a modelling technique for representing cooperative activity and a means of creating working CSCW systems that are characterized by a high degree of flexibility. The Alvey-funded IPSE 2.5 project completed its work at the end of 1989. Further funding has now been obtained on a significant scale from the UK Government (the Information Engineering Directorate's Advanced Technology Programme) to support further development of the technology and to promote its industrial exploitation.

The Introduction of Process Technology (IOPT) project is a major collaborative project involving STL (now ICL), Praxis, ISS and the University of Manchester. It has a number of important aims. The first is the development of the technology itself, specifically to develop the base technology and enrich the process modelling language with higher level constructs for describing collaborative work. A second line of work is the development of an underlying open systems architecture for PSS with improved tool and database interfacing capabilities. While this chapter is not primarily concerned with the engineering aspects of PSS, these technical developments have important implications and are thus briefly outlined.

8.4.1 Tool Integration

There are at least two ways of looking at PSS. The first perspective, which is the preoccupation of this chapter, is to see PSS as a technology for supporting group work (the CSCW perspective). The second viewpoint focuses on PSS as a medium for integrating a wide range of computer artefacts and systems into a homogenous framework (the systems integration perspective). Organizations have made great investments in applications software and many powerful individual office tools are available. While PSS provides some generic facilities, its aim is not to replace specialized tools. Rather, PSS should be seen as a framework for bringing together a wide variety of tools in an integrated environment, supporting people in their individual tasks as well as supporting group coordination. The job of the PSS is thus not to replace tools but to put to hand the right tool at the right time (e.g. the appointment diary, the secretary's preferred word processor, the manager's usual spreadsheet etc.). Mechanisms called tool servers are integral parts of PSS, allowing the incorporation of external (alien) tools and applications.

The vision in IOPT is that a PSS will not simply cover a local work group but that the PSS will subsume the entire organization. In other words, the user, seating himself before any workstation in the organization, should be able to carry on his work, under the benign supervision of the PSS, from wherever it was left off previously. To continue our medical example, when the doctor logs off the workstation in the ward office and returns to her base, she logs on and resumes exactly where she left off. Perhaps the workstation on the ward is an IBM PC connected to the hospital X.25 wide area network and her office system is a SUN workstation connected to a local departmental Ethernet. That should be quite immaterial. With these exacting technical requirements in mind, there is a major effort in IOPT to develop an open systems platform, based on X/Open standards (X/OPEN 1990), in which interfacing capabilities can be developed for a wide range of office tools and databases across a computing infrastructure potentially characterized by many heterogeneous elements (hardware and software).

8.4.2 Designing PSSs

Another important area addressed by IOPT, which is a particular concern of the authors, is the development of a systematic approach (a methodology) to the introduction and design of process support environments. The conventional paradigm of systems development depicts systems development proceeding in a more or less linear and prescribable fashion, from an analysis of requirements, to a precise specification, through technical design to delivery and acceptance testing of a definitive product. This is the so-called life cycle (or waterfall) model and is manifest in one form or another in the structured methods that are now the backbone of current design practice. Hirschheim et al. (1987) have dubbed this paradigm *the technical perspective*. From this perspective, systems (e.g. office information systems, management information systems etc.) are seen as machine-like artefacts and their development as a rational, deterministic problem solving activity. The structured methods might be dubbed Procrustean in memory of the mythical brigand, slain by Theseus, who had the habit of fastening his victims to an iron bed; those who were too short, he stretched, and those who were too long were truncated.

The technical perspective has considerable difficulty in dealing with the all-too-common phenomenon of system failure (Hirschheim and Newman 1988), failure being defined as a significant gap between the expectations of users (managers, end users) and the actual performance of the system (Lyytinen 1988). Hirschheim et al. (1987) have developed an alternative model of system development, which they call *the social action perspective*. This perspective sees system development as a social process characterized by purposeful interaction between designers and users. The success or otherwise of the project reflects "the accumulated quality of these episodes"; consensus formation, rather than precise specification, is seen as the turning point of the design process. The attainment of genuine consensus requires "free and fair debate" and is hindered by differences in knowledge, interests and power between designers, users and managers.

In a similar vein, Lyytinen (1987) has argued that Information System Design (ISD) is essentially "language action", that reality is actively constituted during design by designers and users as a shared knowledge structure that makes sense of organizational life. Their involvement in design obliges users to make explicit the "hidden" structure of organizational life and in a real sense design deepens the understanding of both designers and users. Lyytinen (1988) describes the design process as "pluralistic, ambiguous and conflict-laden" and argues that Soft Systems Methodologies (SSMs), which help to structure ill-defined problems, therefore have an important part to play. Similar views of design as a fundamentally social activity have been advanced by other theorists, who have put forward metaphors for design based on hermeneutics rather than the orthodox engineering paradigm (see Wastell 1988; Wastell and Cronin 1988).

A number of SSMs have been developed which share the common goal of helping people to deal with complex problems. SSMs embrace both a dialectical epistemology (subject and investigator are acknowledged to participate actively in the synthesis of knowledge) and a perspectivist ontology (no single objective reality is assumed). In common, the SSMs insist that the role of the analyst is to seek out diversity and to construct a so-called "rich picture" of the problem situation, accommodating as many world views as possible. One well known SSM is Checkland's soft systems methodology (Checkland 1981), which Lyytinen (1988) discusses in the ISD context.

Another interesting approach is Colin Eden's Strategic Options Development and Analysis (SODA) methodology (Eden 1989). As well as stressing the analytical skills of the investigator, Eden pays considerable attention to the social dynamics of the SODA process and the interpersonal skills required by the investigator. SODA provides a very useful formal notation (the cognitive map) for expressing the logical structure of complex problems and, indeed, some mathematical techniques for processing these structures (e.g. looking for a common structure across a range of representations). Eden is careful to stress that SODA is a group activity whose aim is not to produce a definitive solution but to achieve sufficient agreement that groups "feel confident to take action". The SODA process involves three main stages: first, the analyst conducts individual interviews, producing cognitive maps that articulate each protagonist's world view. These maps are then combined (as far as possible) to produce a merged map. A group workshop is then convened, in which the merged map is taken as the basis for the group discussion.

In IOPT, a design methodology is being sought that is work-orientated, participative and open-ended, and which sees consensus formation as the critical success factor in design. The framework provided by SODA thus provides a very promising paradigm. PSS is not intended to be authoritarian and controlling (although we are aware of the dangerous potential of the technology); the aim is to liberalize work by enabling greater individual freedom and control. The nature of the technology makes sense, and can achieve its intended benefits, only if it is put in the hands of the users themselves. Central to our methodological work is the development of software tools to allow users, using a high level graphical formalism, to display, design and redesign their local processes to suit evolving personal and group requirements.

8.4.3   Language-Action Based Process Modelling

We have referred to a number of formalisms for representing office work, e.g. Petri nets, RADs, dataflow diagrams etc. Clearly, some formalisms capture more semantic complexity than others. In this section, we describe some of our most recent work on modelling, which has been strongly influenced by a new perspective in systems design known as the Language-Action (LA) perspective. In the CSCW field, the LA perspective is associated particularly with the name of Terry Winograd (1988) and in the information systems field, with Kalle Lyytinen (Lyytinen 1987; Auramaki et al. 1988).

The LA perspective presupposes a pluralistic view of human organizations in which order is maintained between conflicting internal interests by contracts which "define how individuals join together and co-ordinate their efforts" (Ciborra 1984). From this perspective, "information systems are needed to set up, control, and maintain the organization's contracts". Information systems are thus regarded as mediating communicative acts (rather than modelling reality in the orthodox view) which form elements in conversations that reflect the day-to-day working of contracts. The task of the analyst is to reconstruct, with users, the structure and rules of these "organizational conversations". Auramaki et al. (1988) describe a complete methodology for designing OISs based on speech act theory, which involves a number of formal techniques for expressing organizational conversations. Inspired by this work, we have developed an embellishment of the RAD, called rather prosaically the SARAD (speech act based role activity diagram), which allows processes to be described in terms of instrumental acts (actual deeds, such as typing a letter) and speech acts (which typically involve one role requesting a service of another, or transmitting information). Detailed treatment of LA modelling and SARADs is outside the scope of this chapter. The interested reader is referred to Wastell (1991).

LA modelling certainly adds greater semantic richness to process modelling. In speech act terms, the outpatient process is remodelled as a network of instrumental acts (e.g. creating an appointment) intertwined with, and coordinated by, speech acts (e.g. the referral letter is seen as a directive speech act, requesting an expert opinion). By revealing the conversational dimension of office work, the LA perspective allows a range of powerful new intellectual tools to be brought to bear. Auramaki et al. argue that "dysfunctional discourses" are a major cause of inefficient office work. The quality of organizational conversations can be analysed along two dimensions: coherence (that the conversation unfolds "logically", e.g. that questions are followed by relevant answers etc.) and discourse completeness. By uttering speech acts, people make *commitments* which bind their future conduct. The idea of commitment is an important one; commitments are the "glue" of cooperative activity. A complete discourse is one in which all commitments (e.g. to give an expert opinion) have been in one way or another resolved. Setting up and monitoring commitments, it will be recalled, is the key purpose of OISs from the LA perspective. Auramaki et al. provide a number of useful graphical tools for analysing discourses for coherence and completeness (commitment networks, reachability trees etc.).

8.4.4 Field Studies of Process Technology and Cooperative Work

Field work is another important ingredient of the IOPT project. An IOPT club has been inaugurated, the role of which is to promote the dissemination of process technology and to coordinate a programme of case studies in organizations. The case studies are a vital part of IOPT. They provide the opportunity to explore a range of practical and theoretical issues relating to the development of the technology and its exploitation. Health care is one area of field work which, as we have seen, has helped further the development of process modelling techniques, and which has provided a test bed for exploring the potential of process technology. Other studies of a similar nature are underway in a range of organizations that have expressed interest in the technology and a willingness to be "guinea pigs".

8.4.4.1 *The Customer Services Case Study*

The case studies are important because they provide the opportunity to evaluate PSS under real-world conditions, complementing our laboratory-based work. One major implementation of PSS is presently under way in the customer services (CS) division of a large manufacturing concern. At the time of writing, PSS is being introduced into one area of CS as a pilot experiment. A full longitudinal evaluation is under way, which we are not yet able to report on. It is, however, instructive to record that PSS has satisfied the CS's functional requirements. The most important of these were the need to introduce PSS incrementally (in particular to incorporate existing databases used by other groups), the need to provide embedded links to other tools (e.g. to an expert system assisting fault diagnosis), to provide support for flexible working and to allow local variations of working procedures. The CS pilot is an important one. If successful, then implementation will proceed to cover the whole of the CS operation, which involves several hundred staff spread across the UK at twenty or so sites. The "process" itself is complex and differentiated. It has discernible stages and involves distinct groups of actors (call registration, first-line support, maintenance engineers, second-line support), each with specialized skills and roles. The process is geographically distributed and indeed many of the work groups are spread across several sites.

8.4.4.2 *Office Automation and Routine Work*

Finally, we will comment on one important general issue for CSCW and OA emerging from the field work in IOPT, the question of the nature of routine work. PSS provides support for processes. By "process" we refer to some routine way of carrying out a desired activity: a definable, generalizable procedure involving people and materials designed to accomplish a well defined objective. The concept of process is clearly associated with the larger concept of bureaucratic organization, i.e. the use of explicit rules and procedures to coordinate the internal operations of the organization (Morgan 1986). The idea that routine office work involves following formal procedures is at the heart of PSS and its OA precursors. But how routine is routine?

In an important paper, Gasser (1986) has addressed the question of "routine" work. From his field observations, Gasser concludes that it is anything but routine. It is quite wrong to regard routine work as the slavish follow-ing of bureaucratic rules and procedures. Much of so-called routine work is skilled problem solving (see also Wynn 1979). Offices are open systems; "anomaly is ubiquitous"; often the correct procedure is not mechanically obvious; indeed, often procedures must be adapted to suit the exigencies of the situation. For these reasons, no formal description can ever completely cover the contingent, ever-varying character of real work. The unanticipat-ed always occurs, requiring resourcefulness and ingenuity. There are always short cuts. "Every real world system requires articulation to deal with unanticipated contingencies: articulation resolves these inconsistencies by packaging a compromise that gets the job done ... the results of this work appear as workarounds or kludges" (Gasser 1986). Gasser takes the "kludge" and the "workaround" not as aberrational but as fundamental to office work, evidence of its skilled nature, of "articulation".

8.4.4.3 *"Routine" Work in Customer Services*

Early attempts to introduce PSS in CS met with fierce opposition. The rea-sons were not hard to find. The system was too prescriptive. "Your system has been designed to be idiotproof, the trouble is we're not idiots", as one user drolly put it. PSS's raison-d'être is to support well defined processes and, indeed, work in CS is governed by clear and detailed work instruc-tions (WI). For example, the procedure for handling customer calls by the diagnosticians who provide first-line support is, crudely, as follows. Several diagnosticians work in a team and they take calls from a common stack which is ordered chronologically within priority level. The rule is to take the top call. Having taken (assigned) a call, the WI prescribe the following call handling process: check details of call – ring customer – note contact made – discuss with customer – note synopsis of problem – route to field service if necessary – suspend or close call. The key performance target is to make contact within 40 minutes.

Let us now look at what happens in practice by examining a typical hour in the life of one of the diagnosticians, DD.

16.00: Three calls on stack. DD looks at top one. It is a "call back" for John [i.e. a customer has been asked to try something; CS to ring back later] scheduled for 15:45. DD decides to take it. Rings customer. Fault has been sorted out. Closes call.

16.05: Looks at stack again. Again takes top call. Another call back for John. Leaves it.

16.08: Looks at next call: software problem. Leaves [for Ted] – s/w not his forte.

16.15: DD checks queue again. Notes one of his call backs is due. Assigns it to himself to "block anyone else taking it".

16.17: Leaves the call back and takes a new hardware call which has appeared from an important client. A laser printer problem. Checks diagnostic database and rings customer. Asks him to check toner and other simple causes. No luck – routes to field service.

16.30: Again checks stack. Three new faults, all from one customer – VDU problems. Assigns all three to himself and rings customer. Brief discussion – probable software fault. Closes two of the faults [i.e. subsumes the trio to one problem], reclassifies as a software fault, adds narrative, and routes to second-line support.

16.48: DD checks stack again. Takes his call back [40 min deadline imminent] even though a "system down" has appeared [top priority]. Rings customer. Still having problems. Customer is exasperated – lots of problems recently. DD thinks Account Manager (AM) should be informed, but no mechanism. John suggests asking field service to alert AM. DD routes to field service with an appropriate message.

What do we see in the above scenario? The idea that DD simply follows procedures is patently absurd. Putting the procedures into action is clearly skilled work. At every turn, judgement and articulation are on show; doing the job well also requires considerable informal knowledge and coordination. In one case, there is a genuine problem over what to do and a workaround is used. On at least four other occasions, procedure is "violated": e.g. when the software call is "handed off", when the "important client" (informal knowledge) is given priority, and when DD comes back to his "call back" ahead of the "system down" call. In all of these cases, DD, far from pleading guilty, would argue – probably vehemently – that he is working consistently with his interpretation of procedure "in the spirit of the law" and in the best interests of efficiency. He knows, for instance, that Ted is better at software problems, and he knows that Ted knows he knows, so he knows he can safely leave the s/w call on the stack and that Ted will pick it up (informal coordination).

8.5 Conclusion

> O chestnut tree, great-rooted blossomer,
> Are you the leaf, the blossom or the bole?
> O body swayed to music, O brightening glance,
> How can we know the dancer from the dance?
>   (W.B. Yeats, *Among School Children*)

PSS is an interesting CSCW technology with a number of notable features. The concept of an executable process model (i.e. process enactment), the emphasis on tool integration and support for change are significant and innovatory ideas which represent a significant step forward over their precursors, especially in the OA field. PSS offers the promise of supporting cooperative work across many domains. However, its application in field studies has raised a number of profound questions about the nature of routine work in offices and the role of computer systems for supporting cooperative work.

With OA technologies, PSS shares a fundamental belief. This belief is important because it is ubiquitous in computer science. It is the belief that human activities (e.g. office work) can be formally described using some sort of graphical notation (RADs, Petri nets, dataflow diagrams) and that these diagrams are in some sense complete, i.e. they capture all that needs to be said and therefore they form a satisfactory and sufficient basis for designing computer systems. But what our field work suggests is that these descriptions fail to capture what is most essential about office work, namely its contingent, problem solving character. Gasser has observed that the designer's view of office work is often naively mechanistic. Indeed, conventional design practices characteristically eschew detail (logicalization), basing design on idealized abstractions of office work. These become reified in inflexible and obstructive office systems. Wynn (1979) makes a similar point from her ethnographical studies of office work. Our field work strongly accords with these views.

What, then, is the relationship between the formal view and actual work practices? Understanding this relationship is clearly crucial. Formal procedures are normative: they define how work ought to be done. In some cases, formal rules may be rigidly enforced and slavishly followed but in general the relationship between procedure and practice is not a simple deterministic one: the application of rules requires interpretation and negotiation. Indeed, working out how to apply the rules, keeping them, as it were, in good repair is a key part of office work. In a real sense, people make the rules work, rather than the other way round (an inversion of Taylorism!). Suchman (1983) states "the procedural structure of organizational activities is the product of the orderly work of the office, rather than the reflection of some enduring structure that stands behind that work". Suchman may rather overstate matters in implying office procedures to be irrelevant. The procedure manual does provide a frame of reference for work. But this is not to say it determines what people do in a mechanistic way; we all know that "working to rule" is not a byword for efficiency! In our view, the relation between rules and practice is dialectical: formal procedures shape but ultimately do not determine practice; practical experience in turn can lead to re-interpretation or reformulation of procedures as contradictions emerge.

Our field studies, such as the CS case study, confirm Gasser's and Suchman's view of the skilled, problem solving nature of apparently routine work and the dangers of being over-prescriptive. Although much of the work in CS is apparently prescribed in detailed work instructions, application of these rules requires considerable interpretation and discretion; sometimes judgements are wrong, requiring backtracking and the exploration of new approaches; often official procedures appear to be violated, but invariably in the interests of efficiency. To repeat our earlier saw, "People make the rules work".

The obvious implication of this is that coordination systems such as those based on PSS need to be extremely flexible. The recognition that offices are open systems motivated the progenitors of PSS to produce a technology on which it was possible to build flexible and adaptable coordination systems. PSS is not a simple tool like Coordinator; it is a system designed to be extensively tailored to the specific situation in which it is used. It works by enacting a model of the processes occurring in that situation. The actual systems built using it can be rigid or flexible, depending on the models created by the designers of a particular system. There is thus a great need for a process design method and supporting tools to aid designers in the production of appropriate models, and as indicated above, this is being urgently addressed in the IOPT project.

Chapter **9**

Computer Supported Teamwork

I.D. Benest and D. Dukić

This chapter briefly describes the emerging Automated Office Metaphor, with particular emphasis on its ability to share captured and computed information, within small project teams. Instruments are formal documents that are used in an unautomated office to assist with the collection of information. They usually exist as paper forms. This chapter emphasizes that it is the organization and design of the electronic equivalent of these instruments that turn the mere sharing of information into a conferencing system that supports small project teamwork. A number of instruments are described, emphasizing both the ease with which they are designed and the way in which they tailor and organize cooperative work. Problems that might arise if this new user interface were to be adopted for serious activity are discussed.

9.1 Introduction

9.1.1 The User Interface and Support for the Task

Twenty-five years ago Kuo (1966) wrote "computation provides depth, clarity and insight", by which he meant that the detailed arithmetic and the precise detail of the equations used to model electronic circuits could be largely left to the computer, while the engineer was able to concentrate on the goal of achieving a design that met a desired specification. The computer was a tool that extended human computational abilities. While it was still necessary to be aware of the effects of finite word size, for most of the time the engineer was able to concentrate on the design goal, rather than on the means of achieving the analyses upon which the design decisions were made.

Today, when application software is designed, effort is still usually concentrated on producing the means, while support for goal achievement is largely ignored, resulting in an overly complex user interface that distracts the end users from their main task. So a computer environment such as the emerging Automated Office Metaphor (Benest and Dukić 1990a), which is designed to support the work of engineers, must provide an infrastructure for tools, a consistent means of user interaction that lacks complexity, a user interface that is in some sense natural, and a provision for handling the clerical aspects of the job. In this way the computer provides the mundane computation (analytic, heuristic) and organizational support, while the user provides the human intelligence, experience, world knowledge and motivation.

9.1.2 The User Interface and Cooperative Work

Generally, individuals do not work in total isolation; they work as part of a team collectively aspiring to a project goal. The team provides mutual support to overcome difficulties that are encountered by the individuals. Unfortunately the members of the team may interrupt each other and this is particularly serious during periods of intense concentration. This interruption is natural, it is not always necessary, sometimes it is thoughtless, but sometimes it can help to synchronize the project team. The proportion of the user's time devoted to intense concentration will grow as the computer takes more of the responsibility for the mundane aspects of the individual's work. So these interruptions will become more serious. This implies that the computer environment that supports the work of the individual should also support the collective work of the team. It also implies that it should help to minimize the number of destructive interruptions within the team, without destroying the cohesiveness that results from spontaneous interaction.

Face-to-face meetings are most productive when it is important for interperson interaction to be fast and intense, and for the arguments to be dynamic and persuasive. Seward et al. in Chapter 10 describe a multimedia environment for supporting face-to-face meetings, and consistent with our suggestion, Diaper in Chapter 6 suggests that such meetings may have a different role and utility from keyboard-based, asynchronous group work (see Rodden, Chapter 1 and Sharples, Chapter 5). Face-to-face meetings cannot be truly supported by the computer where the form of inter-person interaction is via the keyboard. The persuasive inflexion, hesitation and emphasis are missing, and the pace is too slow. Where groups are widely dispersed geographically, there is hope that if the main communication medium is a large-screen television arranged so that participants really see who is looking where, then face-to-face meetings might become a rarity. A computer would set up the audiovisual link and would provide the transmission of computer information, either freshly computed or from store. However, the reality of the situation and the sense of presence will be very hard to transmit, simulate or otherwise provide.

Furthermore, real face-to-face meetings are not always as productive as they could be. For example, meetings can waste time with matters of information that could be more efficiently divulged in a copied, circulated, or electronically mailed form. Unfortunately, these do not easily convey the inter-person discretions that smooth the path to their acceptance. An agreed code and etiquette are necessary (Shapiro and Anderson 1985; and in particular in this book Hewitt and Gilbert, Chapter 3; Gilbert, Chapter 4; Sharples, Chapter 5; and Diaper, Chapter 6). Furthermore, face-to-face meetings at which factual information must be gathered from the team before a decision can be made, are inefficient. Instead, the data should be gathered and distributed prior to the meeting, thus enabling the participants to dwell on the information before the final decision is taken. This is particularly relevant where all team members are present, but not all are directly contributing all the time. In such circumstances it may be necessary for them to be aware of the arguments being discussed, but not necessary for them to take part in the discussion. Therefore, they are partially wasting time being present. It is this latter area of cooperative work that can be supported by a conventional computer system.

9.1.3 Scope of this Chapter

This chapter briefly describes the Automated Office Metaphor, two of its constituent elements, the manner in which management and organization is incorporated, the mechanisms that provide information sharing, and the organizational means that exploit that information sharing to enable support for some aspects of cooperative work. It discusses those areas of cooperative work support that can be assisted within the Metaphor, with possible help from other media such as the telephone. A number of scenarios for cooperative work within the Metaphor are described. The overall design of the system is meant to support the need for individuals to be undisturbed when their work demands quiet and thoughtful solitude, to increase the proportion of the working day where this ideal is met, and to make more open the management of the project. In this way the productivity of the team (and perhaps the quality of the work) should be enhanced. To achieve this enhancement, the computer support should be designed to reduce the number of interruptions that an individual receives, reduce the number of meetings that do not require the dynamics of a face-to-face meeting, and make the project team more aware of who is contributing to which activity.

9.2 The Automated Office Metaphor

The Automated Office Metaphor (Benest 1989) is a high level style of user interface designed to overcome the window chaos (Benest and Dukić 1989) usually apparent with desktop style user interfaces. (We use the term "Metaphor" to mean a high level style of user interface, including the guidelines necessary for consistency, and we use the word "metaphor" in its literal sense.) The Automated Office Metaphor removes the need for the window manager to have a user interface, leaving the window manipulation (e.g. bringing a window to the front, making the window the right size) to be performed by the tool that has to assist with the given task. In certain respects it has a managerial function that organizes the clerical facilities (open, close, pop, resize, etc.) of a window manager.

Fig. 9.1 shows a typical arrangement. Currently there are two constituent elements to the Automated Office Metaphor: the Role Controller (there are four different formats of a Role Controller, three of which are illustrated on the right-hand side of Fig. 9.1) and the Book Emulator (seen on the left-hand side of Fig. 9.1).

9.3 Role Controller

The Role Controller provides user access to software tools. These tools are organized in two ways. First, they may closely align with the user's job description, and, second, they may provide access to very large quantities of information. For example, most people have an implied self-managing role (see Brooke, Chapter 2, for a more extensive discussion on this issue), so that the appropriate Role Controller would provide access to a diary, telephone directory, notebook, planner, etc. If, as part of the job, the user needs to obtain information that is centrally retained (on company clients, for example) then a Role Controller would be provided that enabled access to the information via an alphabetical ordering. A person who is responsible for the maintenance of, for example, four pieces of software would have, in four separate roles, access to the sources and the tools for specifically compiling and binding each program. There is no restriction as to the software that may be run; generally applications would be sited at the same location (totally overlaid), but they could take over the whole screen such as might be required by a computer-aided circuit design environment. By means of a message passing process, the Role Controllers are aware of which tools have been invoked and which one is currently in view.

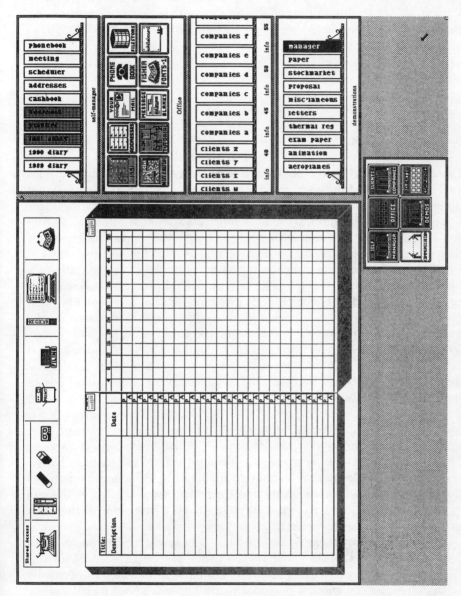

Fig. 9.1 Automated Office Metaphor with activity planner.

Furthermore, although the same tool may be in many roles, only one copy is ever invoked and may be brought to the front via any of the roles that have that tool. Fig. 9.1 illustrates that a number of tools have been invoked, but only one is currently in view. So the Role Controller identifies with Woo et al.'s (1985) definition that "an office role is the set of actions and responsibilities associated with a particular office function" (see also Wastell and White, Chapter 8).

9.4 The Book Emulator

9.4.1 Navigation

The Book Emulator is an alternative form of hypertext system (Conklin 1987), with many of the hallmarks that would categorize it as hypertext, but none of the fundamental user interface problems that grossly nonlinear hypertext systems exhibit. By maintaining a basic linear information presentation format, together with book-like cues that signal location and directional travel, it is predicted that the user is most unlikely to suffer the "getting lost" predicament encountered in hierarchical or generally networked hypertext systems. Since the main travel direction is linear, the cognitive overhead of having to remember the location and semantics of a future path along which it would be desirable to travel is not apparent. Furthermore, two mouse buttons are allocated to changing book-like pages so that the user can go forward or back a page; the page turn is animated across the screen, reinforcing the direction of travel and the fact that a desired move has actually taken place. Maintaining pressure on one of these buttons, enables the user to flick through the electronic book. By so doing, the user can, ostensibly, see all the information contained in the book; there is nothing hidden from view. In this way, there is a very open view on to the information quite unlike the "tunnel vision" effect imposed by the "interlinked mass of spaghetti" (Brown 1989) characteristic of hypertext, where the information is made available only if the user remembers the precise path to take. In addition to the flicked page animation, the size of the book indicated by a splayed page image at the sides of the book grows and shrinks as the user progresses and regresses.

Despite the basic linear presentation, it is possible to jump around the book. There are the standard mechanisms of contents and indexes. Generally, these are located at the front and back of the book, respectively, so that the user can employ personal world knowledge for their location. Flicking to the back or to the front will locate them. Approximate jumps can occur if the user selects within the image of the splayed pages at the sides of the book. Jumping to the very front or very back only requires the user to select at the edge of the splayed page area. The author of each book can also specify "hot-spot" areas anywhere within the book. One particular use of them is to make nonlinear jumps.

The user can also insert bookmarks; if they are placed so that they overlap the top edge of the book, then the user can later select the protruding part and the book will be turned to that marked page. In principle, any number of bookmarks can be inserted and they are persistent across sessions. In fact, there is a maximum number that has been set to a value (50) much higher than it is thought would be demanded by a user. The width of the page imposes a practical limit. Of course bookmarks can be overlapped and can be placed anywhere on a book page. Their depth within the book is (inadequately) signalled by horizontal lines within the splayed pages along the bottom of the book. The intention is to simulate the indentation that would be caused by a bookmark in a real book. Bookmarks cannot be labelled, but the pages they mark can be annotated, particularly if the document is "single-sided" (with every other page blank). Automatic insertion of a bookmark occurs if the user selects an arbitrary hot-spot or selects an item in the contents or index. It replaces the need for users to mark their place (in the contents or index) with the finger. Selecting on these automatically inserted bookmarks causes the user to move to the marked page, and the bookmark is removed. Any automatically inserted bookmark that remains when the book is "put away" is not retained for the next session. This special handling of automatically inserted bookmarks ensures that the user is not required, at frequent intervals, to remove those that are unwanted. Any bookmark can be picked up from the page, placed on another page, or put back on the stack. When an automatically inserted bookmark is picked up it reverts to ordinary status.

So navigation is generally linear (using the two mouse buttons), though it can be nonlinear (using contents, index, bookmarks, arbitrary hot-spots and the splayed page area), but the location cue is linear.

9.4.2 Type of Information and its Production

Information can be text (in any font), lines or pictures with which any diagram or table can be visually specified. The hot-spots enable extra information to be added to the current pages in view. This enables the basic information to be presented without the clutter of qualifying or more detailed explanatory information. This extra detail can take the form of animation (Benest 1990) or pre-recorded speech. In many cases, it is only necessary to change the layout of the book's pages to create a new tool, a task that takes only a short period of time to perform. Even with a tool that requires a computation application (the Book Emulator can be controlled by a parent process and thus act as a front-end to the process), the user interface (interaction and presentation), can be implemented in the same period of time. Thus the interface to a tool (with or without a computation application) can be very rapidly prototyped by the user interface design engineer.

9.4.3 Information Capture

As with hypertext systems, the Book Emulator is not only a means of information presentation, it is also a means of collecting information from the user. The mechanisms by which information is collected are via the keyboard, free hand quill pen using the mouse, highlighter using the mouse, multi-state buttons changed by selecting with the mouse, and schematic drawing using mouse and keyboard. All these annotations are, by default, personal to the user and are retained between invocations of that book.

9.4.4 Information from the Keyboard

Books can be annotated using the keyboard. The text can be freely edited, although text cannot be inserted within existing text; it can only be deleted or overtyped. By judicious use of left and right margins, typing can be restricted to specific areas of a page. Such a mechanism is ideal for form-filling applications, the form being a major office instrument (Yao et al. 1984). The user need only type, the Book Emulator automatically places the current word on to the next line if there is insufficient room for the word on the current line. The page is automatically turned when the typing cursor reaches the end of the right-hand page during typing, and similarly if the cursor reaches the top of the left-hand page while deleting. Single lines can be copied and pasted, both within a book and between books. The typing cursor may be moved with the keyboard cursor keys or with the mouse.

Facilities exist through hot-spots that enable typing annotation to be copied to another location within the book. This enables the author to provide the user with the ability to make short notes, which are then collected together at some other point in the book. Such a technique enables the user to see all the notes together (for an overview), while still being able to see each note in the same location at which it was made.

9.4.5 Free-Hand Sketching, Highlighter and Multi-State Hot-Spots

Using the mouse, the user can annotate as if with a quill pen or can highlight lines of text. Quill pen and highlighter annotations are removable with a rubber.

Multi-state hot-spots visually (and semantically) change their state when selected. The designer (author) of the book determines how many states each hot-spot should have, and what their visual representation should be for each of those states. The states of these hot-spots are retained between sessions and they can be interrogated by an application program. They provide a very useful general function. For example, in a noughts-and-crosses conference book, each of the nine play positions may be implemented as a three-state hot-spot (blank, cross, nought). Repeated selection cycles through these states with wrap-around. They can be used to change the style of the page from, for example, a day planner to a week planner, to graph paper, to blank paper, and so on.

9.4.6 Schematic Drawing

Schematic drawing is also possible. The symbols for the specification are placed in the book on an invisible grid; the presence of the grid makes the placement easier to perform. Rubber band lines are used to connect between symbols; the lines utilize the invisible grid. Once placed, lines can be reselected to move them to a new location, but if selected near one of their end points, the line becomes an anchored rubber band line again. Text can be used to annotate the drawing; the text can be reselected for repositioning as well as for full re-editing (including character insertion). The text can include mathematical notation so that formal specifications of software are possible. If any symbol, line or text is dragged outside the book boundary and tacked down, the item is deleted. There is a limited form of automatic grouping, so that, for example, if a line that has text close by is selected for moving, the text is carried with the line. The schematic information is of sufficient detail to enable, for example, a circuit diagram to be translated automatically into a nodal description suitable for a circuit simulator. The mathematical notation is sufficient for syntax checking and checking proofs.

9.4.7 DrawingBoard

DrawingBoard (Dukić and Benest 1991) is a separate program that can be run as a child process of the Book Emulator. It exploits the skills of the drawing office; in so doing, it minimizes the complexity of the user interface, complexity being a common feature in commercial systems that have a similar output. DrawingBoard produces text and image files compatible with the Book Emulator. When it is run as a child process of the Book Emulator, it edits pictures that it has previously drawn, without editing the fixed aspects of the book page. DrawingBoard can draw lines and arcs of various thicknesses, it can arbitrarily rotate parts of a picture, and it can be used to clean up images previously captured by a video camera. DrawingBoard updates the two pages on view when it terminates. It is by this means that DrawingBoard offers basic authoring facilities for electronic books.

9.4.8 Shared Captured Information

Although these annotations (and the state of the multi-state hot-spots) are by default personal to the user, it is possible that they may be made visible to any number of other specified users, in which case those other users may have observer status, or they may have full read and write permission. Arbitrary text, lines and pictures that are separate from the main page design can also be similarly shared. These are the files used by DrawingBoard, and they can also be used by any separate application to compute arbitrary information such as a graph or table of data and cause it to be displayed in the book, the information automatically being made available to all those sharing.

The facilities for collecting information from the user and allowing these to be shared between users effectively provides the mechanics upon which a conferencing system for text, drawing and pictures can be based, the information being provided by both human and computer conference participants.

9.4.9 Computer Conferencing

The original perception of a computer conferencing tool was that it should provide a means by which debate could take place between participants who were geographically and temporally remote from each other (see Rodden, Chapter 1 and Newman, Chapter 7, in particular). The sharing mechanism abides by this percept. Thus users do not have to be present on-line at the same time. Instead, they can choose a time that is most suitable for them. However, any or all of the participants can be present at the same time and see the information, but only one person can annotate at a time and all others present are informed of who is annotating. When that user finishes, all members are updated with the new annotation within ten to twenty seconds. The system works over a distributed filestore linked by means of a local area network (LAN). Thus, at present, geographical remoteness extends only within a local site, though future advances in inter-LAN connections (Delisle and Pelamourgues 1991) are likely to remove this restriction.

9.4.10 Teamwork Support

A conferencing system should be more than just a shared filestore (see Brooke, Chapter 2); but a tool that supports teamwork must be more than a conferencing system. The design of such a tool must have two characteristics. First, it must provide clerical organization that enables participants to concentrate on the debate and not on the means by which individual contributions are made, collected and conveyed to the rest of the team. In particular this clerical organization should enable the team leader to concentrate on directing the thread of debate. In many respects the clerical facilities focus on the secretarial activities needed in a face-to-face meeting. The second characteristic relates to the order of debate. Because the temporal order in which contributions are made is not necessarily the order in which the thread of debate should be read, there is a need to ensure that the thread is correctly organized; otherwise all users have to identify the correct order while also trying to understand the meaning of the material. This incorrect order is a direct result of allowing users to "attend the meeting" at different times rather than for them all to be present at the same time. This is most pronounced when participants go away for long periods such as holidays.

But teamwork is not solely a matter of discussion and debate. It is also a matter of project planning, progress monitoring and reporting; that is tools, methods and instruments that help a project to keep to agreed time-scales and within available resources (see in particular Gilbert, Chapter 4, and Sharples, Chapter 5).

9.5 Instruments for Teamwork

In an unautomated office, instruments are formal documents that are used to assist with the collection of information. They usually exist as paper forms. As an example, a paper version of a day planner (a form partitioned into fifteen-minute intervals from 8.00 a.m. to 6.00 p.m.) is an instrument that helps clarify and plan an individual's working day.

The instruments described below give an indication of how the sharing mechanism can be exploited in the Automated Office Metaphor. They are largely based upon paper instruments, for four reasons. Firstly, they exploit a long development period with contributions from very many people, and probably represent an optimum in design. They have been shown to be useful, at least in the paper implementation. By exploiting computer technology, initial marginal improvements can be made to their handling, but of course tremendous benefits can accrue from the fact that the information is stored on a computer and thus can be reprocessed. Secondly, the instruments are well known in the unautomated world and so the user's world knowledge can be exploited. Indeed the form is "the central structural abstraction for data flow in an office" (Yao et al. 1984). Thirdly, the instruments are usually forms, so their implementation maps well on to a form-fill style of interface, which lacks the complexity that often accompanies menu-based or command-based styles. Fourthly, when combined (bound) with other instruments, their shape and layout offers a very positive differentiating cue when truly browsing, enabling them to be recognized quickly.

The illustrations offer an indication of possible final designs that might be used. It is emphasized that because the layout of electronic book pages is not a time consuming activity, the precise layout can be modified to reflect the organization, the department, the group and even the individual. There are two basic formats described in this chapter, a book containing multiple copies of a single instrument, or a book containing a few copies of multiple instruments. No authoring system exists to help in the production of these pages, though DrawingBoard (Dukić and Benest 1991) has been developed as a step in this direction.

The instruments illustrated are designed for small teams. Generally such an environment would complement the IPSE and CAD tools available and whatever sharing mechanisms that they provided for cooperative on-line work. However, it is possible for the interface software to such design tools to be replaced by that of the Book Emulator, though the replacement would not be direct. One of the benefits of utilizing the Book Emulator is its ability to freeze states in the iterative design process. In other words it can manage the clerical notes of the project. This means that the steps in the design can be retained by the Book Emulator and those actual steps reviewed (audited) at a later date, together with the results of the final design. This provides a "two-and-a-half-dimensional" view on to the design space. Thus, the standard engineering approach to having designs checked by a colleague can go deeper than merely the finished article. The ability to review in depth a safety critical system that has just proved its fallibility in practice would also be useful. But having the Book Emulator as a front-end immediately provides a sharing mechanism for cooperative work.

9.5.1 White-board

The simplest form of shared activity is the electronic equivalent of the group's white-board that is usually mounted in a central area and visible to the whole team. What information is presented here depends on the team members but generally it is informal, often very newsworthy, and sometimes the best place to put unmemorable material used by the whole team prior to its formal adoption. An electronic book of blank pages suitably titled could be shared by the team and dated items would be introduced as and when necessary. Information that went out of date could be erased, or merely kept; if the latter, an informal record of the team's high spots, deadlines and periods of intense activity would automatically result.

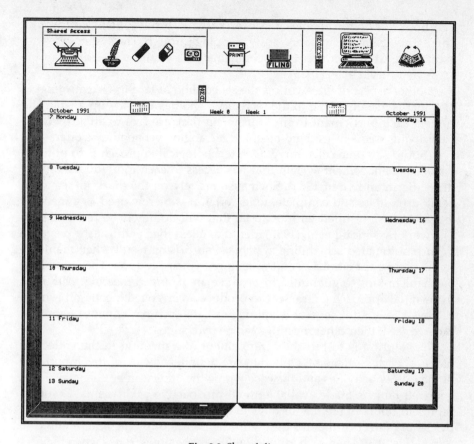

Fig. 9.2 Shared diary.

Alternatively, a single project book would contain a few pages for a central white-board that would need to be kept relevant by one member of the team. Of course, it could be used as the medium for giving a picture to a colleague without the need to specify file names. This instrument maintains the principle of the white-board and does not attempt to expand the metaphor as do Donahue and Widom (1986).

Another shared information medium is the diary (Fig. 9.2), particularly in the secretary/manager team, the manager/sales staff team or where a central room-booking facility is required. The diary is presented through the Book Emulator very much like a conventional paper diary, with one page per week for fifty-three weeks. The normal previous year, current year and next year calendars are provided at the front of the book. Notes in the diary are made using the keyboard annotation facility. Each working day may have up to eight lines of text. This diary clearly offers a different user interface on to information compared with previous systems (Gifford 1980).

The Book Emulator enables the user truly to browse visually through appointments instead of laboriously stepping through. The system does not exhibit the user interference mechanisms such as those identified in the study by Kincaid et al. (1985).

Another aspect of teamwork is the scheduling of face-to-face meetings, a task that is usually given to the secretary, who has to draw up a table and contact each participant to find out when they are free to attend. Where participants frequently attend meetings, arranging yet another is often difficult, not to say time consuming. One technological approach is to utilize a database management system that has access to each individual's on-line diary (Sarin and Greif 1985). Such systems rely on the diary information being up to date and complete, when often it is merely used as a memory jogger and is not filled with material that will definitely be remembered. The work by Kincaid et al. (1985) identifies a less than enthusiastic response to such automated scheduling systems, a surprising result when manufacturers place great emphasis on this feature in their products. The automated mechanism fails to guarantee to produce an arranged meeting. Although the manual approach guarantees to produce an arranged meeting it is often achieved only after several telephone calls to each participant requesting them to see if their other meetings can be rearranged.

The solution is to put the arrangement of a meeting in the collective hands of each participant. Only they are definitely aware of the importance of their other activities and the ease with which they can be changed. Thus, a shared table is made available to all prospective participants. Columns represent hours in the day or days in a fortnight and the rows are filled in by the organizer of the meeting with the names of the people required to attend (Fig. 9.3). Then each individual fills in the times/dates when they are available for the meeting. An advantage is that all attendees can see the organizational difficulties and, where possible, modify their response to accommodate the schedule. The meeting scheduler can be made in a number of guises, depending on the level of secrecy that pervades the organization. For example, an open organization would ensure that all members of a department, via a common meeting scheduling book, could know which meetings were being arranged in their department even though not all people attended or needed to attend every single meeting that took place. Such a system could provide an interesting impact on the social fabric of the organization! In a project team book, a couple of pages would be allocated for arranging such face-to-face meetings.

9.5.2 Limited Discussion Meetings

Face-to-face meetings are most important when the discussion concentrates on collective decision making by means of persuasion, rather than on the simple collection of facts upon which to make a reasoned decision. Intense

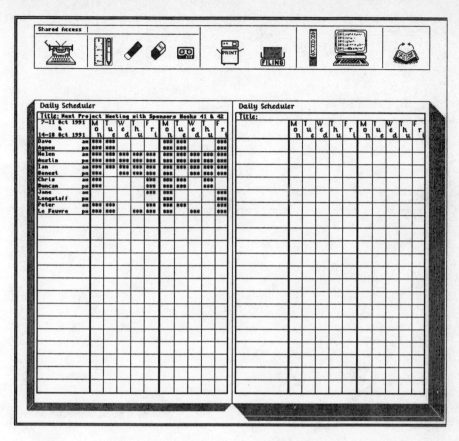

Fig. 9.3 Face-to-face meeting planner.

argument cannot adequately be supported by a computer whose only means of capturing individual's statements is via the keyboard. The instrument described here attempts only to support discussions that consist of capturing points of view, capturing individual's comments on each of those points, and reaching a decision within a few rounds of discussion either by obvious consensus or by voting. The meeting support instrument (Fig. 9.4) consists of double pages with enough sections for all participants to make their contribution at each round of the discussion.

Each person is allocated a section in which to make their contribution. The number of such double pages limits the number of rounds that a given discussion can take; a limit which still ensures that the type of discussion described in the previous paragraph can be transacted. If the team uses one whole book per meeting, the absolute limit would be set to the maximum number of pages in the book (currently set at 100). If the number of participants is large, then each round has to occupy more than two pages. The

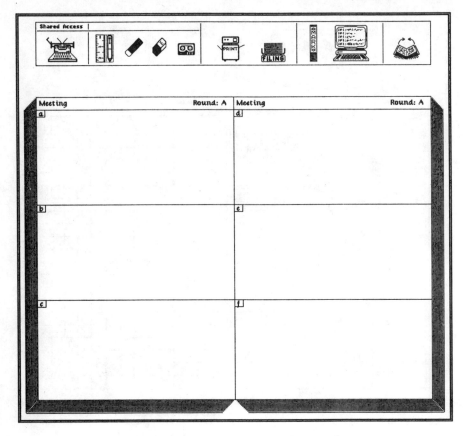

Fig. 9.4 On-line meeting support – first round.

team leader sets the item for discussion, and each participant makes their comment. If necessary the team leader picks up a comment for the next round, inviting the others to pass an opinion. Several comments can be picked up at once and invitations issued on subsequent rounds in parallel. The discussion continues in this vein until consensus is reached. If the discussion looks as though it is going to open up into a more heated debate, then a face-to-face meeting would be called. If a consensus cannot be reached then a proposal is put to the meeting, upon which a vote is taken (see also Rodden, Chapter 1 and Diaper, Chapter 6). Two different forms of voting slip are illustrated in Fig. 9.5. In both cases, each person's vote is clear and might influence the later voters. Shared multi-state hot-spots are employed here, enabling votes to be cast by using the mouse to select a vote area. A secret ballot could always be called by electronic mail (email) (Benest and Dukić 1990b).

This organization has three advantages. First, although it needs positive leadership, it encourages the meeting to "stick to the point" (Maude et al.

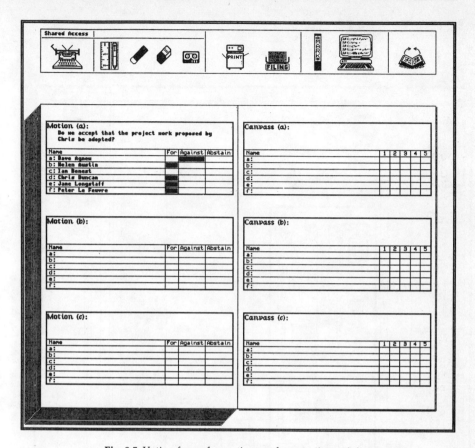

Fig. 9.5 Voting forms for motions and canvassing opinion.

1984). Second, if a member is away for an extended period and the meeting otherwise progresses during that time, then when the absentee returns, responses can still be placed at the correct position within the discussion, ensuring that "old" issues are not muddled with the latest. Third, if the team uses one whole book per meeting, then several items can be discussed in parallel; an index (agenda) located at the front, and suitably annotated by the team leader, would be used to indicate where each item begins.

In comparison with older systems (Palme 1984a; Pankoke-Babatz 1984), it offers an improved ability to browse through earlier discussion, and to see the arguments in a more parallel fashion than that exhibited in the older "serial" systems. Of course if members wished to consult documents relevant to a discussion point, then they have access through their Role Controllers to specific volumes (e.g. the papers for the meeting) all through the same style of interface. If a whole book is devoted to a given meeting, then when the meeting is judged to have finished, the whole book can be filed as the minutes of the meeting without further minutes being written.

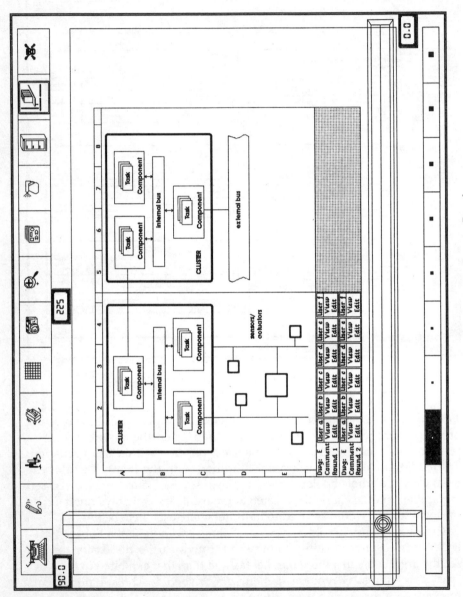

Fig. 9.6 On-line meeting using DrawingBoard.

9.5.3 Limited Discussion Meetings with Drawings

Discussions between designers often revolve around drawings or sketches that in some way encapsulate a design idea more satisfactorily than plain text. Equally, discussions might revolve around mathematical equations. So a system that supports design teams should support such activity (see the forthcoming book in this series, edited by Rosenberg and Hutchison, for a more detailed treatment of the topic of collaborative design). It is debatable whether such discussions do not always invoke intense debate, in which case the only course open is to utilize a face-to-face meeting. However, if debate is short lived then it can be supported under the Automated Office Metaphor. Fig. 9.6 illustrates the view.

There are two ways to draw diagrams: the conventional CAD style of schematic drawing, and the more flexible drawing tool called DrawingBoard (Fig. 9.6). When the drawing is finished each member of the

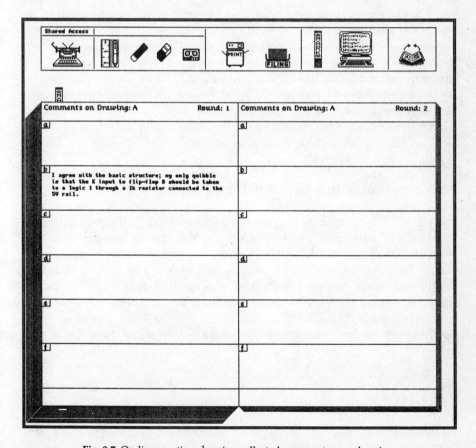

Fig. 9.7 On-line meeting showing collected comments on a drawing.

team may make a seven-line typed comment on each drawing and up to two rounds of discussion are possible. Each person's comments may be viewed (over the grey area) at the bottom of the right-hand page using the active areas on the left-hand page. Thus, comment and diagram are available on the screen at the same time.

Comments may be written by each member while looking at the diagram, and when finished, the comment is moved to collecting pages where all comments in both rounds may be viewed together. So for a detailed comment the other participants can view it with the diagram. But all comments can also be viewed together (Fig. 9.7), thus enabling a very fast overall view of the group's opinion, including those that conflict. (Conflict in the context of collaborative writing is dealt with in detail by Diaper in Chapter 6.) Where there is conflict, rebuttal statements can be made in the second of the two rounds.

Alternatively, a telephone conference might be established to discuss the drawing, and changes would be effected during that discussion period. Components can be "pointed to" by using a grid reference. For example, in Fig. 9.6, the rectangle at grid reference E4 can be orally distinguished by one of the participants. This is an old method of pointing to a symbol in a drawing when the discussants are geographically remote from each other. It is a simple solution to the technical problem of who has control of the cursor for pointing (see also Hewitt and Gilbert, Chapter 3); a mouse and its shared cursor are not employed. A telephone conference between two people cooperatively and intensely discussing a design issue would be very effectively supported in this way; more than two would be technically feasible, but in the authors' view, humanly impossible.

9.5.4 Meeting with a Computational Participant

It is possible to incorporate the computer as a meeting participant, enabling the results of a simulation to be shared. The intention is that the simulator runs on the fastest workstation to minimize the delay in receiving the results. One approach is for the computer process to run entirely independently and when signalled (by means of a multi-state hot-spot), lock the shared files, perform the computation, update the appropriate shared files, and then release the lock. An alternative is for the simulator to run as a parent of one of the Book Emulators. Such a shared simulator is illustrated in Fig. 9.8.

9.6 Discussion

While the sharing mechanism has been tested on numerous small and very specific group discussions, the instruments illustrated in this chapter both

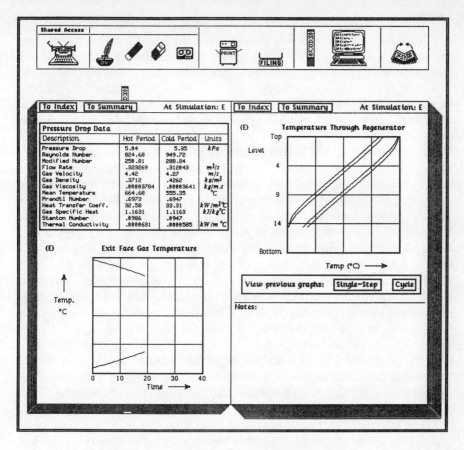

Fig. 9.8 On-line meeting with a computational participant.

singly and collectively need to be tested for their ability to match the task for which they were designed. It thus remains for this to be achieved. However, certain ramifications of the system can be hypothesized, and possible problem areas can be identified. The testing that has been achieved relates to the on-line equivalent of face-to-face undergraduate tutorials consisting of twenty conferences, each with four students answering twenty questions on digital electronics. The monitored performance indicates that the sharing mechanism is successful. (A paper on this facility is at an early stage of preparation.)

9.6.1 Problem Areas

The fixed size area of the typewritten annotations seems to the authors to be desirable, but not necessarily very acceptable to the annotator. If asked to write up an activity, it is common to enquire what quantity/length is required. A fixed size area answers this question. Furthermore, the company/group management gets the amount it requires, ensuring that the employee does not waste time doing more than is required and necessary. It should encourage a well thought out and succinct statement that should be welcomed by the other participants. It thus imposes a required level of efficiency. Yet the fixed area still appears to restrain the freedom for literary expression.

Another irritation is the restriction that only one person can annotate or draw at one time. So all other participants on-line at the same time have to wait before they can make their contribution; and there is no queue mechanism. It is estimated from work reported by Richer (1980) that about ten minutes is necessary for a user to compose a ten-line contribution. That is a long period for others to wait. But it ensures that two or more people cannot update in the same place at the same time, which would pose both a technical problem and a human interface problem. Furthermore, the whole thrust is for discussion that does not require the feedback of an immediate response. Indeed, if all others in a group are waiting for a colleague to make an annotation and the group is local, it calls into question why the group is not meeting face-to-face; certainly a face-to-face meeting would be a better vehicle for the discussion. It would seem that while there is no theoretical limit to the numbers in the team, there must be a practical limit determined by the number of times two people want to annotate at the same time during normal working hours. What that limit is would need to be determined by practice.

Clearly when a decision is called for by voting, it would be interesting to identify the reactions of participants who saw colleagues vote before all had made their comments. In other words, they had made up their minds and were not going to be swayed by their colleagues. The correct etiquette, of course, would be to wait until the voting deadline, read all comments, and then vote.

Another problem is that the computer is able to make seamless changes to information. Because of the consistency of the information, changes to previous comments are hard to detect. This problem is very well illustrated by a chess board shared by two players. Although it is straightforward to provide a mechanism that indicates who is to play next, there is currently no way to indicate what was the last move, a cue that would indicate a change in, or reinforce, the opponent's predicted strategy. A mechanism that generally supported a change indicator (including changes to drawings) is needed.

Perhaps of a more serious nature is the effect of the system upon the team leader. (NB A similar role is suggested in many of the other chapters in this book, although given different names (e.g. "the chair, the secretary or the 'facilitator'", Hewitt and Gilbert in Chapter 3; Sharples's "Host" in Chapter 5; Diaper's "honest broker" in Chapter 6; and Newman's "moderator" in Chapter 7) and there are more or less subtle differences in the purpose and responsibility associated with these roles, depending in part on the group's task, the technology, and so forth.) In many respects, the team leader becomes responsible for clerical activities normally undertaken by lower grade staff, although Gilbert in Chapter 4 suggests that roles can be divided into those of "director", "time-scale watcher" and "absence coordinator", for example, as one means to minimize this problem. The management itself is thrown open to the whole team for inspection and is not the sole prerogative of the manager. These may be seen as degrading the function of the manager, but from the project point of view it must be beneficial. If the team leader should become ill, members of the team can collectively fulfil the monitoring role. The overall technical strategy is also likely to be more visible to the whole team rather than just to the technical manager and as more people will subconsciously consider the whole strategy, flaws are more likely to become visible earlier in the project. It also ensures that the problems of keeping the project on time and within budget, and the technical problems incurred by colleagues, are clear to all, encouraging them to assist in rectifying any difficulties.

9.7 Conclusions

This chapter has briefly described the Automated Office Metaphor that appears to be capable of being a viable user interface to a computer system in place of the traditional command-based or desktop-based interfaces. In particular, it has described the central object within the Metaphor that is seen as an alternative to hypertext and can provide the buttress between the user and the application code. The information that the user enters, be it text, schematics, pictures, or the state of hot-spots, is persistent between sessions. It may be shared with others, including other computer processes. This sharing mechanism provides the technical basis for traditional computer conferencing, but it is the design of the electronic pages that turns the conferencing system into a tool that supports teamwork. The design of these electronic pages is based upon the paper instruments that already exist in the unautomated office.

A book of instruments (Benest and Dukić 1991) for teams of up to six people contains two pages of white-board, four pages for members to request help from others in the team, four day planners, four diary pages, two hour-schedulers, two day-schedulers, four Gantt chart pages, six pages for activity review reports, two year-calendars, eight rounds of textual discussion, six drawing sheets each with two rounds of textual discussion, three motion voting slips, three canvass opinion voting slips, and four pages for a schematic symbol library for drawings appropriate to the team's activity. In addition it contains a selectable index at the front that can be annotated with deadlines and four pages for guidelines on the use of the tool. The true browsing mechanism inherently provided in the tool enables each team member with little effort quickly to scan the state of the project and identify new aspects that have arisen since the last browse. Furthermore, one late monthly activity report is clearly seen by the team and by the person who is late, and it might be sufficient to goad that person into action. Of course, it might have the opposite effect if everyone is late! This book of instruments needs to be evaluated, both in terms of its usability and its usefulness, by a number of small-team projects.

Acknowledgements This work has been partially funded by UK SERC grant number GR/F 37535/IED4/1/1220. The authors are grateful to John Willmott for giving them full access to his simulation software and for his contribution towards the design of the user interface to that software, seen in Fig. 9.8.

Chapter 10

The Pod: A Purpose-built Environment to Support Group Working

R.R. Seward, D. Diaper and C. Sanger

This chapter starts with a summary of work undertaken by Seward (1987) on business trends. This work is first related to a realistic view of the nature and organization of many large commercial and industrial companies. The target user population of particular interest is middle and senior management. The Pod, which provides a unique work environment aimed at providing support to a wide range of managerial groups, is then described. Just how the Pod meets the needs of its managerial users is discussed. The data supporting the claims made for the Pod's success are based on interview and questionnaire data gathered from commercial use of the Pod.

10.1 Introduction

10.1.1 Business Trends

The entry point to this research was the assumption that information technology does support the individual in his or her tasks, but that there is little evidence of its use in the group situation (see, for example, Brooke, Chapter 2), particularly in synchronous, co-existing work groups such as meetings (Rodden, Chapter 1).

A survey was undertaken and over 200 people from a wide range of commercial, business and government organizations were interviewed. The question asked was: "What business trends occurring now or which are likely to occur over the next five years will affect your way of working?" An analysis of the data evidenced the following trends:

- Businesses were moving towards "softer" missions.

- There was more data, and hence more information, particularly external information (see Section 10.2.2), to consider.

- With the easy transport of high value products and know-how, business was increasingly taking on an international dimension.

- The time-scales of business opportunities were getting shorter and were in weeks rather than years.

- The organization was getting flatter; there was a breakdown of the traditional management hierarchy, a loss of so-called middle management and a shift towards more participatory management.

- There was a move towards group working and a need to support this change, as evidenced by office buildings incorporating more group activity space as against individual desk space.

- Finally, there was a confirmation that information technology was an important factor in shaping "the way we do things around here".

Investigation of the methods used by groups of managers highlighted a number of key factors which were subsequently incorporated into the design and implementation of the Pod (see Section 10.3 for a description of the Pod). It became apparent that there were four major steps in most group management activities:

1. *Planning or modelling* involves identifying goals and methods to achieve them. It often uses quite abstract representations of information and could be characterized as being relatively cheap and risk-free. The evidence suggests that this phase of group working is becoming more complex in the light of the business trends identified above.

2. *Decision making* characterized as where the group agrees what it wants to achieve in terms of some form of change and the means of achieving and, hopefully, monitoring the change. It is at this point that the degree of organizational risk relevant to the managerial group is decided.

Note, there may be considerable iteration between these first two steps.

3. *Implementation* characterized as the attempted "engineering" of the changes agreed in step 2. It is here that the major cost to the organization potentially occurs. The implementation of management decisions remains an art or craft (Long 1986; Long and Dowell 1989) and what management science that exists is used rarely and often idiosyncratically. While the bottom line position is that if the estimated and actual costs are similar then management has been effective, there are always

unanticipated effects of organizational change, and, overall, such effects, at least in the long term, tend to make implementing organizational change more expensive than anticipated.

4. *Monitoring and control* naturally follows implementation. Monitoring may range from the very formal to the implicit, and control may be effected as part of the daily management tasks, or by more specialized efforts.

Note, steps 3 and 4 naturally iterate less frequently with the first two steps.

The Pod is intended to provide a complete system (in the general systems theory sense of "system" (Open Systems Group 1972)) that supports discrete examples of steps 1 and 2 above. Indeed, part of the Pod's success undoubtedly lies in the specialized and, to its users, novel nature of its environment. Such a view is predicated on the assumption that people do behave differently when moved to a different environment, even to a more common meeting room. The Pod is basically a carefully designed, technologically sophisticated meeting room.

Additional research suggested that there was a need to limit the group to a manageable size. It was found that between eight and twelve persons con-stituted an ideal group for the planning and decision making steps described above. The knowledge such a group can bring to bear on an issue appears to balance peer group pressure (see also Chapter 6).

It also became evident that if the Pod were to be successful in providing support to group working then it would have to be engineered to support the overlap of perceptual, group behavioural and information technology elements. Our evidence suggests that such a simple model is often used as a basis for discussing with managers their information needs and the kinds of solution that may satisfy them. This model has proved to be widely accept-able and easily understood when used as a means of describing the Pod. Section 10.2 will examine organizational models further and how these affected the Pod's design.

10.2 Organizational Modelling

In the industrial and commercial world, the word "management" has become synonymous with the management of people. This derived from the fact that the demands of a task or tasks have increased to a point beyond the capability of a single individual to perform satisfactorily, mainly through the lack of time or sometimes skill. The manager has, there-fore, to manage this situation by employing others to assist or carry out the task or tasks. Therefore the management need is primarily to manage people, as well as other resources, within a manager's influence or domain.

All this necessitates some form of structure or organization to contain these complex processes.

It appears that the modelling or planning aspects of management are becoming relatively more difficult, wider and complex in scope. On the other hand, the implementation processes are becoming more specialized and narrow in scope. This is not to say that implementation is necessarily easy, or easier, but that the implementation processes are being increasingly helped by supporting technologies.

10.2.1 Pyramidal Models of Organizations

To understand the role of the Pod in its organizational context and to understand its users it is necessary to model the Pod's target organizations. The basic model used is the traditional organizational pyramid, sometimes referred to as the "military model", where line management responsibility flows from apex to base. While radical alternatives have been suggested (e.g. Bjorn-Andersen 1986), this model remains the generic one, although there are local quirks in every real organization. The model is discussed in the context of an industrial or commercial organization, but the general description could be applied equally to, say, a charitable, educational or government organization.

In a conventional organizational pyramid, the Chief Executive Officer (CEO) is at the apex and the operating units are at the base. While this is a gross generalization, it remains a useful model: it at least indicates the relationships that formally exist between the levels of management in a typical organization; the model also suggests the numbers of managers present at each level and it gives some indication of the individual's status and power in the organizational structure and in the decision making processes.

10.2.1.1 *Junior Management*

At the bottom of the organizational pyramid, junior line managers use a very restricted subset of the organization's internal information. Often this merely consists of discrete yet pertinent information derived from data at a transaction level (e.g. Buckley and Long 1985), and only very limited use is made of external information (see Section 10.2.2). Junior line managers make decisions about the detailed and practical interrelationships between resources, such as people and machines. The word "line" implies the implementation of set processes or procedures directed from above. The decision making processes at this level are largely deterministic and the technical systems available to support them are becoming increasingly sophisticated. In many instances, human intervention in this decision making process appears to continue only for historical or highly valid and critical labour-related reasons.

10.2.1.2 Middle Management

Higher up the organization, so-called middle managers are usually interested in the gross performance of particular components or operating units. This means they take a statistical rather than a deterministic approach to their work. Middle managers become interested in individual transaction type data and information only when these are large enough to cause some kind of disturbance in the expected performance of an operating unit. When external information is used, it is largely quantitative, rather than qualitative. The statistical manipulation processes make the information manageable by reducing its variety. The formal models used at this level are characterized by being noncontentious. They are factual and well-proven, as is the information and data they use.

10.2.1.3 Senior Management

For the CEO and other senior managers at the top of the organizational pyramid the *modus operandi* is different: even before setting out to make a decision these managers will commonly have to make initial judgements by answering some fundamental questions. For example, they have to ask themselves: "What is this decision really about?"; "What ball-park am I in?"; "What is the game and its associated rules?"

The CEO and other senior managers are interested only in a very highly summarized and integrated view of the organization's internal information. However, these people place a heavy emphasis on externally derived information.

10.2.2 External Information

Externally derived information available to the organization is significantly different both in source and nature from internally derived information. It is seldom contained in the organization's information base, although it may be available on externally held information bases. However, it is rarely available in a format that is compatible with the organization's internal data management standards. External information comes from a wide variety of sources: not just from commercially available information databases, but also from books, magazines, newspapers, market research data, radio, television, discussions or overheard snatches of other people's conversations. It may be in data, text, image or voice form – or any combination of these. In addition, its accuracy, validity and reliability are variable. External information is often ambiguous and open to various interpretations, and its relevance is debatable. Also, it may be security classified, hence difficult to get at in the first place. It may be confidential, and may bestow power on the individual or group that owns it. Furthermore, it may not be prudent to divulge particular information to the remainder of the organization due to its real or perceived competitive advantage.

10.2.3 Senior Managerial Information Processing Needs

Senior managers have to make judgements about the information available and to question its relevance, accuracy, validity, reliability, etc. and, if the information is judged to meet acceptable criteria, to ask what it means when applied to a particular problem area. At this top level managers have to ask what assumptions or constraints they should make about those aspects for which the information available may be inadequate. In other words, the individual senior manager or the senior managerial group find themselves in a much more ambiguous situation than middle management.

Independently or collectively, senior managers often have to make decisions on the basis of dubious and incomplete information. Therefore, such decisions rely heavily on the judgemental capacity of the decision makers. Such decisions are often strategic and have far-reaching implications, and the risk to individuals and to the organization is potentially high. The situation is further complicated by the fact that in most medium or large organizations, decisions are taken as the result of peer group consensus rather than by individuals. The sheer size and complexity of the organization necessitates this course of action. Thus, it is often the case that though an individual senior manager may have the formal authority to make a decision, he or she does not have the breadth or depth of knowledge to enable that decision to be made. He or she is therefore forced by circumstance (the personal risks of not doing so being too high) to consult with colleagues. In addition, without his or her peers' involvement in the modelling and decision making process, it is unlikely that the necessary commitments to change will be forthcoming.

If it were that simple, a group of senior managers could in all probability cope. The truth is that it is not, and that there is an added complication in terms of personal interpretation. It is an observed phenomenon that a group of managers, when asked to make a decision about the same strategically significant problem, will often each reach a different conclusion. Their conclusions are based, in the main, on the individual's personal judgement. This reflects not only the information which they hold in common with their peers but also their education, training, experience, preferences and beliefs. Furthermore, personal chemistry and participants' views about the reliability and relevance of the opinions expressed by their colleagues are vital ingredients of the mix.

10.2.3.1 *Information Technology Sophistication and Organizational Level*

Historically, junior line managers were among the first people to benefit from the introduction of data processing. In addition to automating clerical tasks, early examples of such systems also provided managers with more timely management information. For example, payroll systems were able to provide labour costs by department; sales ledger systems showed indebtedness by customer with exception reports on customers who exceeded their credit limits or who were slow payers. Today, few such large-scale clerical tasks remain to be automated, and if present-day operational systems do not meet the needs of the users and their organizations, then the shortfall is more likely to be due to lack of resource or management commitment rather than the inadequacies of the information technologies involved.

Developments over the past ten years, notably decision support systems, allow many of the needs of middle managers to be met. Such systems can provide tools to help middle managers identify and monitor trends, to plan projects and make operational forecasts. Knowledge-based systems are also having an impact in this so-called middle management area. The rapid increase in the nature and variety of external information databases could provide them with the quantitative information they need for both modelling and forecasting processes. Any shortfall between the desire and the realization is due to such things as the inaccessibility of corporate information, a historic underinvestment, a conservative culture, lack of education, lack of training and/or lack of time.

But what about systems to support senior management decision making? In reality, few such systems yet exist and those that do ignore one or more of the key characteristics of the decision making processes at this management level.

We are suggesting that there is a positive correlation between the management level in an organization and the necessary sophistication of information processing requirements. Similar correlations with organizational level, we predict, would also be obtained for factors such as:

1. Abstractness of the models employed.

2. Implementation cost of decisions, perceived and actual.

3. Range of sources, media, types, etc. (see below) of information.

The organizational modelling described above suggests that a system to support the top management processes must combine the following attributes:

- *Information* firstly, the ability to access information from a variety of sources, both internal and external to the organization. The trend is towards the external. Secondly, to be able to manipulate and present information from disparate sources in a variety of media and styles. At present there remain format problems, particularly with many sources of external information.

- *Environment* in addition to the functional, information handling capabilities described above, the use of the system, its usability, efficiency, pleasantness, etc. must combine in an environment that supports the kind of behaviour most likely to lead to good decisions. For many, this environment is private and, possibly, secure.

- *Modelling* this involves the group's use of information for modelling: the process of reducing the variety and complexity to a manageable state (i.e. abstraction and reduction) and the ability to make enquiries of these models and of the modelling processes. Enhancing the convergent thinking of the group as modellers and decision makers occurs when they can at least share the same information.

The Pod attempts to possess such attributes because it is designed to maximize, with current analogue and computer technology, the manipulation of accessible information. The Pod does support the presentation of information in a variety of media and styles at different levels of abstraction, depending on the purpose to which the information is to be put. The Pod as an environment has been designed to provide appropriate psycho-social settings for modelling and decision making and actively supports these processes by its information technology.

10.3 The Pod

It is now necessary to describe the physical Pod (see Figs 10.1 and 10.2). It consists of a purpose-built eight-sided windowless room. One of the sides is devoted to a technician's workstation housing a variety of information technology, communications and control equipment. The other sides are information faces that accept images projected from a central dome hung from the ceiling. In the centre of the room is a round table which can seat up to twelve people.

The information faces are used to present controlled information to the group via information technology outputs – graphics in particular. The sequencing of these information faces is controlled either by the presenter or by the technician sitting at his/her workstation.

The facilities provided to users of the Pod allow them to control information from information technology sources using traditional keyboards or mice, as well as from 35 mm slides, video, fax, closed circuit TV cameras, etc. by means of a hand-held infrared controller. This controller also controls the Pod's lighting and sound systems, and enables a quick setup or close down of the Pod if desired. Thus, users can quickly bring to bear any of the Pod's facilities without leaving their seats. Great emphasis is placed on the use of predefined or user controlled light levels to emphasize the information frames to the group.

World-wide, about ten Pods exist and are in constant use. Why are there no more? Partly, the answer lies in the cost, since to build and implement a

Fig. 10.1 The Pod at the ICL Information Technology Centre in Dublin, Ireland, showing the technician's workstation in the background.

Fig. 10.2 The Pod in use at the Decision Analysis Unit at the London School of Economics, London, showing five of the information faces and the projection dome viewed from the technician's workstation.

working Pod costs in excess of £120,000, depending on specification. Partly, it is that the multimedia, multi-element, and even multidisciplinary nature of the Pod concept does not equate to a particular job role within current organizational structures, and that therefore a committed "champion" is required to own and run such a system.

10.3.1 The Pod's Design Concepts

Clearly, it is important to understand what underlying concepts make the Pod work. There are at least six basic concepts that need to be considered, and which were part of the Pod's design:

- First is the Pod as a "shell". The Pod provides a highly visible environment in which to work as a group. There is a strong analogy to the theatre here, in that it provides an open framework in which the users can build "sets" for particular group tasks. The Pod provides the services and scenery while the group provide the actors; the information provides the story line; and the group's goals the plot.

- Secondly, the Pod provides a ready-made, engineered human–environmental interface with a number of control levels. The Pod's air-conditioned environment, lighting and services provides a closed, secure environment. The position and relationship of people around the table, and the use of colour, shape, texture and lighting were all important factors in the Pod's design.

- Thirdly, the Pod is a system that reduces variety. The trick here seems to be reducing the information available to a manageable state. The relationship of people at the centre of the Pod and the data which is around them appears helpful. What appears to be important is to keep both elements in an exciting state and not to reduce either to a point where the answer requires no effort.

- The fourth concept relates to the Pod as a high throughput system. It is compact in size, highly structured to give a number of presets and quick to set up and close down.

- Fifthly is the Pod as a high performance human – computer interface. The Pod's users control the flow of information available to the group, not just its sequence, but also how it is formatted and displayed.

- Finally, the Pod is a high performance normalizer. Here we are back to the concept of theatre: the Pod seems to balance structural and process elements to provide a "no problem environment". It appears to normalize the values of the group, which is perceived as being very important in the process of gaining consensus and commitment within the group.

10.3.2 Evaluating the Pod

An analysis of Pod usage shows that it is used mostly in the following areas:

- For group planning.
- For group reviewing.
- For group activities such as design.
- For group training.
- For meetings and presentations to third parties.

Over a year's use, one particular Pod's users were asked for their reaction to it. In comparison with a normal meeting environment, it was perceived as much better in facilitating the achievement of group tasks and there was more commitment to tasks. Users reported that they had much more confidence in the likelihood of a successful outcome of the task or project at hand. The Pod made it much easier to communicate their objectives, to absorb information and to brainstorm and generate ideas. There was, however, a down side: some people found such an environment too daunting, and considered that it took too long to set up and to learn how to exploit its facilities to best advantage. Overall, it turns out that the Pod is very good at supporting group working where a quality output is required – not urgency. It also appears excellent when democracy and consensus are the norms, as against a telling, dictatorial style. The evidence from the analysis of surveys indicates that the Pod increases both efficiency (by a marked reduction in the time taken to complete a task) and effectiveness (by raising the level of the meeting to a common understanding). Furthermore, it appears that the Pod is perceived as also supporting the engineering of change in the organization, although the accuracy of this perception has not yet been evaluated.

Users' reactions to the Pod suggests that it works because:

- Firstly, the Pod reduces the information complexity to a manageable state by reducing its variety, but at the same time retaining its richness. Such information may originate from individuals in the group or be given to individuals via a number of complementary visual or audio media sources.

- Secondly, the Pod raises the group members to a common higher management level which is often described as: "middle managers thinking and acting like top managers; top managers thinking like the Board". Thus, better communication and understanding is engineered vertically as well as horizontally through the organization concerned.

- Thirdly, the Pod negates extraneous systems noise not just because it is a physical, enclosed system but by the removal of unwanted and undesirable systems noise.

- Fourthly, the Pod increases focus by engineering through good design, lighting and boundary definitions.

- Fifthly, the Pod increases group unity, trust and common purpose, this being reflected in both the efficiency and effectiveness of the output when completing the task. This is brought about by taking into account good group behavioural practices in the Pod's structural design.

A common initial reaction to using the Pod are words such as "It's magic". Overall, and this cannot be easily evaluated in an empirical manner, there is a suggestion that it is the synergistic combination of the Pod's diverse resources and elements, rather than any single feature, that makes the Pod a success.

10.4 Conclusion

Currently the Pod is the Rolls-Royce, state-of-the-art, local, synchronous, multimedia, CSCW management support system. Its success is important because it implies that systems can be designed to support the more senior managerial processes, just as much existing information technology supports the more junior level tasks. What cannot be discovered from directly analysing the Pod is what are the minimum central features that the mass-produced, production line version of the Pod would have to possess. As a minimum the Pod provides an early standard against which future systems in this CSCW area can be evaluated.

Chapter **11**

Usability Trialling for CSCW Technology: Lessons from a Structured Messaging Task

A. Kirkwood, S. Furner, W. Ablard, B. Clark, K. Dickerson, A. Mercer, S. O'Donnell, Y. Siu and O. Williams

The shape of public communications networks is changing. Information technology integrated with communications services will provide opportunities for new forms of distributed work groups to develop. It will be possible to distribute work roles geographically for an activity and link them together through communications and computing facilities. The work itself need not take place by the participants working in a real-time conferencing mode. Group activities that involve passing various types of text-based document are a common feature of office life in any organization. This type of asynchronous group activity can be supported at relatively low transmission rates using conventional electronic mail (email) systems if simple text documents are used. This paper draws on the work being carried out at British Telecom's (BT) laboratories on usability engineering trials of Computer Supported Cooperative Work (CSCW) systems. It focuses primarily on the results obtained from a small trial of COSMOS II, a structured messaging system. The COSMOS II project follows on from the COSMOS collaborative project (see also Rodden, Chapter 1 and Gilbert, Chapter 4) which was carried out as part of the Alvey programme. The aim of this small trial was to identify issues that would need to be addressed if a full-scale trial of this type of CSCW system went ahead. The results of the COSMOS II trial, and the lessons learned from it, are presented here.

11.1 Structured Messaging

Simple computer messaging systems are now an established feature of the electronic workplace. They offer facilities such as the transfer of email, program code or other information between people using the system. Within organizations much of the information flow is dependent upon the requirements of the job role of the individual using the system. Specific items of information need to be viewed and commented on by specific job functions and stored at known locations for future reference.

The communications specific to a work group task provide a requirement on the technology being used. It is not desirable to broadcast every item of mail to everybody on the system. A simple general mail system aims to control the volume of mail through directing it to sender-defined recipients. The use of a communications structure aims to go a stage further and provide a messaging facility that will automatically deal with the distribution of messages according to the task being carried out.

The COSMOS demonstrator (see Clark and O'Donnell 1991 and James & Churcher 1988 for descriptions of the COSMOS demonstrator and project) provides a messaging service based around the roles and the messaging that individuals perform in a work group (see in particular, Sharples, Chapter 5; Wastell and White, Chapter 8). The structure identifies the communication that the roles undertake in order to support the functioning of the work group.

The COSMOS role definitions and communications structure are not arbitrarily decided, but are produced as the result of analysing the tasks that the role players are expected to perform. Where it is being used to automate existing messaging in a work group, the task analysis is used as a simple requirements capture methodology.

Grudin (1989) identified that the failure to learn from the experiences of trialling groupware systems like COSMOS was often a result of the extreme difficulty of evaluating groupware systems in the real environment. Multiuser applications are more susceptible to the social, political, economic and motivational factors at work within a user group than single-user applications, and Brooke in Chapter 2 looks at the differences between single-user and CSCW applications. All users of groupware systems have to be able to participate effectively if the application is to have a chance of success.

11.2 Cooperative Tasks Supported by COSMOS II

The evaluation was based around the performance of two defined tasks. These tasks were selected from a small number of candidate tasks identified as a result of an in-depth study of the trial group's activities during the feasibility stage of the COSMOS II project. Candidate tasks were rejected because:

- They were unable to be completed within the confines of the trial, i.e. joint production of papers.
- They were unable to be supported effectively with this implementation of COSMOS II.

The tasks that were left were not as representative of the trial group's activities as would have been liked. Although not performed as frequently as preferred, the tasks selected did provide a good test of the capabilities of COSMOS II. They were:

- Project checkpoint reporting.
- General mailing.

Project checkpoint reporting was selected because it required regular written contributions from every project member. The trial participants used a paper-based system for reporting project progress information twice a

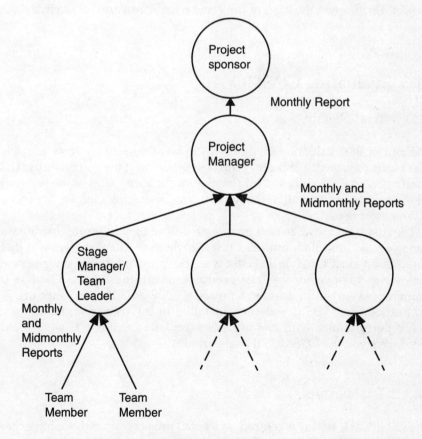

Fig. 11.1 Participant view of the flow of reports between participant roles in trial.

month. The reports were passed along the line management hierarchy (see Seward et al., Chapter 10). The reports themselves were a project management tool that the participants used to identify progress and potential problems (see Fig. 11.1). The mid-month report was used essentially for collecting financial information.

One of the advantages of the original COSMOS system was that it was intended to be user configurable. That is, it would be simple for individual users to change the reporting structure to accommodate any changes in the allocation of roles within the group. It also meant that users would be able to set up their own structures to meet their own communication and information needs. However, due to implementation problems this feature could not be provided in the COSMOS II system that went to trial.

The information gathered on the requirements for the general mail service did not specify a communications structure. It identified the task in which it was likely that an email system would be useful and the types of files it would be expected to transport, e.g. spreadsheet, graphics etc. A general mail structure had been developed within the original COSMOS project. This formed the basis of the general mail structure for the trial.

11.3 Evaluating COSMOS II

11.3.1 Trial Design

The aim of the evaluation method was to be as non-intrusive as possible. Too much paperwork and other interference during the course of the trial would potentially reduce the cooperation of the users. Most of the self-completed paperwork and all of the interviewing was scheduled for the end of the monitoring periods.

The first monitoring period investigated how the trial group carried out the trial tasks, and their attitudes towards those mechanisms prior to their automation on COSMOS II. This was the pre-trial monitoring period. Following this period, the trial group were introduced to COSMOS II. Training was given to users to show how COSMOS II could support the trial tasks. COSMOS II was then installed in the trial environment and users' performance with and attitudes towards COSMOS II were monitored. This was the COSMOS II trial period.

11.3.2 Trial Group

The COSMOS II trial was centred on a small project team developing expert systems, split between two locations, London and BT Laboratories at

Martlesham Heath. The group at BT Laboratories was further split between two locations on site for the pre-trial monitoring period, but for organizational reasons they were merged into one office for the COSMOS II trial period.

The user group had nine personnel for the pre-trial monitoring period, but was reduced to eight for the COSMOS II trial period. The group was selected because they were experienced computer users working as a close team, but split initially over three locations. The trial group were also human factors experts who had an interest in both the CSCW concept and the issues that were involved. This was also a very real test of COSMOS II, as the trial group was a business unit operating under real commercial and organizational constraints in the highly competitive telecommunications market.

11.3.3 Pre-Trial Monitoring Period

The pre-trial period lasted approximately ten weeks and investigated the ways in which the tasks were carried out in the group prior to their automation on COSMOS II. A wide number of office tools and procedures were used to support the tasks during this phase, most notably post (internal and external), telephone, fax, meetings and an internal email system.

Subjects were asked to record on a specially designed form the frequency, type and content of written reports that they sent and received during this phase. This was achieved by attaching the form as a front sheet to every report sent and requiring both sender and recipient to fill in a section.

Towards the end of this period subjects were given a structured questionnaire to record their attitudes towards the current systems and procedures they used for the two trial tasks. Following analysis of the questionnaires subjects were then interviewed individually to draw further information about their responses. These interviews were semi-structured, lasted from 30 to 45 minutes, and were recorded using a small tape recorder. The evaluation tools used were evolved from those suggested at the end of the original COSMOS project (Lea et al. 1989).

11.3.4 User Support and Training for COSMOS II Trial Period

User support and training were provided to the trial participants. Checkpoint reporting for project management was supported by training, consisting of a seminar lasting about an hour. This was a mixture of lecture room training and practical demonstration. At the seminar, the participants received an overview of the COSMOS II project and instructions on how to use their equipment to produce their monthly and mid-monthly project checkpoint reports. At the seminar the participants were given:

- Copy of overhead projector slides (OHPs).
- Booklet describing the COSMOS II project.
- User guide.

The OHPs were intended to act as a simple guide to the basic use of the system. They were designed so that the procedure for writing a report was split down into a series of simple tasks. There were also some hints and tips on avoiding obvious problems and an overview of advanced features such as the inclusion of text files from external word processors. The user guide was a more comprehensive document that went into further detail on the subjects covered in the OHPs.

11.3.5 COSMOS II Trial Period

The COSMOS II trial period lasted approximately ten weeks and investigated performance of the trial tasks supported by COSMOS II. During this period subjects were asked to record each time they used COSMOS II, for whatever reason, and to describe the type of usage they had carried out. At the end of the period subjects were given a questionnaire based on the one distributed during the pre-trial monitoring period. There were, however, additional sections to cover specific issues related to the functionality of COSMOS II. Again, following analysis of the questionnaires, subjects were given an individual interview.

11.4 Technical Implementation

The COSMOS II system was installed on SUN 4 machines. Although these were not the machines that the trial group would have normally used for the preparation of text, they were used for software development and prototype demonstrators. It needs to be emphasized that moving from a technical demonstrator to a system that can provide a service for customers to use is a large step. The differing, sometimes conflicting, requirements of these two roles can introduce significant technical difficulties in migrating a system from one role to another. It must be possible to reliably reconfigure the functionality of the demonstrator to cope with the practical problems of office activities.

It is a mistake to believe that a commercial system is simply research software with a few minor changes. Research software by its very nature is often not concerned with some of the essential properties of commercially released systems; reliability, maintenance, security etc. An adequate implementation of these properties often requires a major redesign, e.g. of the abstract data types (Diaper 1990; Pressman 1987: Sommerville 1989).

COSMOS II was never intended to be a commercial system. It was piloted to identify the issues that would need to be addressed, should a large-scale trial of this type of CSCW system be carried out by BT. The problem of migrating the demonstrator into a practical office tool raised the following key issues:

- Speed of operation.
- Reliability.
- Ease of use.
- Functionality.

11.4.1 Speed of Operation

For the trial it was necessary for the COSMOS II system to be ported across from its original development platform of a SUN 3 to the newer SUN 4. This was carried out to speed up the system response time offered to the user, and to enable COSMOS II to be integrated into a software environment employed by the trial group.

11.4.2 Reliability

The reliability of the system was a major problem. A significant effort was spent identifying the aspects of the system functionality that were unstable and how they were to be dealt with. In some cases it was necessary to trade off functionality against reliability. The approach taken to this was to make an initial assessment of the operating problems. These were then prioritized according to their significance for the trial task. This identified where maximum effort needed to be expended in order for the trial to progress, and those features that could be traded off against technical implementation constraints.

11.4.3 Functionality

The migration from the demonstrator to a practical prototype resulted in the addition of functionality to the basic COSMOS II system. The SUN OpenWindows text editor was integrated into the COSMOS II prototype to enable the users to produce their technical reports. Procedures were also developed to enable the inclusion of external text files created by other office automation equipment used by the trial group. The COSMOS II system was enhanced to enable it to make use of UNIX mail. Also, provision was made for the use of other messaging systems such as X.400 in the future. The UNIX mail interface enabled messages originating in COSMOS

II to be sent out from the trial group to a recipient on a local email system used at BT Laboratories.

11.5 Trial Results

11.5.1 Questionnaire Findings

In almost every aspect of its use, COSMOS II proved to be much less popular in the execution of the trial tasks than the original post/phone/fax/ email based system (see Sharples, Chapter 5, and Diaper's comments in Chapter 6). This feeling was applied to high level usage issues like ease of use, flexibility, efficiency, reliability, speed and accessibility as well as the specific difficulties individual users experienced.

Table 11.1 gives an overview of users' responses to some of the usability statements on the COSMOS II questionnaires. Of the 26 usability statements on the questionnaire, not one indicated that COSMOS II had been better than or even close to the original office procedures it replaced. A further 14 statements relating to the specific properties of COSMOS II similarly produced a consistently negative view across the trial group. The theme underlying the responses to these statements is that the COSMOS II system as it was implemented, turned the trial tasks from being fairly transparent procedures, to an unacceptably large overhead in terms of time and effort.

Table 11.1 Individual and mean responses by usability statements from the questionnaire PT, pre-trial period; COS, COSMOS trial

Response		Usability statement											
		Simple to use		Accessible		Quick		Efficient		Flexible		Reliable	
		PT	COS	PT	COS	PT	COS	PT	COS	PT	COS	PT	COS
Strongly agree	+2	2	0	2	0	2	0	3	0	1	0	3	0
Agree	+1	7	1	6	0	6	0	3	0	6	0	3	1
Uncertain	0	0	2	1	1	1	2	3	3	2	0	2	4
Disagree	–1	0	3	0	3	0	3	0	2	0	3	1	1
Strongly disagree	–2	0	2	0	4	0	3	0	3	0	5	0	2
Means		2.2	–0.75	1.11	–1.37	1.11	–1.12	1.0	–1.0	1.0	–1.62	0.88	–0.62

11.5.2 Interview Findings

The information collected from the user interviews provided a wealth of anecdotal evidence of the COSMOS II system's impact on the trial group. Some key themes emerged from this information.

Users felt their expectations of the systems performance had been raised by the approach of the COSMOS II project team. This led to disappointment when they were confronted with the system for use during the trial. COSMOS II was mounted on two SUN 4 workstations, one in London and one in the group office at BT Laboratories. This meant that seven users were using the same machine to send and receive messages to and from each other. This accessibility problem was compounded by the SUN workstation also being used for software development as part of the trial group's ongoing project work. The tasks selected for the trial were felt to be too infrequently performed and unrepresentative of the group's day to day activities. This was a problem that had been identified during a feasibility analysis of the project. However there were no other tasks that could be supported effectively within the confines of the trial.

COSMOS II's lack of user configurability meant it could not change in response to changes in the project reporting structure during the trial. A change to the reporting structure was made on at least one occasion, which caused local disruption while COSMOS II was reconfigured by the project team.

The feedback (see also Hewitt and Gilbert, Chapter 3 and Gilbert Chapter 4) provided by COSMOS II was too limited to be helpful to the users. The psychological feeling of feedback was felt to be much stronger in the old post/telephone/fax/email system. Sending a message or project report on COSMOS II was a long and arduous process. Users felt it was too much of an overhead in terms of time and effort and consequently most users used COSMOS II only when they were obliged to. For some users the length of the trial was felt to be an inadequate test of the system's performance. On the other hand they were relieved when the trial was over as it meant they didn't have to use COSMOS II any longer.

It was not all bad news from the trial. A bonus of having an email link between the trial sites in London and Ipswich was that it was possible to transfer program code quickly. Previously code had been transported by car or train and this mail link drastically reduced the time required to check for and correct bugs in the developed code.

The overall impression gained from the interviews was that users lost faith in COSMOS II's abilities to carry out its role effectively very early on in the trial.

11.6 Discussion of Trial Results

The results indicate the obvious technical difficulties COSMOS II had supporting users' attempts to carry out the trial tasks. The lack of configurability proved to be one of the stumbling blocks towards better usage of the system. Because users couldn't set up their own reporting structures they were unable to send messages across the project reporting hierarchy, and as a result felt isolated.

In comparison to mailing systems currently available on the market, COSMOS II is very primitive. There are no distribution lists, no copy facility, read receipts or urgency markers. This level of functionality is something that users in the trial group had come to expect from their experiences with other mail systems and may have resulted in a further loss of confidence in COSMOS II. Typically, simple messaging systems are not sufficient for long-term regular users of computerized communications systems (Hiltz and Turoff 1981).

Most commercial systems offer a wide range of messaging facilities. COSMOS II, as implemented in this trial, exhibited only a subset of the facilities normally available in such messaging systems. The trial showed that employing a messaging system with just a narrow subset of those facilities reduced its usefulness, and therefore limited its usage.

11.7   Lessons Learned from the COSMOS II Trial

The experiences of both the COSMOS II project team and the trial group have produced some important lessons in the following areas:

- Going from a demonstrator to a real working system.
- The task domain for the trial.
- Configurability of structured messaging systems.
- Compatibility and accessibility of structured messaging systems.
- Management of expectations.
- Risk management.

11.7.1 From Demonstrators to Real Working Systems

When trialing a prototype system it is essential that it is robust enough to function acceptably under the pressures of a real working environment. The step from demonstrator to working system is a long and often very difficult one. Before taking this step it should be considered whether it would be more appropriate to build a working system from scratch.

In this trial, mainly as a result of time constraints but also owing to financial constraints, the COSMOS II system implemented was developed from demonstrator software, produced as a result of the original COSMOS collaborative project in 1988–1989. This meant that the system used for development inherited the bugs and faults that are invariably a part of demonstrator systems. Much of the development time in this project was necessarily spent sorting out those software problems just to make COS-MOS II functional.

The lesson learned from this experience is that the amount of time and effort required to turn demonstrator software into a reliable working system is often too long, and reduces the time available for improving the range and quality of the functionality of the final system.

11.7.2 Task Domain

The domain of tasks supported by a structured messaging system should, hopefully, represent some of the day-to-day activities of the user group. If day-to-day activities are not supported, users' contact with the system will be limited. The system will then be perceived as having limited use and its subsequent level of usage will potentially suffer.

The project reporting and general mailing tasks were selected because they were felt to give the COSMOS II system installed the best test of its capabilities. Project reporting occurred once every fortnight and general mailing was at the discretion of the users. The impression gained from the interviews was that users carried out the project reporting task at the required times because they felt obliged to. However, their use of the general mail facility, which was at their own discretion, was extremely limited. Users stated that if the tasks supported by COSMOS II were more closely linked to their day-to-day activities they may have used it more.

Users also felt that the tasks selected were not particularly collaborative. Initial investigations during the feasibility stage of the project suggested a number of activities as possible candidates for trial, i.e. joint production of reports or papers for publication. The reasons tasks like this were not implemented were because it was felt that COSMOS II would not be able to cope with them, because they were too complex, or required more flexibility than COSMOS II could offer.

11.7.3 Configurability of Structured Messaging Systems

In a fully configurable structured messaging system each user would be able to set up their own structures to reflect their own reporting requirements and communication needs. The structures could then be altered whenever required to take account of any changes in the users' needs. Structured messaging systems that are not configurable are of limited use in a dynamic business environment.

Configurability was the key function that may have raised COSMOS above the level of other structured messaging systems. The reasons that it could not be implemented were that the software was not robust enough and the structure editor and other facilities required to support configurability were not sufficiently developed.

11.7.4 Compatibility and Accessibility of Structured Messaging Systems

COSMOS II was installed on SUN 4 workstations. However, the standard desktop computer used by the seven members of the trial group at BT Laboratories was the Apple Macintosh. It had been identified in the feasibility stage of the COSMOS II project that it would be advantageous to have COSMOS II installed on the users' desktop computers. However, it was realized early on that this would be too difficult technically to accomplish in the time available. The SUN workstation was chosen as the next best option. This meant that seven users were using the single SUN workstation to send and receive messages to and from each other. This does not fit either the users' model of how messaging systems in general operate, or the users' model of how the tasks themselves were accomplished in real life. This is also discussed in more detail by Brooke, Chapter 2 and by Wastell and White, Chapter 8.

If COSMOS could have been mounted on the users' own desktop computers employed for office tasks, accessibility to the system would have been improved dramatically, and there would have been a better match with the users' model for accomplishing the tasks COSMOS II was employed for.

11.7.5 Management of Expectations

Raised expectations of system performance can be damaging to its acceptance by a user group if the performance is below the level of those expectations.

In this trial, a user-centred approach was taken. The COSMOS II team set out to involve and inform users of the status of the system as it was being developed and installed. During the training sessions it was emphasized that the system was not as robust as might be hoped, nor did it have the user configurability that was part and parcel of the original COSMOS concept. Despite this, users felt they had been given an unreasonable expectation of the performance of COSMOS II.

This raises a problem in the introduction of trial prototypes to potential users. Striking a balance between the similarly unfavourable outcomes of overselling and underselling is not easy. Even with an approach which is sensitive to these effects, the outcome in terms of expectations is not always predictable.

11.7.6 Risk Management

Trials based in real working environments are an excellent test of a prototype's usefulness and acceptableness to its user group. However, real working environments operate under the constraints of commercial pressures and organizational changes, and must respond dynamically to accommodate those changes. This can often be to the detriment of the trial in progress in that environment. Trial managers can make predictions about what is likely to happen during the trial, but have very little power to influence those changes to reduce any potentially adverse effects on the trial.

11.8 Recommendations

As a result of the experiences and lessons learned from the COSMOS II trial we can make the following recommendations to assist researchers and practitioners in this area:

- Build in facilities to simplify "ruggedization" of prototypes or demonstrators to simplify migration to practical applications trials.

- To encourage usage, tasks supported by COSMOS II type systems should reflect day-to-day activities, as well as the less frequent but more information rich collaborative tasks.

- Configurability is essential if a structured messaging system is to be operated effectively in a dynamic business environment. Beyond that, the introduction of user configurability would be desirable.

- Where possible, use the standard desktop computers of the environment in question to support configurable structured messaging systems.

- When developing structured messaging systems, support the users' model of how tasks are carried out.

- The introduction of any system should be sensitive to the potential effect on users' expectations.

- The planning of an evaluation trial in a real working environment should take account of all potential risks that might impact on the trial from that environment.

11.9 Conclusions

The trial and evaluation of COSMOS II taught us a great deal about the evaluation of CSCW systems in a real working environment. Unfortunately, the benefits of the COSMOS II approach could not be realized at the trial site due to implementation problems. However, groupware that exploits the benefits to be obtained from structured messaging are becoming commercially available.

As organizations move toward multi-user, rather than single-user applications to support their activities, there is a need to provide the network services to support them. The future role for BT in the area of CSCW is to provide the network services to support the increasing number of groupware/CSCW products that are rapidly emerging, and to encourage the further development of more sophisticated systems.

References

Achtert WS and Gibaldi J (1985) The MLA Style Manual. MLA, New York

Ackerman MS and Malone TW (1990) Answer Garden: a tool for growing organisational memory. In: Lochovsky FH (ed) Proceedings of the Conference on Office Information Systems (COIS-90), Cambridge, MA, 25–27 April. ACM, New York

Ahuja SR, Ensor JR and Horn DN (1988) The Rapport multimedia conferencing system. In: Allen RB (ed) Proceedings of the Conference on Office Information Systems (COIS-88), Palo Alto, CA, 23–25 March. ACM, New York

Apple (1987) Human Interface Guidelines: The Apple Desktop Interface. Addison-Wesley, New York

Ariav G and Ginzberg B (1985) DSS design: a systemic view of decision support. Communications of the ACM 28(10)

Auramaki E, Lehtinen E and Lyytinen K (1988) A speech-act based office modelling approach. ACM Transactions on Office Information Systems 6: 126–152

Bannon L and Schmidt K (1991) CSCW: four characters in search of a context. In: Bowers JM and Benford SD (ed) Studies in Computer Supported Cooperative Work: Theory, Practice and Design. North-Holland, Amsterdam

Barlow J, Rada R and Diaper D (1989) Interacting WITH Computers. Interacting with Computers 1(1): 39–42

Barrett JA and Brooke JB (1989) Usability, change and adaptable systems. Paper presented to European Space Research and Technology Centre workshop on human factors engineering, 21–23 November, Noordwijk, Holland

Bass BM (1980) Team productivity and individual member competence. Small Group Behavior 11(4): 431–504

Bass BM (1981) Stogdill's Handbook of Leadership. Free Press, New York

Bench-Capon T and McEnery A (1989) People interact through computers not with them. Interacting with Computers 1(1): 31–38

Benest ID (1989) Towards an office automation metaphor. In: Proceedings of the First World Electronic Media Symposium, Geneva, Switzerland, October. International Telecommunications Union, Geneva, pp 151–155

Benest ID (1990) Computer-assisted learning using dynamic electronic books. In: Kibby M (ed) Computer Assisted Learning. Pergamon Press, Oxford, pp 195–203

Benest ID and Dukić D (1989) High-level user-interface objects. In: Salvendy G and Smith MJ (ed) Designing and Using Human–Computer Interfaces and Knowledge Based Systems. Elsevier, Amsterdam, pp 597–604

Benest ID and Dukić D (1990a) Some design issues in the automated office metaphor. In: Conference Proceedings of the European X Window System User Group, Guildford, UK, Autumn. European X User Group, Cambridge, pp 56–69

Benest ID and Dukić D (1990b) Tools that support human–human communication in the automated office. In: Diaper D, Gilmore D, Cockton G and Shackel B (ed) Human–Computer Interaction: Proceedings of INTERACT '90. Elsevier, Amsterdam, pp 853–859

Benest ID and Dukić D (1991) Computer support for the group in computer based technical projects. In: Queinnec Y and Daniellou F (ed) Designing for Everyone and Everybody. Taylor and Francis, London, pp 549–551

Benyon D (1992) The role of task analysis in systems design. Interacting with Computers 4(1): 102–123

Bilange E, Fraser N, Gilbert N, Guyomard M, Heisterkamp P, McGlashan S, Siroux J, Unglaub J, Wooffitt R and Youd N (1990) Functional specification for the Sundial Dialogue Manager. ESPRIT project 2218

Bjorn-Andersen N (1986) Understanding the nature of the office for the design of third wave office systems. In: Harrison MD and Monk AF (ed) People and Computers: Designing for Usability. Cambridge University Press, Cambridge, pp 65–77

Bracchi G and Pernici L (1984) The design requirements of office systems. In: ACM Transactions on Office Information Systems 2(2) April 1984, ACM Press

British Telecom (1989) User Interface Style Guide RD 0024. British Telecom, Martlesham Heath, UK

Brobst SA, Malone T, Grant KR and Turbak FA (1986) Toward intelligent message routing systems. In: Uhlig R (ed) Computer Message Systems '85. Proceedings of the 2nd International Symposium on Computer Message Systems. North Holland, Amsterdam

Brooke JB (1991) Usability, change, adaptable systems and community computing. In: Bullinger H-J (ed) Human Aspects in Computing: Design and Use of Interactive Systems and Work with Terminals. Elsevier, Amsterdam, pp 1093–1097

Brooks P (1991) Wide area IP in the UK academic community. In: Beer MD (ed) UKUUG Summer 1991 Conference Proceedings, Liverpool University, pp 62–67

Brown PJ (1989) Do we need maps to navigate round hypertext documents? Electronic Publishing 2(2): 91–100

Buckley PK and Long JB (1985) Effects of system and knowledge variables on a task component of "teleshopping". In: Johnson P and Cook S (ed) People and Computers: Designing the Interface. Cambridge University Press, Cambridge, pp 76–91

Burrage M and Torstendahl R (1990) The Formation of Professions. Sage, London

Business Week (1991) I can't work this ?#!!@ thing! 29 April

Carasik RP and Grantham CE (1988) A case study of CSCW in a dispersed organisation. In: Soloway E, Frye D and Sheppard SB (ed) Proceedings of the Human Factors in Computing Systems Conference, CHI-88, Washington. ACM, New York, pp 61–66

CCITT (1987) Draft Recommendation on Message Handling Systems, X400, Version 5, November

Checkland P (1981) Systems Thinking, Systems Practice. Wiley, Chichester

Ciborra CU (1984) Management information systems: from decision-making to exchange. In: Bemelmans ThMA (ed) Beyond Productivity: ISD for Organisational Effectiveness. North-Holland, Amsterdam, pp 135–145

Clark B and O'Donnell S (1991) Computer supported cooperative work. British Telecom Technology Journal 9(1): 47–55

Conklin J (1987) Hypertext: an introduction and survey. IEEE Computer 20(9): 17–41

COSMOS (1989) Specification for a configurable, structured message system. Report 68.4, COSMOS Project, Queen Mary College, London

Croft WB and Lefkowitz LS (1984) Task support in an office system. ACM Transactions on Office Information Systems 2(3)

Croft WB and Lefkowitz LS (1988) Using a planner to support office work. In: Allen RB (ed) Proceedings of the Conference on Office Information Systems (COIS-88), Palo Alto, CA, 23–25 March. ACM, New York

Crowley T, Milazzo P, Baker E, Forsdick H and Tomlinson R (1990) MMConf: an infrastructure for building shared multimedia applications. In: Proceedings of the Conference on Computer-Supported Cooperative Work (CSCW-90), Los Angeles, CA, 7–10 October. ACM, New York

CSMIL (1990) ShrEdit 1.1, a shared editor for the Apple Macintosh. Cognitive Science and Machine Intelligence Laboratory, University of Michigan

Danielson T, Panoke-Babatz U, Prinz W, Patel A, Pays PA, Knut S and Speth R (1986) The AMIGO project: advanced group communication model for computer-based communication environment. In: Peterson D (ed) Proceedings of the Conference on Computer Supported Cooperative Work (CSCW-86), Austin, TX, December. ACM, New York

De Cindio F, De Michelis G et al. (1986) CHAOS as a coordinating technology. In: Peterson D (ed) Proceedings of the Conference on Computer Supported Cooperative Work (CSCW-86), Austin, TX, December. ACM, New York

Delisle D and Pelamourgues L (1991) B-ISDN and how it works. IEEE Spectrum 28(8): 39–42

Delisle NM and Schwartz MD (1986) Neptune: a hypertext system for CAD applications. In: Proceedings of the 1986 ACM-SIGMOD International Conference on the Management of Data, Washington, DC, 28–30 May. ACM, New York, pp 132–143

Denning PJ (1982) Electronic junk. Communications of the ACM 25(3)

Diaper D (1987) Designing systems for people – beyond user-centred design. In: Software Engineering. Proceedings of the Share European Association (SEAS) Anniversary Meeting, Edinburgh. SEAS, pp 283–302

Diaper D (1989) Task analysis for knowledge descriptions (TAKD): the method and an example. In: Diaper D (ed) Task Analysis for Human–Computer Interaction. Ellis Horwood, Chichester, pp 108–159

Diaper D (1990) An organisational context for expert system design. In: Berry D and Hart A (ed) Expert Systems: Human Issues. Chapman and Hall, London, pp 214–236

Diaper D (1992) Look before you leap; the hypertext bandwagon. (in preparation; may be obtained from the author)

Diaper D and Addison M (1992) Task analysis and systems analysis for software engineering. Interacting with Computers 4(1) 124–139

Dodd WP, Maude TI, Pullinger DJ and Shackel B (1985) Software infrastructure for the BLEND "Electronic Journal" experiment. In: Shackel B (ed) Human–Computer Interaction: Proceedings of INTERACT '84. North-Holland, Amsterdam, pp 933–936

Donahue J and Widom J (1986) Whiteboards: a graphical database tool. ACM Transactions on Office Information Systems 4(1): 24–41

Dukić D and Benest ID (1991) DrawingBoard: adopting the drawing office metaphor for page composition. In: SUN '91 Conference Proceedings, Birmingham, UK, September. Sun UK User Group, Buntingford, pp 227–239

Eden C (1989) Using cognitive mapping for strategic options development and analysis. In: Rosenhead J (ed) Rational Analysis for a Problematic World. Wiley, Chichester

Ellis CA and Nutt G (1980) Office information systems and computer science. ACM Computing Surveys, 12(1), March

Ellis CA and Nutt G (1988) Office information systems and computer science. In: Greif I (ed) Computer Supported Cooperative Work: A Book of Readings. Morgan Kaufmann, San Mateo, CA

Ellis CA, Gibbs SJ and Rein GL (1991) Groupware: some issues and experiences. Communications of the ACM 34(1): 39–58. Also published as MCC Technical Report STP-414-88

Fanning T and Raphael B (1986) Computer teleconferencing: experience at Hewlett-Packard. In: Peterson D (ed) Proceedings of the Conference on Computer Supported Cooperative Work (CSCW-86), Austin, TX, December. ACM, New York

Farallon Computing (1987) Timbuktu: the next best thing is being there. Farallon Computing Inc, Berkeley, CA

Fish RS, Kraut RE, Leland MDP and Cohen M (1988) Quilt: A collaborative tool for cooperative writing. In: Allen RB (ed) Proceedings of the Conference on Office Information Systems (COIS-88), Palo Alto, CA, 23–25 March. ACM, New York, pp 30–37

Flores CF and Ludlow J (1981) Doing and speaking in the office. In: Fick G and Sprague R (ed) DSS:Issues and Challenges. Pergamon Press, London

Freeman C (1974) Economics of Industrial Innovation. Penguin, Harmondsworth

Garret LN, Smith K and Meyrowitz (1986) Intermedia: issues, strategies and tactics in the design of a hypermedia document system. In: Peterson D (ed) Proceedings of the Conference on Computer Supported Cooperative Work (CSCW-86), Austin, TX, December. ACM, New York

Gasser L (1986) The integration of computing and routine work. ACM Transactions on Office Information Systems 4: 205–225

Gifford DK (1980) Violet, an experimental decentralized system. In: Naffah N (ed) Integrated Office Systems – Burotics, IFIP. North-Holland, Amsterdam, pp 27–41

Goldberg A (1984) Smalltalk-80: The Interactive Programming Environment. Addison-Wesley, Wokingham

Green TRG (1991) Describing information artifacts with cognitive dimensions and structure maps. In: Diaper D and Hammond N (ed) People and Computers VI. Proceedings of the HCI '91 Conference, 20–23 August 1991. Cambridge University Press, Cambridge

Greif I (ed) (1988) Computer Supported Cooperative Work: A Book of Readings. Morgan Kaufmann, San Mateo, CA

Grudin J (1989) Why groupware applications fail: problems in design and evaluation. Office: Technology and People 4(3) 245–264

Grudin J (1990a) Interface. In: Proceedings of the Conference on Computer-Supported Cooperative Work (CSCW-90), Los Angeles, CA, 7–10 October. ACM, New York

Grudin J (1990b) The computer reaches out: the historical continuity of interface design. In: Chew JC and Whiteside J (ed) Proceedings of the Human Factors in Computing Systems Conference, CHI-90, Seattle, WA, 1–5 April. ACM, New York

Gust P (1988) Shared X: X in a distributed group work environment. Presented at the 2nd Annual X conference, MIT, Boston, MA, January

Hahn U, Jarke M, Eherer S and Kreplin K (1991) CoAUTHOR: a hypermedia group authoring environment. In: Bowers JM and Benford SD (ed) Studies in Computer Supported Cooperative Work: Theory, Practice and Design. North-Holland, Amsterdam

Hewett TT (1991) Importance of failure analysis for human–computer interface design. Interacting with Computers 3(1) 3-8

Hewitt B (1989) Pilot study of Timbuktu to evaluate aspects of floor control. Internal Report, Department of Computer Science, Queen Mary and Westfield College

HICOM Executive (1988) A report on the HICOM Service Report submitted to DEC in fulfilment of the terms of DEC External Research Agreement Contract UK-014

Hiltz SR and Turoff M (1978) The Network Nation: Human Communication via Computer. Addison-Wesley, Reading, MA

Hiltz SR and Turoff M (1981) The evolution of user behaviour in a computerized conferencing system. Communications of the ACM 24(11): 739–751

Hiltz SR and Turoff M (1985) Structuring computer-mediated communication systems to avoid information overload. Communications of the ACM 28(7)

Hirschheim RA (1985) Office Automation: A Social and Organisational Perspective. Wiley, Chichester

Hirschheim RA and Newman M (1988) Information systems and user resistance: theory and practice. Computer Journal 31: 398–408

Hirschheim RA, Klein H and Newman M (1987) A social action perspective of information systems development. In: DeGross J and Kriebel C (ed) Proceedings of the 8th International Conference on Information Systems (ICIS). ACM, New York, pp 45–56

Hutchins EL, Hollan JD and Norman DA (1986) Direct manipulation interfaces. In: Norman DA and Draper SW (ed) User-centred System Design. Lawrence Erlbaum, Hillsdale, NJ, pp 87–124

Hutchison D and Walpole J (1991) Distributed systems and objects. In: Blair G, Gallacher J, Hutchison D and Shepherd D (ed) Object-Oriented Languages, Systems and Applications. Pitman, London, pp 223–243

James P and Churcher J (1988) COSMOS – A project in structured messaging. British Telecom Technology Journal 6(4): 37–43

Jirotka M, Luff P and Gilbert GN (1991) Participation frameworks for computer mediated communication. In: Bannon L, Robinson M and Schmidt K (ed) Proceedings of the Second European Conference on Computer Supported Cooperative Work (EC-CSCW '91), Amsterdam, September. Kluwer, Dordrecht

Johnson P (1987) Using Z to specify CICS. In: Proceedings of the SEAS Anniversary Meeting. Software Engineering 1: 303–333

Johnson TJ (1972) Professions and Power. Macmillan, London

Kiesler S, Siegel J and McGuire TW (1984) Social psychological aspects of computer-mediated communication. American Psychologist 39: 1123–1134

Kincaid CM, Dupont PB and Kaye AR (1985) Electronic calendars in the office: an assessment of user needs and current technology. ACM Transactions on Office Information Systems 3(1): 89–102

Kirkwood A (1990) Monitoring the performance of ESCFE, pre-COSMOS. Internal Report, British Telecom, Martlesham Heath, UK

Kraemer KL and Kling JL (1988) Computer based systems for cooperative work and group decision making. ACM Computing Surveys 20(2)

Kraut RE, Galegher J and Egido C (1988) Relationships and tasks in scientific research collaborations. In: Greif I (ed) Computer Supported Cooperative Work: A Book of Readings. Morgan Kaufmann, San Mateo, CA, pp 741–769. Also published in Human–Computer Interaction (1989) 3: 31–57

Kreifelts T and Woetzel G (1986) Distribution and error handling in an office procedure system. In: Proceedings of the IFIP WG 8.4 Conference on Office Systems Methods and Tools, Pisa, Italy. North-Holland, Amsterdam, pp 197–208

Kuo F (1966) Network Analysis by Digital Computer. Proceedings of the IEEE 54(6): 820–829

Laird JE, Newell A and Rosenbloom PS (1987) Soar: an architecture for general intelligence. Artificial Intelligence 33(1): 64

Lane IM, Mathews RC, Chaney CM, Effmeyer RC, Reber RA and Teddie CB (1982) Making the goals of acceptance and quality explicit: effects on group decisions. Small Group Behaviour 13(4): 542-554

Lantz KA (1986) An experiment in integrated multimedia conferencing. In: Peterson D (ed) Proceedings of the Conference on Computer Supported Cooperative Work (CSCW-86), Austin, TX, December. ACM, New York

Lauwers JC and Lantz KA (1990) Collaboration awareness in support of collaboration transparency: requirements for the next generation of shared window systems. In: Chew JC and Whiteside J (ed) Proceedings of the Human Factors in Computing Systems Conference, CHI-90, Seattle, WA, 1–5 April. ACM, New York

Lay MM and Karis WM (ed) (1991) Collaborative Writing in Industry: Investigations in Theory and Practice. Baywood, Amityville, NY

Lea M, Wilson P and Young R (1989) Recommendations for the application, further development and evaluation of COSMOS. Report 71.4 Ext/ALV. COSMOS Coordinators Office, Queen Mary College, London

Lederberg J and Uncapher K (1989) Towards a national collaboratory. Unpublished Report of an invitational workshop at the Rockefeller University, 17–18 March

Lee J (1990) SIBYL: a tool for managing group decision rationale. In: Proceedings of the Conference on Computer-Supported Cooperative Work (CSCW-90), Los Angeles, CA, 7–10 October. ACM, New York

Leland MDP, Fish RS and Kraut RE (1988) Collaborative document production using Quilt. In: Proceedings of the Conference on Computer Supported Cooperative Work (CSCW-88), Portland, OR, September. ACM, New York, pp 206–215

Lochovsky FM, Hogg JS, Weiser SP and Mendelson AO (1988) OTM: specifying office tasks. In: Allen RB (ed) Proceedings of the Conference on Office Information Systems (COIS-88), Palo Alto, CA, 23–25 March. ACM, New York

Long J (1986) People and computers: designing for usability. In: Harrison MD and Monk AF (ed) People and Computers: Designing for Usability. Cambridge University Press, Cambridge, pp 3-23

Long J and Dowell J (1989) Conceptions of the discipline of HCI: craft, applied science, and engineering. In: Sutcliffe A and Macaulay L (ed) People and Computers V. Cambridge University Press, Cambridge, pp 9–34

Lyytinen K (1987) Two views of information modelling. Information and Management 12: 9–19

Lyytinen K (1988) Stakeholders, information system failures and soft systems methodology: an assessment. Journal of Applied Systems Analysis 15: 61–81

Malone TW (1987) Computer support for organisations: towards an organisational science. In: Carroll JM (ed) Interfacing Thought. MIT Press, Cambridge, MA

Malone TW and Lai K (1988) Object Lens: a spreadsheet for cooperative work. In: Proceedings of the Conference on Computer Supported Cooperative Work (CSCW-88), Portland, OR, September. ACM, New York

Malone TW, Grant KR and Turbak FA (1986) The Information Lens: an intelligent system for information sharing in organisations. In: Proceedings of the Human Factors in Computing Systems Conference, CHI-86, Boston, MA. ACM, New York pp 1–8

Mantei M, Hewett T, Eason K and Preece J (1991) Report on the INTERACT '90 Workshop on Education in HCI: transcending disciplinary and national boundaries. Interacting with Computers 3(2) 232–240

Marchionini G and Schneiderman B (1988) Finding facts vs browsing knowledge in hypertext systems. IEEE Computer, 21(1): 70–79

Maresh J and Wastell DG (1990). Process modelling and CSCW: an application of IPSE technology to medical office work. In: Diaper D, Gilmore D, Cockton G and Shackel B (ed) Human–Computer Interaction: Proceedings of INTERACT '90. Elsevier, Amsterdam, pp 849–852

Maude TI, Heaton NO, Gilbert GN, Wilson PA and Marshall CJ (1984) An experiment in group working on mailbox systems. In: Shackel B (ed) Human–Computer Interaction: Proceedings of INTERACT '84. North-Holland, Amsterdam, pp 396–400

Molich R and Nielson J (1990) Improving a human–computer dialogue: what designers know about traditional interface design. Communications of the ACM 33(3)

Morgan G (1986) Images of Organization. Sage, London

Neuwirth CM, Kaufer DS, Chandhok R and Morris JH (1990) Issues in the design of computer support for co-authoring and commenting. In: Proceedings of the Conference on Computer-Supported Cooperative Work (CSCW-90), Los Angeles, CA, 7–10 October. ACM, New York, pp 183–195

Newman J and Newman R (1992) Two failures in computer-mediated text communication. In: Sharples M (ed) Computers and Writing: Issues and Implementations. Kluwer, Amsterdam, pp 33–49

Newman J, Reynolds C and Wilson P (1990) HICOM: an interactive scientific community. In: Colloquium on CSCW: Computer Supported Collaborative Work, London. Institution of Electrical Engineers Digest 132, 1-2, 7

Newman R and Newman J (1993) Social Writing: Premises and Practices in Computerized Contexts. In: Sharples M (ed) Computer Supported Collaborative Writing. Springer-Verlag, London

Norman DA (1988) The Psychology of Everyday Things. Basic Books, New York

Nunamaker JF, Dennis AR, Valacich JS, Vogel DR and George JF (1991) Electronic meeting systems to support group work. Communications of the ACM 34(7)

Olson M and Lucas H (1982) The impact of office automation on the organisation. Communications of the ACM 25(11): 838–847

Olson J, Olson G, Mack L and Wellner P (1990) Concurrent editing: the group's interface. In: Diaper D, Gilmore D, Cockton G and Shackel B (ed) Human–Computer Interaction: Proceedings of INTERACT '90. Elsevier, Amsterdam, pp 835–840

Open Systems Group (1972) Systems Behaviour. Harper and Row, New York

Opper S (1988) A groupware toolbox. Byte 13: 275–282

Page S (1992) Why industrial reports are missing from conferences. HICOM Open Forum, uk.ac.lut.hicom

Palme J (1984a) COM/PortaCOM conference system. Design goals and principles. In: Shackel B (ed) Human–Computer Interaction: Proceedings of INTERACT '84. North-Holland, Amsterdam, pp 271–272

Palme J (1984b) You have 134 unread mail do you want to read them now? In: Smith HT (ed) IFIP Conference on Computer Based Message Services, Nottingham University. North-Holland, Amsterdam

Panoke-Babatz U (1984) The computer conferencing system KOMEX. In: Shackel B (ed) Human–Computer Interaction: Proceedings of INTERACT '84. North-Holland, Amsterdam, pp 269–270

Patterson JF, Randal LS and Steward R (1981) Advisory decision aids: a prototype. Technical Report PR 80-27-312. Decision and Designs Inc, McLean, VA

Patterson JF, Hill RD and Rohall SL (1990) Rendezvous: an architecture for synchronous multi-user applications. In: Proceedings of the Conference on Computer-Supported Cooperative Work (CSCW-90), Los Angeles, CA, 7–10 October. ACM, New York

Pava C (1983) Managing new office technology: an organisational strategy. Free Press, New York

Pemberton L and Sharples M (1988) Textual structures in a Writer's Assistant. In: Collins JH, Estes N and Walker D (ed) Proceedings of the Fifth International Conference on Technology and Education, Edinburgh, March, vol 1, pp 296–299

Piccardi S and Tisato F (1989) Conference Desk: an experiment and model for application sharing. Technical Report, Systems Software Laboratory, Direzione Olivetti Ricerca, Milan, January

Poggio A, Garcia Luna Aceres JJ, Craighill EJ, Moran D, Aquillar L, Worthington D and Hight J (1985) CCWS: a computer based multi-media information system. IEEE Computer 18(10): 92–106

Posner LR, Baecker RM and Mantei MM (1991) How people write together. Technical Report, Computer Systems Research Institute and Department of Computer Science, University of Toronto, 6 Kings College Road, Toronto, Ontario, Canada M5S 1A1

Pressman RS (1987) Software Engineering: A Practitioner's Approach, 2nd edn. McGraw Hill, New York

Prinz W and Speth R (1987) Group communication and related aspects in office automation. In: Shicker P (ed) Proceedings of the IFIP TC 6/WG 6.5 Working Conference on Message Handling Systems, Munich, 27–29 April, North-Holland, Amsterdam

Pullinger D (1985) BLEND – 4: User–System Interaction, British Library LIR Report 45

Pullinger D (1989) Moral judgements in designing better systems. Interacting with Computers 1(1): 93–104

Reynolds C (1990) The HICOM Information Service for HCI Professionals, CSIRO Technical Report TR-FD-90-10, North Ryde, New South Wales

Richer I (1980) Voice, data and the computerized PABX. In: Naffah N (ed) Integrated Office Systems – Burotics, IFIP. North-Holland, Amsterdam, pp 55–69

Rimmershaw R (1992) Technologies of collaboration. In: Sharples M (ed) Computers and Writing: Issues and Implementations. Kluwer, Dordrecht

Robertson A and Project SAPPHO Research Team (1972) Success and Failure in Industrial Innovation. Centre for the Study of Industrial Innovation, London

Root RW (1988) Design of a multi-media vehicle for social browsing. In: Proceedings of the Conference on Computer Supported Cooperative Work (CSCW-88), Portland, OR, September. ACM, New York

Rosenberg D and Hutchison C (eds) (1993) Design Issues in CSCW. Springer-Verlag, London

Rosenberg LC (1991) Update on National Science Foundation funding of the "Collaboratory". Communications of the ACM 34(12): 83

Sarin S and Greif I (1985) Computer-based real-time conferencing systems. IEEE Computer 18(10) 33–45

Scheifler RW and Gettys J (1986) The X window system. ACM Transactions on Graphics 5(2)

Schneiderman B (1987) Designing the User Interface: Strategies for Effective Human–Computer Interaction. Addison-Wesley, Reading, MA

Searle JR (1975) A taxonomy of illocutionary acts. In: Gunderson K (ed) Language, Mind and Knowledge, University of Minnesota, Minneapolis, MN

Seward R (1987) The support of managerial groups – a new development. MPhil thesis, Lancaster University

Shackel B (1982) The BLEND system – programme for the study of some electronic journals. Ergonomics 25(4) 269–284

Shackel B (1986) BLEND – 5: The Computer Human Factors Journal, British Library LIR Report 47

Shackel B and Pullinger D (1984) BLEND – 1: Background and Developments, British Library LIR Report 29

Shackel B, Pullinger DJ, Maude TI and Dodd WP (1983) The BLEND-LINC project on "Electronic Journals" after two years. Computer Journal 26(3): 247–252

Shapiro NZ and Anderson RH (1985) Towards an ethics and etiquette for electronic mail. Rand Report R-3283-NSF/RC, Rand Corporation, Santa Monica, USA, July

Sharples M, Goodlet J, Beck E, Wood C, Easterbrook S, Plowman L and Evans W (1991) A framework for the study of computer supported collaborative writing. Cognitive Science Research Paper 190, School of Cognitive and Computing Sciences, University of Sussex

Shepherd A, Mayer N, Kuchinsky A (1990) Strudel – an extensible electronic conversation toolkit. In: Proceedings of the Conference on Computer-Supported Cooperative Work (CSCW-90), Los Angeles, CA, 7–10 October. ACM, New York

Shuttleworth M (1988) HICOM: enter a new communications network. Behaviour and Information Technology 7: 216–218

Sluizer S and Cashman PM (1984) XCP: an experimental tool for supporting office procedures. In: Proceedings of the 1st International Conference on Office Automation, Silver Spring, MD, October. IEEE, Washington, pp 73–80

Smith H, Hennessy P and Lunt G (1991) The activity model environment: an object-oriented framework for describing organisational communication. In: Bowers JM and Benford SD (ed) Studies in Computer Supported Cooperative Work: Theory, Practice and Design. North-Holland, Amsterdam

Sommerville I (1989) Software Engineering, 3rd edn. Addison-Wesley, Wokingham

Steeb R and Johnston SC (1981) A computer based interactive system for group decision making. IEEE Transactions on Systems, Man and Cybernetics 11(8): 544–552

Stefik M, Foster G, Bobrow DG, Kahn K, Lanning S and Suchman L (1987a) Beyond the chalkboard: computer support for collaboration and problem solving in meetings. Communications of the ACM 30(1): 32–47

Stefik DG, Bobrow G, Foster G, Lanning S and Tatar D (1987b) WYSIWIS revised: early experiences with multiuser interfaces. ACM Transactions on Office Information Systems 5(2): 147–168

Suchman L (1983) Office procedures as practical action. ACM Transactions on Office Information Systems 1: 320–328

Suchman L (1988) Designing with the user. In: Winograd T (ed) ACM Transactions on Office Information Systems 6: 173–183

Sun Microsystems (1987) NeWS Manual 800-1632-10, Revision A, March

Trigg R, Suchman L and Halasz F (1986) Supporting collaboration in NoteCards. In: Peterson D (ed) Proceedings of the Conference on Computer Supported Cooperative Work (CSCW-86), Austin, TX, December. ACM, New York, pp 1–10

Tueni M, Li J and Fares P (1988) AMS: A knowledge based approach to task representation, organisation and coordination. In: Allen RB (ed) Proceedings of the Conference on Office Information Systems (COIS-88), Palo Alto, CA, 23–25 March. ACM, New York

University of Michigan (1990) ShrEdit 1.1: A Shared Editor for the Apple Macintosh. Cognitive Science and Machine Intelligence Laboratory, University of Michigan

Viller S (1991) The group facilitator: a CSCW perspective. In: Bannon L, Robinson M and Schmidt K (ed) Proceedings of the Second European Conference on Computer Supported Cooperative Work (EC-CSCW '91), Amsterdam, September. Kluwer, Dordrecht

Warboys B (1990) The IPSE 2.5 project: a process model based architecture. In: Bennet K (ed) Software Engineering Environments: Research and Practice. Wiley, New York

Warboys B and Veasey P (1989) Twenty years with support environments. ICL Technical Journal 6: 447–466

Wastell DG (1988) Phenomenology and participation: alternative principles for IS development. Lecture Notes in Medical Informatics 35: 717–722

Wastell DG (1991) Process support technology, cooperative work and information system development. In: De Gross JI, Benbasat I, De Sanctis G and Beath CM (ed) Proceedings of the 11th International Conference on Information Systems (ICIS). ACM, New York, pp 93–100

Wastell DG and Cronin E (1988) Soft systems methodologies in the design of information systems: insights from hermeneutics and Habermas's theory of communication. In: Computers in Clinical Medicine. British Medical Informatics Society, London

Wastell DG, Acheson J, Cotter L, Schady W and Lucas S (1987) Computing in clinical departments: implications for the design of hospital information systems. Health Policy 8: 347–354

Watabe K, Sakata S, Fukuoka H and Ohmori T (1990) Distributed multiparty desktop conferencing system: Mermaid. In: Proceedings of the Conference on Computer-Supported Cooperative Work (CSCW-90), Los Angeles, CA, 7–10 October. ACM, New York, pp 27–28

Wilbur SB and Young RE (1988) The COSMOS project: a multi-disciplinary approach to design for computer supported group working. In: Speth R (ed) EUTECO '88: Research into Networks and Distributed Applications, Vienna, Austria, 20–22 April. North-Holland, Amsterdam

Wilson PA (1988) Key research in computer-supported cooperative work. In: Speth R (ed) EUTECO '88: Research into Networks and Distributed Applications, Vienna, Austria, 20–22 April. North-Holland, Amsterdam

Wilson PA (1989) Some notes on a European network or collaboratory for research and development. In: European Workshop on CSCW in Research Laboratories, ISPRA, Italy, 4–5 December

Wilson PA, Maude TI, Marshall CJ and Heaton NO (1984) The active mailbox – your on-line secretary. In: Smith HT (ed) IFIP Conference on Computer Based Message Services, Nottingham University. North-Holland, Amsterdam

Winograd T (1987) A language/action perspective on the design of cooperative work. Technical Report STAN-CS-87-1158, Department of Computer Science, Stanford University. Also published in Human–Computer Interaction 1988 3(1): 3–30 and in Greif I (ed) (1988) Computer Supported Cooperative Work: A Book of Readings. Morgan Kaufmann, San Mateo, CA, pp 335–366

Winograd T (1988) Where the action is. Byte, December, 256–258

Winograd T and Flores F (1986) Understanding Computers and Cognition. Ablex, Norwood, NJ

Woo CC, Lochovsky FH and Lee A (1985) Document management systems. In: Tsichritzis DC (ed) Office Automation Concepts and Tools. Springer-Verlag, London, pp 21–40

Wulf WA (1989) The National Collaboratory – A White Paper. National Collaboratory Workshop, National Science Foundation, Washington DC

Wynn E (1979) Office conversation as an information medium. PhD thesis, University of California at Berkeley

X/Open (1989) X/Open portability guide. Prentice-Hall, Englewood-Cliffs, NJ

Yao SB, Hevner AR, Shi Z and Luo D (1984) FORMANAGER: an office forms management system. ACM Transactions on Office Information Systems 2(3): 235–262

Zloof M (1982) Office by example: a business language that unifies data and word processing and electronic mail. IBM Systems Journal 21(3)

Subject Index

Name Index

Printing: Weihert-Druck GmbH, Darmstadt
Binding: Theo Gansert Buchbinderei GmbH, Weinheim